A Gathering of Feathers

Individuals with the Feather surname buried in Lenox Memorial Cemetery,
Preston County, West Virginia 1832-2023
and
Minutes from Feather Family Reunions, 1909-1972

Researched, Compiled and Written by Carl E. Feather

Feather Cottage Media

A Gathering of Feathers:
Individuals with the Feather surname buried in Lenox Memorial Cemetery, Preston County, West Virginia 1832–2023
and
Minutes from Feather Family Reunions, 1909–1972

By Carl E. Feather, author of *My Fathers' Land* and *Wandering Back-Roads West Virginia* book series.

Published by The Feather Cottage
6 Seaford Lane, Bruceton Mills WV 26525
thefeathercottage.com / carl@thefeathercottage.com

Original material copyright 2024 Carl E. Feather / Feather Cottage Media

All rights reserved. No part of this book may be reproduced in any form or by any electronic or mechanical means, including information storage and retrieval systems and audio books, without permission in writing from the publisher, except by reviewers, who may quote brief passages in a review.

ISBN: 979-8-9907539-0-7
Library of Congress Control Number (LCCN): 2024911259

Printed and bound in USA
First printing, June 2024

AI was not used to produce the contents of this book.

All photos in this book, unless otherwise attributed, are by the author, Carl E. Feather, and copyrighted.

Front cover photo: Gravestones of Jacob Feather and Mary Connoly, Lenox Memorial Cemetery, Lenox, Preston County, West Virginia

All photos in this book, unless otherwise credited, are by Carl E. Feather.

Also by Carl E. Feather

Mountain People in a Flat Land:
Appalachian Migration to Northeast Ohio, 1940–1965
Ohio University Press

Covered Bridges of Ashtabula County, Ohio

Hidden History of Ashtabula County, Ohio
Arcadia

Ashtabula Harbor, Ohio:
A History of the World's Greatest Iron Ore Receiving Port

Pleasure Grounds: 150 Years of Geneva-on-the-Lake,
Ohio's First Summer Resort

My Fathers' Land: Palatinate Immigration
to North-Central West Virginia

Wandering Back-Roads West Virginia (4 volumes)

Wandering Preston County, West Virginia

Wandering Tucker County, West Virginia

Wandering Route 50, West Virginia

Feather Cottage Media

order online at amazon.com
or purchase autographed copies at thefeathercottage.com

James C. Feather Jr. and his wife, Irena Ervin Feather. Jame's C. and the author's second great-grandfather, Adam H., were siblings, and James and Irena raised his great-grandfather after Adam and his wife died.
From the collection of Wendy Feather McLaughlin.

Dedication

To all the Feathers who have come before us,
to their pioneering spirit and grit,
and to their faith that continues to offer
the hope of eternal life in our Fathers' Land.

Let the pleasant memories of his life prove a stimulant in the conduct of ours, and let us look beyond to the great fact of immortality and be comforted with the thought that after life's fitful fever, he sleeps well.

From the obituary of M.L. Feather,
who died December 14, 1913, on his sixtieth birthday.

Support Lenox Memorial

Lenox Memorial Cemetery depends upon donations for upkeep of the grounds. Your donations will be greatly appreciated and ensure continued maintenance of this hallowed ground for descendants of Jacob and Mary Feather, as well as many other Palatines who settled in Preston County, Virginia, later West Virginia.

As a purchaser of this book, you are already supporting this effort; the author is donating a portion of the profit to the fund.

Checks should be made out to Lenox Memorial Cemetery Fund and mailed to:

Lenox Memorial Cemetery
c/o Lenox Store
10737 Brandonville Pike
Albright WV 26519

Contents

Acknowledgments: 9
Introduction 11
A Gathering in Lenox 17
Maps 22
Feather Burials in Lenox Memorial
(listed alphabetically by **first** name)
A 27
B 37
C 40
D 50
E 59
F 67
G 67
H 69
I 73
J 78
L 102
M 107
N 122
O 123
P 123
R 125
S 128
W 130
Z 134
"Feathers" burials 136
Minutes of reunions: 138
Bibliography 155
Reunion endnotes 157
Index 159

Lenox Memorial Cemetery is also known as Lutheran Church Cemetery and Crab Orchard Cemetery. It is located south of Lenox, off Brandonville Pike.

Acknowledgments

The author is grateful to Wendy Feather McLaughlin and her husband, Bob, for contributing obituaries and the recollections of her grandmother, Wanda Hillery Feather, to this work, and for their ongoing friendship and encouragement.

Gratitude also goes to Ed Fisher and the 100th James C. Feather Reunion attendees whose participation in the cemetery walk put the author on the path of creating this book. A special thanks to Ed for providing a second set of eyes during the editing stage of the book.

Thanks goes to the many researchers who, over the years and through diligent pursuit of obituaries and details, posted to websites such as Findagrave and Geni information about Feather ancestors. Special recognition goes to Patty Ringer Brown, who manages many of the family entries on the Geni website.

The Bolinger family at the Lenox Store maintains the cemetery records of Lenox Memorial and provided the author access to the map and register.

Janice Sisler Cale provided a basic listing of burials in Lenox Memorial Cemetery in her book, *In Remembrance: Tombstone Readings of Preston County, West Virginia.*

To the late Edna (Davis) Rogers goes a huge hug of gratitude for giving us her exhaustive work, *Genealogy of the Jacob and Mary (Connnoly) Feather Family.*

Thanks to Carrie Wimer of the Ashtabula County District Library, who researched the death of Earl Feathers for this work.

My wife, Ruth, patiently listened to my discoveries as I delved into the stories behind the tombstones. She is my greatest blessing in this earthly life.

My father, Carl J. Feather, for supporting my work and life in so many ways. He is the kind of person that makes me proud to be a Feather.

To the Lord Jesus Christ for once again sustaining me through a book project and giving me the health to complete it.

A Gathering of Feathers

Lenox Memorial Cemetery at Crab Orchard, Preston County, West Virginia.

Crab Orchard Road at the intersection with Lutheran Church Road..

Introduction

The remains of more than 100 individuals with the surname of Feather/Feathers are interred in the Lenox Memorial Cemetery at Lenox, Preston County, West Virginia. The place is truly a "Gathering of Feathers," as were the lively family reunions held at Crab Orchard throughout the 20th century. This book is a compilation of these two gatherings of the quick and dead Feathers.

One of the earliest burials (1832) at Lenox Memorial was Jacob Feather (Vätter), whose grave is marked with a headstone and Revolutionary War bronze plate. His wife, Mary (Connolly/Connery), is likewise honored. The graves of many of their children and grandchildren surround them on the sloping parcel.

Jacob immigrated to the colonies in 1775 from Frankenthal in the Palatinate. He came with his parents—Joseph Christian and Anne Marie Vätter—and sister, Anna Clarissa (Clara), all three of whom are buried in the Schneider Cemetery at Casselman, Somerset County, Pennsylvania.

Lenox Memorials' dozens of tombstones containing a "Feather" moniker attest to the pervasiveness of this family in the rural Crab Orchard/Lenox community during the 19th and 20th centuries. It is hallowed ground for those of us who trace our lineage back to this union of Jacob Vätter and Mary Connoly, who were married in 1791.

The Feather presence in what became West Virginia began with Jacob's purchase of 75 acres along Muddy Creek circa 1803-1805. At that time, this land was in Monongalia County, Virginia, whose courthouse records provide us with documentation of the early land transactions. Between 1809 and 1818, Jacob and Mary purchased up to 314 acres in the Crab Orchard community. Some of this is conjecture based upon tidbits in newspaper and history-book prose rather than courthouse documentation. Preston County land records from its inception in 1818 were destroyed in an 1869 courthouse fire, depriving us of a clear picture of how much land was owned by Jacob

A Gathering of Feathers

Jacob Feather's bronze marker at Lutheran Memorial Cemetery.

and Mary and its exact location. An opaque curtain hangs over those 51 years when it comes to land transactions in Preston County.

The author's book, *My Fathers' Land*, provides a history of Jacob Feather's immigration in 1775, his Revolutionary War service, years in Somerset County, Pennsylvania, and eventual migration to what became West Virginia. It is a family history told through the lands that the Feathers, Harshes, and other Palatinate families owned in West Virginia. Land at a bargain price was the Palatinate immigrant's primary motivation to risk life and resources on the hazardous Atlantic passage. For Jacob and many other young, male Palatines, it also involved risking their lives in a war for the freedom of this newly adopted land.

Extant tax records from 1860, the year Mary died, indicate that many Feather children and grandchildren had established farms and homesteads in the Crab Orchard community, as well as in the areas of Cranesville, Bruceton Mills, and Kingwood. More than 1,000 acres were owned by second- and third-generation Feathers in the Portland/Pleasant districts alone. Yet, driving down Lutheran Church and Coal Lick roads in 2024, the only outwardly visible nods to this family's extensive presence are "Feather Lane" and the stones in this cemetery.

There were many other first- and second-generation immigrants who found the land in Crab Orchard to their liking. Reckarts, Rodeheavers,

Introduction

Mary Connoly Feather's bronze marker at Lutheran Memorial Cemetery.

Haugers, Howdershelts, Ringers, Hartmans, Welches, and Kellys are abundant here, as well. Their labors and stories became intertwined with those of Jacob's and Mary's offspring, and this book briefly explores their histories, as well. In general, it may be said that the young Palatinate males tended to marry women of English and Irish heritage, whose families had migrated from eastern Tidewater Virginia, New England, and eastern Pennsylvania.

Writing about the German Whetsell family in Preston County, Oren Frederic Morton observed in the second volume of his 1914 *A History of Preston County*, that these German pioneers "have intermarried with families of English origin, as in the case of the Felton, Feffers, Taylors and Heradons; with Scotch families, as in the case of the Bucklews and Calverts; also with the French Trembleys and Scotch-Irish Freelands. All this but exemplifies what is generally true of Preston county, the Prestonians of the present day being usually result of the fusion of several different stocks into a new type, that of a genuine American."

A Gathering of Feathers

The Wesley Chapel United Methodist Church continues to serve the community at Crab Orchard, about one mile south of the Lenox Memorial Cemetery. Many of the folks buried in Lenox Memorial had their funeral service held in this chapel. The fancy outhouse behind the church was partially funded from a collection taken at a Feather Family Reunion.

About this book

The first section of this book deals with Feather burials in Lenox Memorial Cemetery on Lutheran Church Road, Lenox (Crab Orchard community). Preston County, West Virginia, United States of America. The author has attempted to provide more than dates and names about these people; unfortunately, in few cases further information that would put "flesh on the bones" could not be located.

As you read these biographies, particularly those from the 19th century, keep in mind that probably 90 percent of the deceased who are profiled were subsistence farmers who had little in way of worldly goods and wealth, and even less in education and professional status. Being honest, owning land from which to take their living, worshiping God, and caring for family were sufficient legacies for them. Comparing their obituaries to those of 21st century Americans, we see a striking difference in the metrics for a meaningful life. For the 19th-century ancestors, character and faith took precedence over accomplishments, degrees, and employment. The earliest obituaries focus on when they became a believer in Christ and were

Introduction

Many Feather funerals were conducted in the Lutheran Church at the cemetery that once bore its name. It is now known as Lenox Memorial Cemetery.

baptized, and how well they followed their savior and gallantly accepted their sufferings "unto death."

For the researcher, the dearth of anecdotes, photographs, diaries, and documentation about the subtle details of their lives is frustrating. What little we can gather about it comes largely from the county's newspapers, *The Preston County Journal* and Kingwood *Argus*. Information about a few of the more prominent folks buried in Lenox Memorial was garnered from county history books and other resources listed in the bibliography.

This book's second section consists of minutes from the Feather Reunions that began in 1909 with an event at the old homestead farm and continued into the 1970s. Admittedly, these summaries border on being trite and repetitious, leaving us thirsting for more details and less fluff. Nevertheless, they provide us with a panorama of a family and nation undergoing cultural and economic vicissitudes that eventually led to the event's demise.

A Gathering of Feathers is intended to supplement *My Fathers' Land* and provide additional information about Feather burials in Lutheran Church Cemetery and the annual Feather reunions (1909-1972). This information was compiled for the 100th reunion of the family of James C. Jr. and Irena

Feather, held July 7, 2024 in the Lenox Community Center. A walk of the cemetery was part of the occasion's very full agenda.

The author's interest in this branch of the family comes through way of adoption. The oldest child of the author's third great-grandparents, Christian and Catherine Feather, was Adam H., a brother to James C. Feather, Jr. James C. and Irena took on the responsibility of raising Adam's underage children after Adam H. died in 1888 (his wife had died the prior year). My great-grandfather, James Walter Feather, spent his teenage years under the instruction and care of James C. and Irena.

James Walter and his brother, Oliver, broke with the family tradition of farming in their early adult years. They found employment in the timber industry, which took them away from their Lenox roots. Oliver went to Randolph County; James Walter wandered to Grant County, where he met his future wife in a timber town. He and this boardinghouse cook from Eglon, Estella Harsh, married and eventually took up farming in Union District, Preston County, but James Walter never forgot his Lenox roots. The Feather reunion records indicate that he returned for the annual family gathering and even served as president of the group. One of his grandchildren told the author that he always contributed a roll of bologna to the reunion's spread of food, the contribution most likely purchased at the Rubenstein Market in Thomas, where he peddled his excess farm products.

A Gathering in Lenox

Lenox Memorial Cemetery was originally known as the Lutheran Church Cemetery, a reference to the house of worship established there in the 1850s. The cemetery is on Lutheran Church Road, which is west of the Brandonville Pike, south of Lenox. There is a sign along Brandonville Pike pointing toward the cemetery, ¼-mile from the highway. Coordinates are 39.55970, -79.59280.

The Lutheran congregation at Crab Orchard was the product of the community's many Palatinate (German) immigrants who settled on the east side of the Cheat River. By 1832, they and adherents of the German Reformed faith had erected a simple, common house of worship on the land that was set aside for a cemetery, the earliest burial in which was 1814. Originally part of the Mount Carmel parish, the Lenox parish—known as "Zion"—was realigned with a new Brandonville parish in 1851. The building, measuring 35-by-45 feet, was dedicated in January 1864.

An article published in *The Preston County Journal* of November 30, 1882, stated that preaching occurred at "the Lutheran Church near this place on last Friday evening by the Rev. W. D. Beerbower, and on Saturday evening by the Rev. J. L. Tressler, of Petersburg, Pa. The church was rededicated to the service of God on Sunday at 10:30 a.m. Mr. Tressler preached the dedicatorial [sic] sermon . . . the repairs of the church cost five hundred dollars, of which one hundred and seventy-six dollars was raised on Sunday at the dedication in a very short time. The people of this place boast of having the nicest church on the Brandonville Circuit."

Despite that impressive showing of support, by 1914 Zion had only 12 baptized, nine confirmed, and nine community members on its rolls. The parish became inactive during World War I, but this landmark house of worship survives under the ownership and care of the Lenox Memorial Cemetery Association.

Important dates and facts

For readers unfamiliar with Preston County and its history, the following information will assist in interpreting the biographies.

⁂ Bedford County, Pennsylvania, where Jacob and Mary Vätter lived prior to coming to Preston County, is northeast of Preston County. Somerset County was created from Bedford in 1795. Milford Township, where the family lived, was in the Somerset County section.

⁂ Preston County was created from Monongalia County, Virginia, in 1818.

⁂ West Virginia, formerly the western lands of Virginia, was admitted to the Union as a separate state on June 20, 1863.

⁂ Virtually all Preston County land records from 1818–1869 were claimed by an arson fire. County land records from the era when it was part of Monongalia County are available in that courthouse in Morgantown.

⁂ Kingwood is the county seat of Preston County.

⁂ Crab Orchard (one word in old newspaper accounts) is located in the area south of the Lutheran Church Cemetery, with its center being Wesley Chapel on Coal Lick Road, which intersects the Brandonville Pike at a ghost town once known as Willey. Coal Lick takes a sharp turn to the south at its intersection with Crab Orchard and Lutheran Church roads. Coal Lick's south end is at Route 26, near Albright. Refer to the map on page 16.

⁂ Major waterways in this area are Lick Run, a tributary of Roaring Creek; Crab Orchard Run; and Muddy Creek. All of these flow to the Cheat River.

⁂ Albright was the post office at which most Crab Orchard residents received their mail, thus their address on death and marriage certificates was often given as "Albright." Lenox is the closest town, however.

⁂ Drift, shaft, and strip mines were extensive on these lands in the late-19th and 20th centuries. Strip mining destroyed virtually all heritage structures once associated with these farms. In many cases, this destructive mining practice changed the topography of the land itself.

⁂ Some members of the Feather family chose to add an "s" to their surname. Those entries are included where it is known they descended from Jacob and Mary.

⁂ Most of the people profiled in this work were subsistence farmers. In the first generation after Jacob, most received only a rudimentary education provided in a one-room schoolhouse at Crab Orchard or Lenox. Parents paid the teacher's salary and school was in session only during the months the farm could operate without the children's labors.

❦ The cemetery under consideration goes by several names: Crab Orchard Lutheran Cemetery, Craborchard Cemetery, Lutheran Cemetery, and Lenox Memorial Cemetery. They are all the same place.

❦ Other cemeteries in the region where Feather descendants are buried include Albright, Maplewood (Kingwood), Parnell (Cuzzart), and, in Eglon, Maple Spring and Eglon Community.

❦ Throughout this work, reference is made to Roger's *Genealogy* book. The full title of this work, which appears to be out of print, is *Genealogy of the Jacob and Mary (Connoly) Feather Family of Preston County, West Virginia*. Copyrighted by Edna (Davis) Rogers, it was published by Feather Genealogic Company, Morgantown, West Virginia, and printed by McClain Printing Company, Parsons, West Virginia, 1980. The printer had no current contact information for the copyright holder.

❦ As you read about the marriages that occurred between Feather "cousins," keep in mind that Crab Orchard was a small community and the pool of eligible mates was quite small. Indeed, as Edna (Davis) Rogers observes in her *Feather Genealogy* book, "Whenever persons have a common ancestor, no matter how remote, they are related to each other; therefore, it is not surprising to learn that most of us with Preston County ancestors are cousins."

Establishing lineage

This work is based upon the family of Jacob and Mary (Connoly/Connery) Feather (Vätter) and their children. Jacob's parents were Joseph Christian (1733–1799) & Ann Marie Wismanns Vätter (1737–1800), who are buried in the Schneider Cemetery, Casselman, Pennsylvania. Mary's parents are unknown. the children of Jacob and Mary *who survived to adulthood* were:

❦ John Solomon (1794–1870), who married Mary Ervin. They had extensive land holdings on Cheat Hill, Roaring Creek, the Reckart farm, and Cheat Hill—more than 1,000 acres (1861);

⚜ Jacob Feather Jr. (1796–1847), who married Mary Sisler, Susan Mah Wolfe, and Mary Silgens. His lands were on Green Run near Kingwood;

⚜ Eve Catherine (1798–1897), who married John Lewis;

⚜ Adam Feather (1800–1884), who married Mary Summers and Sabra Eusebia Summers (sisters). He owned the homestead on Roaring Creek;

⚜ Christian Feather (1802–1883), who married Catharine Dunham; he owned a toal of 68 acres straddling Pleasant and Portland districts;

⚜ Zaccheus Feather (1805–1891), who married Elizabeth Ervin. He owned 46 acres on Roaring Creek and 110 acres on Conner Run;

⚜ Sarah Feather (1807–1893), who married James Beatty and eventually relocated to Iowa;

⚜ James Feather (1809–1886), who married Catharine Jane Lewis and Christeen Summers. James had 145 1/2 acres at Crab Orchard;

⚜ Jane Virginia Feather (1812–1876), who married Israel Shaffer. They lived in the Kingwood area and are not represented in Lenox Memorial;

⚜ Joseph B. Feather (1816–1896), who married Lydia Hartman. Joseph was a Bruceton Mills resident and successful businessman. He had extensive land holdings in the Pine Swamp/Cranesville area and on Muddy Creek.

Conventions and methodology

In the entries that follow, the lineage of the individual is provided immediately after the name and dates. A name that is **bold-faced** on first reference indicates a burial in Lenox Memorial Cemetery.

Throughout the work, females who lost the Feather surname but are buried in Lenox Memorial are recognized with bold attributes and discussed in the text, but may not have a listing. The individuals who are listed have Feather as their surname or married a Feather. Burials of infants and children bearing the Feather surname are under the Infants & Children entry only and are recognized under their parents' entries, where applicable.

In the index, women are listed by their maiden name, with their married name in parentheses. In listings of children, the "Feather" surname is assumed for males but listed before the married surname for females.

The list of names was compiled from the Findagrave website by searching for entries with "Feather" in the name, from Janet Sisler Cale's *Preston County Cemeteries* book, and by walking the cemetery in April and May 2024. The

Along Lutheran Church Road, Crab Orchard, 2024. Amish families have moved into the community, reviving old farms, and returning horses and buggies to the byways.

map and listing of burials for the cemetery, maintained at the Lenox Store, were consulted, as well. The author was conservative in assigning section, row, and grave numbers to the listings. Some do not have headstones or what remains of them is illegible. Others are simply listed as "unknown" or "Feather," in which case it would be a guess as to who is buried there. The name "Mary" is used on several listings without an adjacent spouse, and there are many "Marys" in the family, so we can't know for sure which one is being referenced.

For those who want to dive deeper in the cemetery records, the map is provided in high resolution on the author's website. Access it at https://thefeathercottage.com/a-gathering-of-feathers/.

Lenox Memorial Cemetery map

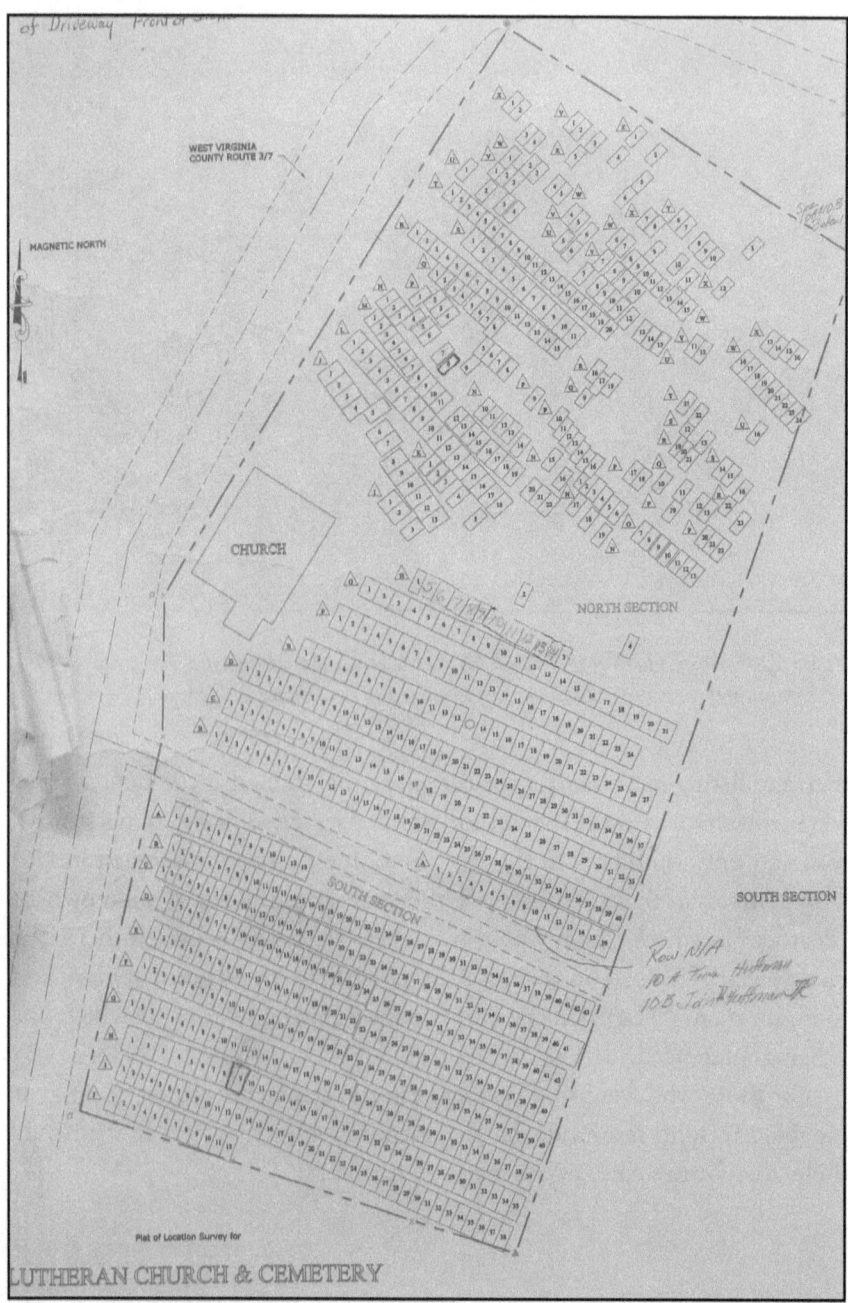

Lenox Memorial Cemetery is laid out in north and south sections, with the north being the oldest. Rows are designated with an "N" or "S," followed by the row letter. A high resolution version of the map is at https://thefeathercottage.com/a-gathering-of-feathers/.

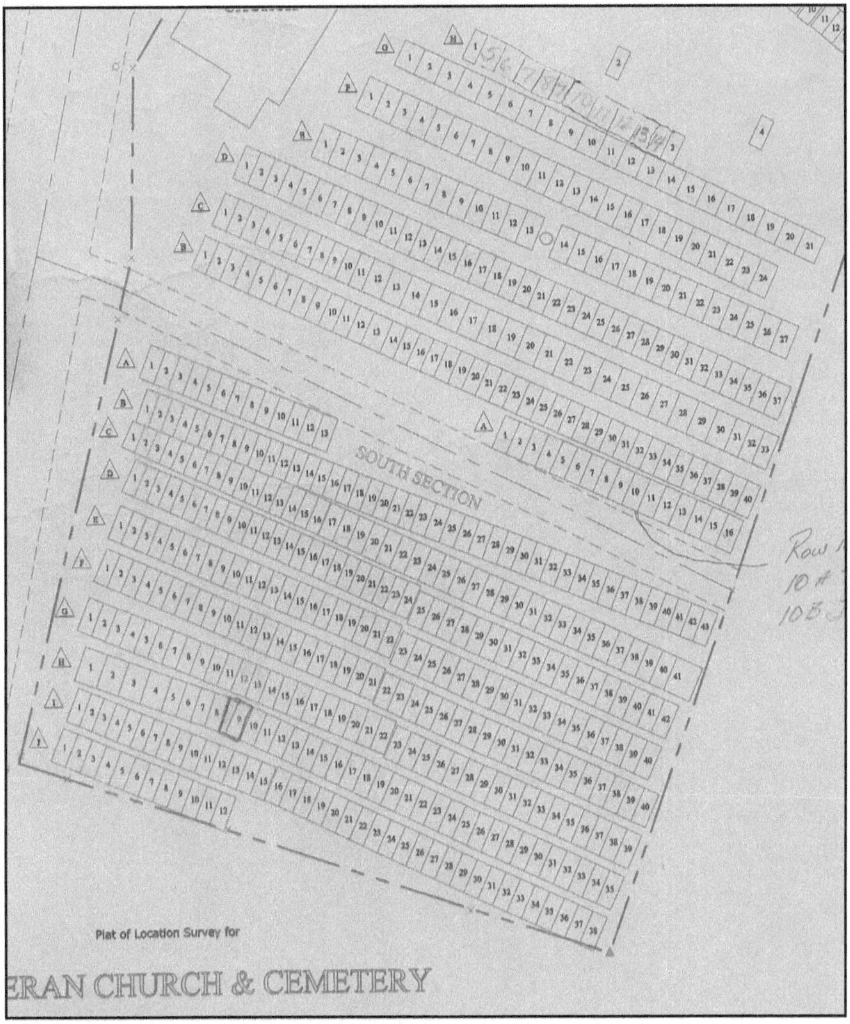

Lenox Memorial Cemetery map, south section

South section of Lenox Memorial Cemetery. These maps are available at https://thefeathercottage.com/a-gathering-of-feathers/.

Lenox Memorial Cemetery map, north section

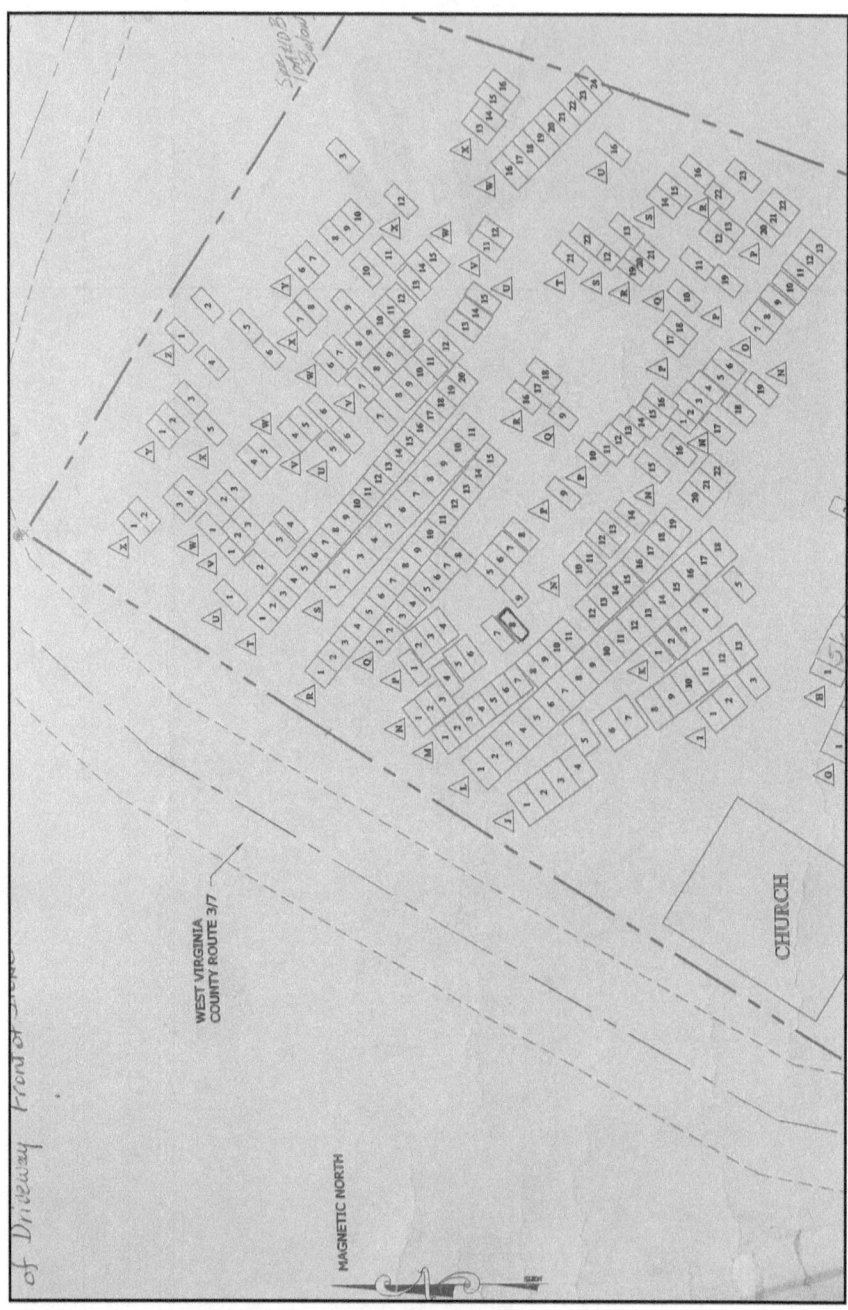

The north end of the cemetery, where most of the Feather burials occurred. Rows are marked using letters of the alphabet. These locators are included in each profile when it was possible to establish a positive reference to the limited information in the cemetery records.

Preston County map, 1876

An 1873 map of Preston County, West Virginia. The Feathers settled in the southern section of Pleasant District and much of Portland in the area of Crab Orchard, Willey and Muddy Creek Post Office.

Crab Orchard map

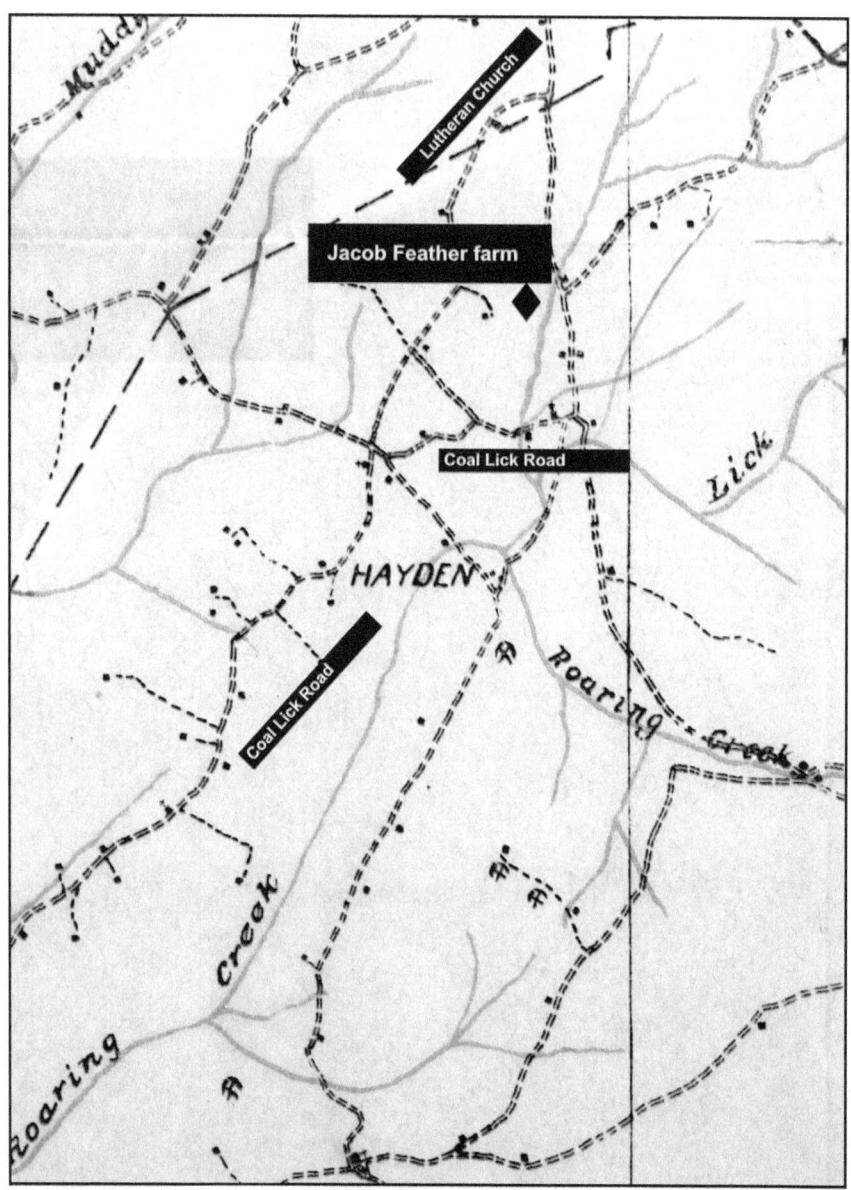

This map shows the communities of Lenox and Crab Orchard that are often referred to in the text. Jacob's and Mary's land was on "Little Roaring Creek" as indicated on the map. The cemetery was north of this land; the Wesley Chapel M.E. Church to the south. The map is a detail of a Preston County map published by Robert D. Hennen & E.S. Taylor of Morgantown, W.Va., in 1917. W.Va. and Regional History Center.

Feathers in Lenox Memorial Cemetery

Adah Blanche Ringer Feather
August 28, 1886–August 16, 1958
North section, family headstone with smaller individual stones

The wife of **Brantson Claude Feather,** Adah was a daughter of **Harrison "Harry"** (1850–1921) and **Virginia Ellen Cuppett Ringer** (1858–1948). Adah was born at Lenox and died in Kingwood.

Her father was a son of **John** (1823–1884) and **Susan Bishoff Ringer** (1824–1899). John Ringer was the son of Philip, one of five brothers who migrated from Mercer County, Pennsylvania, to Preston County, Virginia, in 1832. Their father was a German immigrant. Philip lived in the area of Centenary, Pleasant District. Their presence pervades the story of Preston County and the Feather family; the index of Roger's *Genealogy* book lists nearly five dozen persons with that surname.

According to Wiley's *History of Preston County*, The "old Philip Ringer farm" contained 450 acres. The Ringer mill was on land formerly owned by John Green and located between the Brandonville and Kingwood turnpikes, one mile from Josephine Furnace. Many Feather descendants also lived, farmed, and attended school in this neighborhood.

Susan Bishoff Ringer (1824–1899) was a member of the Evangelical Lutheran Church at Lenox. Her parents were **Henry** (1798–1872) and **Lydia Elizabeth Albright Miller Bishoff** (1803–1891). The Bishoffs/Bischoffs and Albrights were pioneer families of Preston County. Henry's father, Johannes Bischoff III (1773–1823) was born in Adams County, Pennsylvania, and migrated to Preston County. He is buried in the Aurora Pioneer Cemetery, Aurora (unmarked grave). The Bishoff's immigrant ancestor, Johannes

Heinrich (Johannes Bischoff III's grandfather), was born 1713 in Germany and immigrated to Philadelphia aboard the *Samuel* when he was 20.

The Cuppets (Adah's maternal grandmother) were of German extraction, as well. Their immigrant ancestor was John Cuppy (1730–1802). Adah's Cuppett ancestors migrated to Glade Farms, Preston County, from Bedford County, Pennsylvania, circa 1822. Jefferson Cuppett (1832–1896), Adah's maternal grandfather, was a businessman who lived near Valley Point.

Adam Feather
April 25 1800–July 30, 1884
Lineage: Jacob & Mary
Row North P / 17

Adam Feather, Jacob's and Mary's fifth child, was born in Somerset County, Pennsylvania. He married **Mary Summers** (1804–1827), who was a daughter of John Summers and Mary Frankhouser Summers. After Mary's death, Adam married her sister, **Sabra Eusebia Summers** (1807–1858). He had two children by Mary and seven by Sabra Eusebia.

Based upon the birth locations of their children, Adam and Mary lived in Maryland during their marriage, which ended with her death in 1827. He relocated to Pennsylvania after marrying Sabra Eusebia. Circa 1845, he returned to Preston County to work and live on the homestead farm with his widowed mother. It appears that his older brother, John Solomon, originally inherited the homestead farm from his father. But, in the mid-1840s, John S. purchased the neighboring Reckart farm, which drew Adam and Sabra Eusebia to Preston County to work the land. Their last child, Sabra Jane Feather, was born in Preston County November 16, 1851. She married Rufus Benton Rodeheaver.

Adam's death announcement was published on page 3 of *The Preston County Journal* of August 7, 1884:

> FEATHER—Adam Feather mention of whose death was made in our last impression, was born April 25, 1800 and was therefore in his 85th year. He had been a member of the Lutheran Church for over 50 years, and after suffering intensely for over a month he

died in great peace. "Uncle Ad," as he was familiarly known, lived, we believe, all his life in the Craborchard. His father, Jacob Feather, who was born in Germany, came to Preston County from Somerset County, Pa., in 1789 (incorrect date), and shortly afterward settled upon the farm where Adam lived at the time of his death. The family has been one of remarkable longevity. Of the brothers of the deceased, John lived to be 76 years and Christian 80, and of those living are James and Ezekiel who have passed their threescore and ten years, and Joseph, who is in his sixties. The others of the family, Sarah, Jane, Eve and Jacob lived to a good old age. Mr. Feather was the father of the Rev. Joseph B. Feather, of the M. E. Conference of W. Va., and Mr. John S. Feather, of Willey.

Adam H. Feather
October 20, 1841–April 21, 1888
Lineage: Christian & Catherine, Jacob & Mary
Row North Q/ 8

Adam H. was the oldest son of **Christian** and **Catharine Dunham Feather**. His small marker only provides information about his Civil War military service, "Co. B 14 WVa. Inf."

He and at least two of his Feather cousins enlisted in the 14th W. Va. organized at Camp Wiley, Wheeling, in August and September 1862. He served in Company B, which consisted of men from Preston County. Other Feathers enlisted in this company were **Daniel C. Feather, son of Zaccheus** and **Elizabeth**, and John B., son of Abraham and Elizabeth, grandson of **John Solomon** and **Mary**.

The company fought its first major battle at Cloyd's Mountain in Virginia, May 9, 1864, a fierce engagement exacerbated by the Confederates' disdain for companies of Virginians who had stayed loyal to the Union and formed a new state. A poorly timed order to retreat resulted in many Company B members being shot or captured.

The cousins were imprisoned at the infamous Andersonville, Georgia, hellhole. Daniel C. and Adam H. were eventually exchanged for Confederate prisoners. John B. died in Andersonville Prison September 5, 1864, at the age of 18. He is buried in the Andersonville National Cemetery.

Adam H. returned to civilian life at Crab Orchard in the spring of 1865. He married **Mary Jane Broomhall** on August 27 of that year. Mary Jane and Adam had six children; two of them died in infancy/childhood and are likely buried in Lenox Memorial without markers. Consumption (tuberculosis) swept through the family in the 1880s, claiming children and parents alike. The surviving four children were orphaned. Their children are listed under Mary Jane's entry.

Adam's brother and his wife, **James C. Jr.** and **Irena,** took on the responsibility of raising his orphans and caring for Adam's small farm, now part of the Larry Feather farm. Irena purchased Adam's land in a chancery case settlement for $155.00. Court documents arising from that case indicate that Adam was heavily indebted and had lived a very difficult life trying to make a living from this small parcel. Further, his health was probably impaired from illnesses/injuries resulting from his military service and imprisonment.

Alva Clifton Feather
1873–March 5, 1933
Lineage: James & Martha, John Solomon & Mary, Jacob & Mary
Row North C / 28

A son of **James Connery** and **Martha V. Rodeheaver Feather, Alva Clifton Feather** took Nettie Herndon for his first wife. He married his second, **Alta** (Atta on stone) **Lovingstein,** in 1897; she was 25, he was 34. His siblings were **Harvey Arlington Feather** (1864–1939); Alitia May "Allie" Feather Crane (1866–1944), Parnell Cemetery; and Bessie Ada Feather Hayden (1872–1957), Westmoreland County Memorial Park, Greensburg, Pennsylvania.

West Virginia Births, 1853–1930, accessed on the FamilySearch website, notes one birth to Alva and Alta, Morris Stanhope Feathers, born September 23, 1904, in Keyser, Mineral County, W.Va. Rogers' *Genealogy* does not recognize the birth. The 1900 U.S. Census places Alva and Atta living in Keyser with Alva employed as a carpenter. His occupation was the same in the 1920 U.S. Census, but the family was living in Terra Alta and their son, "Norris," was age 14. It appears that they were living in his parents' household at the time; James Connery reported his occupation as farmer.

Norris died February 15, 1961, in Los Angeles, California. His wife, Bernyce Hill Feather, of Harrison County, died December 15, 1947, at the age of 40. They had two children, James C. (wife Carol), and Margaret A. "Peg" Feather Egensperger (1834–2014), who served as mayor of Mayfield Heights, Ohio. A marriage license was issued to Norris and Marie M. Grucza in Cuyahoga County, Ohio, in December 1953. Norris is buried in Forest Lawn Memorial Park, Los Angeles County, California, but Bernyce, who died in Cleveland Heights, Ohio, is buried in Harrison County, W.Va.

Amanda (Jane) E. Feather Peaslee
January 4, 1852–1930
Lineage: Zaccheus & Elizabeth; Jacob & Mary
Row North N / 1

A daughter of **Zaccheus** and **Elizabeth Ervin Feather**, **Amanda E. Feather** married **John K. Peaslee** (1845–1906). The 1880 U.S. Census places Amanda and John in Pleasant District and "keeping house" as her occupation. John was a farmer.

They had two children, **Howard Franklin** (1873–1942), who married Leeta May Sisler (1877–1972), and **Benjamin Zeke** (1875–1920), who married **Charlotte Dessie Hileman** (1873–1940). Howard Franklin lived on the family farm in Lenox.

The Peaslees were "Yankees from New Hampshire," Quakers who came to America in the 1600s. John K. was born in New Wilmot, New Hampshire, a son of Benjamin Wells and Hepsibah Pike Peaslee. He had seven brothers, all of whom settled in Etam, Preston County.

Amanda Jane Ringer Feather
November 8, 1860–March 31, 1937
Row North R / 2

Amanda Jane Ringer Feather was the daughter of **John Ringer** (1823–1884) and **Susan Bishoff Ringer** (1824–1899). She married **Martin Luther Feather**, son of **Zaccheus** and **Elizabeth Feather** (Roger's *Genealogy*, inverts Martin Luther's first and middle name.) Their one child, **Bertha B. Feather**, (1883–1909), married **Harvey Calvin Moss** (1882–1957). The death date was never added to his stone—and with good reason. But first, Bertha's story.

Numerous briefs in local newspapers during the years leading up to the wedding suggest that Bertha was a popular young lady who enjoyed a very active social life in Preston County. Harvey, according to news briefs in 1907 editions of *The Preston County Journal*, worked as a clerk in the department store of Harley & Gustkey in Independence and was an agent for the B&O Railroad at Independence and Terra Alta.

Martin and Amanda were married July 15, 1908. *The Preston County Journal* reported on their wedding in its August 6, 1908, edition.

> **A Pretty Home Wedding**
>
> Mr. Harvey Moss and Miss Bertha Feather were united in the holy bond of matrimony on July 15, at the home of the bride's at 8:30 p.m. by Rev. J.W. Engle of Terra Alta.
>
> The bride wore a beautiful dress of white silk with a boquet [sic] of carnations. Miss Ada ringer played the wedding march while the happy couple escorted by W.A. Whitehair and Miss Isa Kelly, marched from the rear to the front of the house where the guests were waiting.
>
> The groom presented the bride with a handsome ring as a wedding ring and Rev. Engle officiated with the ring ceremony.
>
> Many congratulations were extended the happy wedded couple after which they were all escorted to the tables upon the lawn to partake of refreshments which were so bountifully and so generously offered by the parents. There were 118 served with ice cream, cake, banannas [sic], oranges and water melons, after which they departed for their homes. The happy couple were presented many handsome and costly presents which were received graciously with many thanks. Last of all the serenaders [sic] made their appearance and gave an old time serenade followed by their congratulations, after which they were served with plenty at the expense of Mr. Feather.

The following spring, Bertha and Harvey were expecting their first child. From page 2 of *The Preston County Journal* of May 13, 1909:

> Mrs. H.C. Moss Dead—Mrs. H.C. Moss, the young wife of the assistant agent of the Baltimore & Ohio railroad at Terra Alta, died Friday evening at her husband's home of a kidney affection [sic],

Harvey & Bertha Moss wedding, continued

aggravated if not induced by approaching motherhood. She was the only child of Mr. and Mrs. Martin Luther Feather, of Lenox, and would have been twenty-six years old the fourteenth day of next August.

Mrs. Moss had been ill for several weeks, and last Friday suddenly became worse. A series of convulsions brought her to the verge of death, and a consultation of physicians was held. It was evident that the only hope lay in an operation, and this hope was very slight. Shortly after noon the operation was performed by Dr. W. F. Daily, of Terra Alta, assisted by Dr. Legge, of Oakland, and Dr. B. F. Scott, of Terra Alta. The one chance in a million for life was against the patient and at six o'clock, without having regained consciousness, she died. Her parents were with the young husband at her bedside.

Mr. and Mrs. Moss were married at the Feather home in Lenox by Rev. J.W. Engle, pastor of the large and influential Methodist Episcopal church of Terra Alta, July 15, 1908. They went to Terra Alta immediately to make their home. Mrs. Moss was a young woman of ideal Christian character and was sincerely loved by many friends.

The funeral was held Sunday, the day set apart by proclamation of Governor Glasscock in honor of the Mothers, living and dead, of West Virginia. Services were held at the house in Terra Alta in the morning by the Rev. Engle, and the body was then conveyed by Undertaker A.R. Fike to the Lutheran church in the Crab Orchard, where additional services took place. It was one of the largest funerals ever known in the county. A score or more carriages went out from Terra Alta, and the whole countryside attended. The interment was at the Crab Orchard Lutheran cemetery.

Twenty years after Bertha was buried in Row N/R, grave 4, Lenox Memorial, Harvey Calvin Moss was living in Baltimore, Maryland, and working as an insurance agent for Prudential Life. He was married to Minnette H. Kondner. She died November 5, 1936. He married again, to Ethel Harrison. She died May 24, 1949. Widowed three times, Harvey C. Moss died in December 1957. He is buried in Elder 176 plot, Loudon Park Cemetery, Baltimore, where Minnette and Ethel are buried, as well.

His presence in Lenox Memorial is in name only.

Amanda Jane Albright Feather
January 27, 1850–July 31, 1912
Row North J / 4

Amanda Jane Albright Feather was the wife of **David O. Feather**. Her parents were Daniel and Sarah "Salome" Engle Albright.

Two Albright brothers, David (1785–1858) and Daniel (1799–1858), arrived in Monongalia County from York, Pennsylvania, shortly before the War of 1812. Their father, Bernhardt Albright (1750–1815) was born in Saxony, Germany. His wife was Anna Maria Speck (1756–1840), born in Bavaria, Germany.

Amanda's father, also named Daniel, was a son of the settler Daniel, who first settled in Crab Orchard, then later moved to Cranesville. David settled in the area where Roaring Creek joins the Cheat River, north of Albright, which takes its name from these brothers.

Amanda's father was born near Guseman on July 10, 1826 and died in Terra Alta April 17, 1898. Her mother was born April 21, 1831, and died April 13, 1889 from a stroke. Amanda Jane was the couple's firstborn child; there were nine children born to the couple; Amanda was the only one to marry a Feather or be buried in Lenox Memorial.

Her father was a Civil War veteran, having served as a sergeant in Company F of the 17th W.Va. Infantry. According to Daniel Albright's obituary, he and his wife lived on High Street in Terra Alta and was a highly respected citizen of the community. He remarried July 1, 1890, to Jennie Poling of St. George, Tucker County, and had four more children before dying in 1898.

David O. and Amanda Feather had only one child, Clinton Daniel Feather (1870–1932), who is buried in Maplewood Cemetery.

Andrew Elias Feather,
December 12, 1865–April 4, 1947
Lineage: Isaac B. & Elizabeth (Reckart), Zaccheus & Mary (Ervin),
Jacob & Mary
Row North E / 17

Andrew Elias Feather married **Dallie A. Kelly**, in 1896 (the county records recorded the bride and groom as "Dallia A. Kelly" and "Andrew E. Feaster."

She died in 1919 at the age of 42, and Andrew remarried, to Julia (Deahl) DeBerry, whose husband, Clark Martin DeBerry, died in 1922. She had one child, Dempsey Ernest (1904–1962) by Clark Martin; Andrew Elias did not have any children by either wife. His second wife is buried at Parnell Cemetery, Cuzzart, next to her first husband.

Andrew owned 64 acres on Muddy Creek, Pleasant District, in 1910. On the 1930 U.S. Census, Andrew listed his occupation as a farmer. His household consisted of his wife, Julia, and a step-son, Gilbert DeBerry, 22, who also was a farmer. Their neighbors included David C. Feather, Daniel DeBerry and Thomas Feather Jr., as well as several Rodeheaver families.

Andrew died at his home near Cuzzart following a lengthy illness. Dallie is buried next to Andrew in grave 18.

Anna May Lee Feather
May 27, 1896–November 30, 1985
Row South C / 13

The wife of **Paul Harold Feather**, **Anna May Lee** was born in Davis, Tucker County, W.Va., and died in Kingwood. Her parents were Samuel Ellsworth Lee (1863–1950) and Elma Jane Nedrow Lee (1871–1934), who are buried in Beech Run Cemetery. Samuel was a farmer in Pleasant District.

Anna May's paternal grandfather was Nicholas J. Lee (1835–1916), who was born in Preston County and married Lydia Bower (1833–1871), and Sevilla "Savilla" Liston (1848–1941). He was a farmer.

Anna May had a brother, William F. Lee, who died at the age of 12. *The Preston County Journal* of February 15, 1906, describes the incident.

> **Accidentally killed. Young man steps in front of train and is killed—two other young men badly hurt.**
>
> Last Saturday evening a distressing accident occurred just below Riggs Factory at Terra Alta, in which a son of Sam Lee was killed. Young Lee, along with two sons of Samuel Nedrow's were on their way to Terra Alta, and they met a train, not knowing there was a train coming in the opposite direction they stepped over to the other track and were overtaken by the train. The Lee boy was killed, being

terribly mangled, while the two Nedrow boys were thrown off the track and rendered unconscious for several hours.

William F. Lee is buried in Beech Run Cemetery, Preston County.

Anna S. Kelley Feather
1862–1930
Row North S / 15

The wife of **John Mark Feather** is identified in Rogers' *Genealogy* as **Anna Sirissi Kelly,** but the marriage license was issued to John M. Feather, 22, and Annie R. Kelly, 28 (September 1897). According to Rogers, she was born September 18, 1862, and her husband was born February 1, 1875, an age difference of almost 13 years, not the six years recorded on the marriage license. The origin/meaning of her middle name is a mystery. It can be a Thai or Spanish surname, suggesting Anna was previously married.

She was a daughter of **John T.** and **Martha A. Rodeheaver Kelly** (1839–1909) of Lenox. John T. died May 30, 1875, but his birth date has not been established.

Anna's husband was a farmer, his land being in Crab Orchard near the **Joseph B. Feather/Elmer B. Feather** farm. The 100-acre Roaring Creek farm was in Anna S.'s name. In the 1910 U.S. Census, they reported one son, 8-year-old **Earl Smith Feather(s),** in the household.

When the 1930 U.S. Census was taken, they were living in Morgantown. Anna died later that year.

Anna's brother, Winfield Scott Kelly (1861–1920), married Sarah Feather, a daughter of **Zaccheus** and **Elizabeth.** Winfield was a farmer in Lenox; while supervising a harvest on the farm in August 1920, he suffered sunstroke. He was sent to Baltimore for treatment, which was unsuccessful, and died a few days later.

Atta (Alta) Lovenstein Feather
1872–1930
Row North C / 29

Atta (Alta) Lovenstein was the second wife of **Alva C. Feather** and a daughter of David (1832–1888) and Mariah J. Houston Lovenstein. Her sisters were Esther, Bertha, Hannah, and Francine; brothers were Charles, Andrew, Archibald, and Marcus. Her parents are buried in Terra Alta Cemetery. Her father was a telegraph operator at Terra Alta for more than 25 years and died from stomach cancer. Although her stone spells her name "Atta," Roger's *Genealogy* and her marriage license used "Alta."

Benjamin Gilbert Feather
April 16, 1877–March 21, 1918
Lineage: Isaac B. & Elizabeth (Reckart), Zaccheus & Elizabeth (Ervin),
Mary & Jacob
Row North E / 12

Benjamin Gilbert Feather married **Effie E. Livengood** on March 16, 1904, at Cuzzart. They had four children: Dale Lloyd, Bertha Mildred, Paul Dana (1909–1981), and Virginia E.

A death certificate for a Benjamin G. Feather is on file in the District of Columbia records. The certificate shows his occupation as a farmer and residence as Cranesville.

From *The Preston County Journal* of March 28, 1918:

> Preston County Man Succumbs to Injury: Washington, D.C., March 21 (1918)—Twelve days after receiving injuries in an altercation at Cranesville, Preston County, W.Va., Benjamine G. Feather, 40, died in a hospital here today. He was a brother of F. J. Feather, bank cashier, also of Preston county.

We credit the above dispatch to the *Wheeling Intelligencer*. Will some of our correspondents enlighten us as to the truthfulness of the above dispatch(?) We know of no F. J. Feather, bank cashier, in this county.

Roger's *Genealogy* does not list an "F. J. Feather" as one of Benjamin's siblings. The closest match would be Thomas Jefferson Feather. No report of the alleged altercation at Cranesville was published in the county's newspaper in the weeks prior to his death, nor was an obituary published.

Brantson Claude Feather
June 25, 1885–August 3, 1958
Lineage: Elmer & Minerva Bell (Feather), Joseph B. & Mary (Atkinson), Adam & Sabra Eusebia (Summers), Jacob & Mary
North section, family headstone with smaller individual stones

B. Claude Feather was the only son of **Elmer B.** and **Minerva Feather**. He was born June 25, 1885, in Lenox, and married **Adah Blanche Ringer**, daughter of **Harrison** and **Virginia Ellen Ringer**, on October 20, 1909.

Adah Blanche also was an only child, and the wedding was a major event for Crab Orchard. From *The Preston County Journal* of October 28, 1909:

> **Married:** At the home of the bride's parents, Mr. and Mrs. Harrison Ringer, near Lenox, at eight thirty o'clock Wednesday evening October 20, 1909, a very pretty wedding was celebrated, when Miss Adah Blanche became the bride of Mr. B. Claude Feather.
>
> Miss Isa Ringer, cousin of the bride played the bridal chorus from Lohengrin as the bridal procession led by Miss Nita Peaslee, foster sister of the groom, and Mr. Klet Forman best man . . . entered the parlors where the ceremony was performed in a very impressive manner by the Rev. Jos. B Feather, grandfather of the groom. Quite a number of the relatives and near friends were present.
>
> After the ceremony and congratulations were over, the party went to the dining-room where delicious refreshments were served. All the arrangements were perfect and passed off without a hitch. Quite a number of very nice presents were received. At a late hour

the company dispersed to their homes to meet the next day at the home of the groom's parents, where a grand reception awaited them. The bride and groom are very well known and popular young people.

The groom is the only son of Mr. and Mrs. Elmer Feather and the bride is the only daughter of Mr. and Mrs. Harrison Ringer. On Friday morning they left for Morgantown, Fairmont and Moundsville to visit friends. The best wishes of their host of friends go with them.

The couple had three children. Their son, **Willis B.**, died in infancy. His stone identifies him as "son of B. C. & A. B. Feather." A daughter, Mary Waunita (1915–2009), married Preston County businessman and farmer Ward Fike Thomas. She is buried in Shady Grove Union Cemetery, Brandonville. Her sister, Pauline Virginia, married Walter J. Kelly and lived in Camden, Maine.

The 1910 U.S. Census identified Brantson as a public school teacher. He also worked the family farm. B. Claude's father, **Elmer B. Feather,** owned the homestead property that his father, **Joseph B.** had purchased from **Adam Feather,** Jacob's and Mary's son. Brantson Claude sold the farm for $4,000 to Archie Dewitt in 1949 but continued to work the land. During the years the land was owned and controlled by Dewitt, it suffered the from the damaging practice of strip mining, which resulted in the destruction of whatever homestead structures may have remained at the time of B. Claude's passing. Foundations of a barn and possibly a machine shop and cabin were on the land as of 2023.

The Feather Reunion was held the Sunday following B. Claude's death in 1958. The reunion minutes attribute his cause of death to a farming accident, but no newspaper documentation of that incident could be located. His death certificate recorded his occupation as farmer.

Obituary from *The Preston County Journal* of September 11, 1958:

> B. Claude Feather, 73, of Clifton Mills, died Wednesday night, Sept. 3 at his home. A native of Albright, he was born June 25, 1885. His wife, Adah B. Feather, died last August 16.

He was a member of Wesley Chapel Methodist Church and Independent Order of Odd Fellows, Kingwood Lodge No. 107.

Survivors are two daughters, Mrs. Ward Thomas of Bruceton and Mrs. Walter Kelly of Camden, Maine, and four grandchildren. Services were held at 2:30 p.m. Saturday by the Rev. Harry Young . . .

Carl Dakin Feather
January 13, 1905–January 19, 1982
Lineage: Ezra A. & Flora M. (Park), Jacob F. & Nancy (Wilhelm), Zaccheus & Elizabeth (Ervin), Jacob & Mary
Row South B / 20

Carl Dakin Feather was born in Magnolia, Putnam County, Illinois. His mother, Flora M. Park, was the second wife of **Ezra A. Feather**.

Ezra's first wife was Clara P. Guseman (1863–1896), who "was in poor health a number of years," according to her obituary of April 27, 1896. She died in Clark County, Missouri, and is buried in Williamstown, Lewis County, Missouri. She and Ezra had two children: Perry Alva Feather (1889–1983) and **Clarence Theodore Feather** (1892–1973).

His first child with Preston County native Flora M. Park, (1884–1970), was **Lena Blanche**. She died in infancy. The home was blessed with **Carl Dakin** in 1905. His younger siblings, Hazel (1908–1914) and Orval (1906–1914), who were born in Menota, Illinois, died in childhood and are buried in Hope Town Cemetery, Lostant, LaSalle County, Illinois.

Ezra died February 15, 1914, and was buried next to Orval and Hazel. Flora died in 1970. She never remarried and stayed in Illinois.

Carl D. moved to West Virginia as a young man. In the 1930 U.S. Census, he was living with his half-brother, Clarence Theodore, in the Portland District. Both were farmers.

The documentation suggests that Carl never married. Half-brother Perry A. Feather is buried in Terra Alta Cemetery.

Catherine Dunham Feather
July 15, 1821–August 20, 1898
Row North P / 8

Catherine Dunham married **Christian Feather** (1802–1883), date unrecorded. Catherine was 19 years younger than Christian.

Her parents were Jacob (1794–1865) and Catherine Goodnight (Gutknecht) Dunham (1794–1870), who were married October 21, 1819, in Berkeley County, Virginia. Inexplicably, Catherine, their first child, was born in Wymps Gap, Pennsylvania. The Fayette County landmark/town is on the Preston/Monongalia counties border.

By 1824, when their son Jacob Mackey was born, the family was back in Berkeley County, where their next three children—Amos, Samuel Goodnight, and David—were born. Circa 1836, Jacob sold his land in Virginia and moved to Fayette County, Ohio, where their last child, David Dunham (1836–1909), arrived. After several years in Ohio, the family relocated to Tipton County, Indiana.

How did Christian and Catherine, who was born in Wymp's Gap and grew up in Berkeley County, come to know each other with these large gaps in distance and age? While we do not have a marriage date for the couple, perhaps Catharine had no interest in moving west with her family and chose to stay behind in the mountains, which would have necessitated marrying someone already established there and able to support her.

An intriguing scenario is that Christian's family and that of Catherine's maternal grandfather became acquainted in Germany and maintained contact in the New World. Her maternal great-grandfather was Johann Leonard Berkheimer (1722–1804), who immigrated to America with his parents and siblings from Frankenthal, Rhineland-Palatinate, when he was child. Their journey was aboard the *Samuel* and they arrived in Philadelphia August 11, 1732. Her paternal grandfather, Christian Gutknecht (1722–1795), was born in Alsace, France, near the Palatinate region (his ancestors were from Switzerland but died in France). In the 18th century, the entire region was in political and religious flux, forcing families to frequently relocate to a more accommodating protectorate in accordance with the winds of war and religious persecution.

Whatever the circumstances that brought them together, it was fortuitous for descendants of Jacob and Catherine Goodnight Dunham, who would become the fourth great-grandparents of Barack Obama Jr. Descendants of Christian and Catherine can claim this common ancestry with a U.S. president, as well.

Christian and Catherine had a penchant for naming their children after Christian's aunts and uncles (Mary Jane, Adam, Jacob, James, Sarah, and Joseph B.). They favored the middle name "Luther," as well, assigning it to Jacob and Martin. In the first instance, the choice may have been driven by the proliferation of Jacobs in the second and third generations. **Martin Luther Feather** (1865–1939) took the matter one step further to distinguish himself from his cousin, **Martin Luther Feather,** son of Zaccheus and Mary, by using the plural form of his surname.

The full list of their Christian's and Catherine's children is under the **Christian Feather** entry.

According to a short death notice for Catherine, "Mrs. Crese Feather mother of Isaac, Jacob, and James Feather, of near Valley Point," died at her home near Clarksburg. That was most likely the home of her son, Amos Conaway Feathers (1855–1921).

Catherine Jane Lewis Feather
October 27, 1809–August 25, 1839
Row North W / 2

Born at Crab Orchard, **Catherine Jane Lewis** was the first wife of **James Feather,** with whom she had three children (see James Feather entry for names). They were married July 14, 1831. Family researchers have not determined her parents' names, only that she was a Lewis.

She and James had three children: Jacob (designated the third) (1832–1862), Malinda Jane White (1834–1888), and Joseph Czalmon (1837–1920). Her burial location in Lenox is based upon conjecture. On the cemetery register, it is just "C. Feather," buried next to a James Feather.

Catharine Jane Welch Feather
December 1, 1829–June 23, 1884
Row North L / 13?

The daughter of John F. Welch (1802–1871) and Barbara Hazelett Welch (1802–1880), Catharine Jane Welch married **Harrison Feather** in 1850. She was his first wife; her grave is marked only "Feather" on the register. Harrison was buried in grave 14.

Many descendants of Jacob Welch (1775–1845) are buried in Lenox Memorial. Catherine's father was the son of Jacob and Eve Hunt Welch of Allegany County, Maryland. Of Irish descent, Jacob purchased 233 acres in the Blooming Rose region above the Youghiogheny River in Maryland. Catharine Jane's father and uncle, Andrew Jackson Welch, established the line in Preston County. Her siblings who are buried in Lenox Memorial are **Thomas Jefferson** and **Clarissa Jane Feather Welch, Jacob Harrison, Persis A. Welch Childs, Joseph J.** and **Virginia Gribble Welch, Marila A.**, and **Mariah Ann** who married **Jacob Emery Feather**.

The Welch family had extensive land holdings at Crab Orchard and were members of the Lutheran Church in that community. Descendants continue to farm the land along Coal Lick Road.

Charles Wade Feather
June 20, 1918–April 29, 1983
Lineage: Clarence T. & Ora Frances (Stanton), Ezra A. & Clara (Guseman) Jacob F. & Nancy (Wilhelm), Zaccheus & Elizabeth (Ervin), Jacob & Mary
Row South B / 19

Charles Wade Feather was born in Terra Alta and died in Clarksburg. According to the 1930 U.S. Census, the family lived in Portland District and had the Kelly and Wolfe families as neighbors. Charles was listed as a farmer in the 1940 U.S. Census and was living with his parents on the farm. He often went by "Wade" in these documents and used the plural form of his surname.

He served in the US Army during World War II. His military draft registration card lists his father as his employer and address as Terra Alta. His grave is marked with a bronze military service plate.

Charles married Loretta Agnes Bishop (Duckworth) in June 1949. Her parents were Gay Alton (1892–1963) and Anna Hazel Teets Bishop (1897–1979). She was born June 1, 1931, and died October 30, 1968. Loretta is buried in the Terra Alta Cemetery.

Their children were **Clarence Wade Feather,** (1950–2018), and Linda Lucille Feather, born June 15, 1951.

Christena Summers Feather
November 1, 1818–May 26, 1885
Row North W / 2

Born in Pennsylvania, **Christena Summers Feather** was the second wife of **James Feather** (1809–1886).

Christeny and James brought 11 more members into the third generation of Feathers in Preston County: **Mary Anna Feather Teets** (1843–1919), Catharine Annie Feather (1843–1851), John Wesley (1845–1851), David Summers (1847–1930), Adam (1848–1851), Hannah Feathers Engle (1851–1929), Ada (1848–1851), Sarah Margaret Scott (1850–1876), Hanna Eliza (1851–?), Martha Ellen "Mattie" Feather VanMeter (1853–1932), Elizabeth Emmer Friend (1855–1906) and Samuel Equatious Feather (1860–1942).

Astute readers will note that 1851 was horrible year for James and Christena. They lost at least four children—Catherine Annie, John Wesley, Ada, and Adam—that year, and it is possible Hanna Eliza was lost then, too. It is likely these infants/children are buried in Lenox Memorial. The only adult child of James and Christena to be buried in Lenox is Mary Anna and her spouse, **Albert Teets** (1841–1918).

Christian Feather
August 15, 1802–January 1, 1883
Lineage: Jacob & Mary
Row North P / 7

Christian Feather was the last of Jacob's and Mary's children to be born in Somerset County, Pennsylvania, before their move to Monongalia County.

Christian farmed a parcel on the Pleasant/Portland districts border, land that was eventually purchased by **Irena Feather**, wife of **James C**. Very little has been recorded of his life. **William Feather** wrote a brief sketch in the *Preston County History* published in 1979.

> "Christian Feather, son of Jacob, and his wife Catherine, settled on a one-hundred acre tract of rocky hillside land built a simple log cabin where they raised their fourteen children. They were real pioneers, living off the land by growing their own food and the flax they spun and wove into cloth to make their clothing. An open fireplace was used for cooking and baking and to keep the cabin cozy."

Their children were: **Adam H.** (1841–1888), **Mary Jane** (1843–1845), Joseph B. (1844–1891), **Jacob Luther** (1846–1935), **James Christian Jr.** (1848–1937), Sarah Elizabeth Feather Childs (1850–1942), John Solomon (1851–1926), Rachel Rebecca Feather Wolfe (1853–1930), Amos Conaway (1855–1921), Isaac Emerson; (1857–1946), and **Martin Luther Feathers** (1865–1939).

Most of their sons continued the family tradition of farming the land of Portland and Pleasant districts. A notable exception was Amos, who, according to his death certificate, was a coal miner/laborer.

The simplicity of Christian's life as a hard-working farmer is summed up in this one-sentence notice that appeared in *The Preston County Journal* of March 15, 1883.

Death notice:
FEATHER—At his residence in the Crab Orchard, Portland District, on Tuesday, March 13, of rheumatism, Christian Feather, in his 81st year.

Clarence Theodore Feather
January 23, 1892–October 30, 1973
Lineage: Ezra A. & Clara P. (Guseman), Jacob F. & Nancy,
Zaccheus & Elizabeth, Mary & Jacob
Row South B / 18

Clarence Theodore Feather was born in Preston County but spent a portion of his childhood in Missouri. When the 1930 U.S. Census was taken, he was living in Portland District, Preston County, as a head of household with a wife, **Ora**; son, **C. Wade**; and half-brother, **Carl D.**, in the household. His

Clarence Theodore Feather, continued

occupation was farming, likewise listed on the 1950 U.S. Census, with Carl D. living in the Terra Alta household.

His mother, Clara Phelicia Guesman Feather, was Ezra Feather's first wife. Clara was born November 19, 1863, in Preston County and died April 27, 1896, in Missouri. She was a daughter of Jacob J. (1835–1916) and Christine Susan Wolfe Guseman (1795–1880).

As the grandson of a Guseman, Clarence T. was heir to significant Preston County heritage. Jacob J.'s father was Jacob Henry (1786–1878), son of Private Abraham Guseman (1753–1821), a pioneer settler in Preston County's Muddy Creek area. The Guseman family had a mill and store on Muddy Creek; a community bearing their name was centered around their enterprises. Abraham Guseman came into this wilderness bearing the scars of having served in the Revolutionary War—he suffered a shot to the leg and a stroke to his head from a saber. He moved to Monongalia County, Virginia, in 1798, and built a mill on Decker's Creek. The day the mill was completed, he was killed in an accident there.

Jacob Henry Guseman, Clara's grandfather, was born in Martinsburg, Berkeley County, Virginia February 14, 1786. He married **Christine Susan Wolfe** (1795–1880) and died in Preston County March 15, 1878. Morton's *History of Preston County* has this to say about Jacob Henry:

> Mr. Guseman was a very large man with a strong frame, and he was a hard worker. He owned and operated a large farm, ran a tannery, a fulling mill, and oil mill, a grist mill, a saw mill, had a big store, and as a merchant and manufacturer did a big business. When merchandise was hauled from Baltimore, his teams would be started off and about one week afterwards he would mount a horse, overtake his wagons on the way, and by the time they would reach their destination the stock of goods would be purchased and ready for their return.

Clara and Ezra were married October 28, 1886, at the residence of the bride's parents in Pleasant District. Perry Alva and Clarence Theodore were born in Preston County, but at some point after 1892, the family headed west. It is possible that the couple went to Missouri based upon her father's glowing reports of western lands seen during his Civil War military experience.

Jacob J. Guseman joined the 6th W.Va. Cavalry and in the months following the Confederate surrender was assigned to the plains of Kansas, Nebraska, South Dakota, and Colorado. He was mustered out in May 1866.

Tragedy accompanied the newlyweds on their journey west. Clara died at home in Clark County, Missouri, April 27, 1896, at the age of 32. Her obituary in the West Virginia *Argus* (Kingwood) of May 7, 1896, stated that she had been in poor health for several years and left behind a husband and two little sons (Perry Alva, Clarence Theodore). She was buried in Williamstown Cemetery, Lewis County, Missouri.

Ezra returned to Preston County and married Flora M. Park (1884–1970) June 17, 1900, at Cranesville. In the 1900 U.S. Census, Ezra, Perry, and Clarence were living in Jacob's and Nancy's household in Portland District. Ezra's occupation was farming. When Clarence registered for the draft in 1917, he gave his address as Terra Alta and job as farming for Jacob Feather "near Cranesville."

In the fall of 1902, Ezra and Flora relocated to Lostant, Illinois, but Perry and Clarence remained in Preston County. After several moves around the region, the boys' parents settled down in Lostant in December 1913.

Four children were born to them: **Lena Blanche** (infant, 1902), **Carl Dakin** (1905–1982), Orval (1906–1914), and Hazel (1908–1914).

As it did in Missouri, death visited Ezra's home as a determined harvester. Orval died January 26, 1914, after an illness of four weeks that turned into pneumonia and overtaxed his weak heart. He was 7 years old. A week later, Hazel, age 5, died. Funeral services were held in their home. Orval and Hazel were buried in Hope Town Cemetery, Lostant, Illinois. Then came the final blow from this icy scythe: Ezra died February 15, 1914, at the age of 48, just 13 days after Hazel died. His occupation was listed as farmer on his death certificate.

From Ezra's obituary, publication most likely in a Lossant newspaper:

> The deceased had been in failing health all winter. He was a Christian man and his faith in Christ enabled him to bear patiently his sorrows and sufferings. He was a man of uprightness, honesty and integrity. He was a member of the Lutheran church and belonged to the Odd Fellows; a number of the lodge being present at the funeral. ...

Those left to mourn his death are the beloved wife and little son, Carl; also two sons in W. Va., by a former marriage, Perry Alva and Clarence Theodore, and his parents at Terra Alta.

It was a great satisfaction to the deceased that his father, Jacob Feather, and his son, Perry, came in time to be with him the last few days he lived. Mrs. Feather's brothers have been her faithful helpers, one of them being here to assist throughout the sickness and death of the three members of the family (Orval, Hazel, and Ezra).

Ezra was buried in Hope Town Cemetery, Lostant, LaSalle County, Illinois. Although from Preston County, Flora stayed in Lostant, where she is buried in an unmarked grave. She died in 1970.

Clarence Wade Feather
March 12, 1950–September 29, 2018
Lineage: Charles Theodore & Ora (Stanton), Ezra A. & Clara (Guseman), Jacob F. & Nancy (Wilhelm), Zaccheus & Elizabeth (Ervin), Jacob & Mary
Row South B / 19

Obituary:

Clarence Wade Feather, 68, of Terra Alta, died Saturday, September 29, 2018 at home surrounded by his loving family.

He was born March 12, 1950, in Terra Alta, a son of the late Charles Wade Feather and Loretta (Bishop) Duckworth.

Clarence graduated in 1968 from Terra Alta High School. He retired in 2015 from the Green River Group where he worked as a heavy equipment operator. He served on the Terra Alta town council and loved going to auctions and spending time on the farm. He was a classic car buff, especially Chevy, and enjoyed watching the Barrett-Jackson car auctions.

Clarence is survived by his loving wife of 45 years, Brenda (Watring) Feather; three daughters, Shannon Friend and Craig of Grafton, Crystal Hardesty and Jamie of Terra Alta and Valerie Moyer and Matt of Reedsville; three grandchildren, Sydney Friend, Wyatt Moyer and Eli Moyer; three sisters, Linda Friend and Sam of Cranesville, Hope Bowman and Rick of Mt. Lake Park, MD, and Ruth Hauger and Mike of Terra Alta and several nieces and nephews.

He was preceded in death by his in laws, Ray and Blanche Watring; two nephews, Michael Friend and Danny Joe Rhodes and a brother and sister in law, Charlie and Linda Himelrick.

Family and friends will be received at the Arthur H. Wright Funeral Home in Terra Alta, on Tuesday, October 2, 2018 from 2–4 and 6–8 p.m. The funeral service will be 2 p.m. on Wednesday, October 3, 2018, at the funeral home with Rev. Gene Turner officiating. Interment will follow in the Lenox Memorial Cemetery formerly the Lutheran Cemetery in Lenox.

Clarissa (Clara) Jane Feather Welch
December 26, 1832–January 3, 1901
Lineage: Zaccheus & Elizabeth (Ervin), Jacob & Mary
Row North S / 7

Clarissa (Clara) Jane Feather Welch was born the same year that her grandfather, Jacob, died. It is likely that she was named in honor of her grandfather's sister, Anna Clarissa Feather, who immigrated to Philadelphia with Jacob and their parents and is buried in the Schneider Family Cemetery, Casselman, Pennsylvania.

Clarrisa Jane married **Thomas Jefferson Welch** and they had 10 children, including an unnamed female infant born May 6, 1869, who died two days later and is buried in Lutheran Memorial. Three other daughters also died in infancy/childhood: **Ida M.**, born and died March 3, 1872; **Catharine**, September 6, 1859–July 5, 1862, and **Barbara E. Welch**, April 2, 1858–December 23, 1860. The children are buried in North S, but some of the graves are marked "unknown" or simply "Welch" on the register.

Her adult children buried at Lutheran Memorial include **Jacob Wesley** (1856–1924), **Roama** (1853–1912), and **McClure Welch** (1864–1891). A daughter, Virginia "Jennie" Welch (1863-1918), married Alpheus Earl "Alpha" Strawser in 1884 and relocated to Wyoming circa 1888. Their son, Ira B. Strawser, died September 24, 1918, at Camp Funston, Kansas.

Dallie A. Kelly Feather
May 8, 1876–March 2, 1919
Row North E / 18

Dallie A. Kelly Feather was the spouse of **Andrew E.** (1865–1947). Andrew and Dallie did not have any children.

Her family's presence in Preston County goes back to John and Elizabeth Askins Kelly, who migrated from Loudoun County, Virginia, in the 1700s. John settled on the north bank of Beaver Creek. Most of the Kelly family pushed farther west, to Muskingum County, Ohio, but two brothers, Joseph and William remained behind in Monongalia County.

Joseph M., born May 15, 1794, in Pennsylvania, was Dallie's grandfather. Her parents were Joseph Meshack Allen (March 5, 1840–May 29, 1898) and Malinda Ryland Kelly (March 18, 1844–June 13, 1928). Both are buried in the Kelly Cemetery at Afton, Preston County.

(The Rev.) Dana Wilbur Mercer Feather
December 27, 1886–January 21, 1914
Lineage: Joseph & Mary Louisa (Mercer),
Adam & Sabra Eusebia (Summers), Jacob & Mary
Row North F / 3

The only child of the **Rev. Joseph Feather** and his second wife, **Mary Louisa "Lou" Mercer Feather** (1855–1919), **Dana Feather** married a cousin, **Mary Jane "Mollie" Welch** (1886–1980), who was a daughter of **Jacob Wesley** and **Matilda Jane Dunn Welch (Row North C, 14, 15)**. Jacob Wesley's mother was **Clarissa Feather,** daughter of **Zaccheus**. Dana's line was through **Adam**.

The couple had one child, Beatrice Lucille Feather, born (1911–1996) Beatrice married George Augustus Flynn on February 25, 1939, in Winchester, Virginia. George (1909–1966) was born in Salem, W.Va., and died in Cumberland, Maryland. He and Beatrice had two sons: Dana Paul Flynn and Robert Michael Flynn. Dana Feather's obituary:

Rev. Dana W. M. Feather, continued

Dana W. B. Feather is buried next to his mother, Joseph B. Feather's second wife.

Rev. Dana W.M. Feather, youngest son of the Rev. J.B. Feather, of near Albright, this county, died Saturday evening in one of the hospitals in Baltimore, Md., where he had been taken for treatment some four weeks ago. Rev. Feather has been the preacher in charge of the Brandonville circuit for the past three years of the Methodist Episcopal church, but his health failing him last year he gave up his work and took a supernumerary relation at the conference held in Buckhannon, hoping that the year's rest would restore him to his usual health. After reaching Baltimore for treatment the physicians found that he was suffering from an attack of appendicitis and an operation was performed but other complications set in which made it impossible to save his life.

The deceased was born December 27, 1886, making him at the time of his death a little past twenty-five years of age. August 11, 1900, he was married to Miss Mollie Welch to which union one child was born. Rev. Feather was a bright young man and highly esteemed by all who knew him. He was a graduate of the Fairmont Normal school; in the third year of his conference course; an able preacher, a close student and everybody's friend.

The funeral services were conducted Tuesday afternoon from the Lenox Luthern church, in charge of Rev. E. P. Idieman of Albright, assisted by Dist. Supt. Rev. W. E. Reed of Oakland, Md., Rev. W. W. Morris of Bruceton, Rev. Albert Engle of Brandonville and Rev. A. D. Craig of Kingwood, all of whom made short addresses. It was probably the largest funeral ever held in that section of the county, showing the high appreciation and character of the deceased. Interment was made in the cemetery adjoining the church..

Daniel C. Feather
February 12, 1842–January 14, 1922
Lineage: Zaccheus & Elizabeth (Ervin), Jacob & Mary
Row North Q / 5

Daniel C. Feather was a Civil War veteran and a prominent citizen of Lenox and Terra Alta. He married **Deborah Ann Chidester** on April 25, 1869, in Logan, Ohio. He owned 94 acres on Roaring Creek.

The following obituary was published on page 4 of *The Preston County Journal, Kingwood,* January 19, 1922.

Daniel C. Feather was born Feb. 12, 1842, at Lenox, Preston county, and died January 14, 1922 at Terra Alta. Funeral services were held in the M.E. church at Terra Alta, and burial in the Lutheran cemetery near Lenox. His wife, Deborah A. Feather of Terra Alta, four sisters, Mrs. Sarah Kelley of Terra Alta, and Mrs. Amanda Peaslee, Mrs. E. B. Feather and Miss Eve Feather of Lenox, and one brother John S. Feather of Logan, Ohio, survive him.

Daniel C. Feather was one of a family of five sons and seven daughters born to the union of Zaccheus Feather and Elizabeth Ervin Feather, one of the largest and earliest pioneer families of Preston County. He was reared on the farm still occupied by the family at Lenox and secured his early education in the county school at that place. When the Civil war broke out, he answered his country's call and enlisted in Company B, 14th W. Va. Volunteer Infantry, Aug. 15, 1862. In the battle of Cloyd Mountain, May 9, 1864, he was shot through the body, a wound that never entirely healed

Daniel C. Feather, continued

and from which he was a patient sufferer through all the remaining years of his life. He was taken from the field by the ambulance corps of the enemy and placed in Emery and Henry college hospitals where the Confederate surgeons gave him such kindly and skillful treatment that he never ceased to praise them. When sufficiently recovered he was exchanged and sent to Annapolis, Md., where he was discharged, April 11, 1865.

On April 25, 1869, he was married in Hocking county, Ohio, to Miss Deborah Ann Chidester, a native of West Virginia, who was reared and educated in Preston county, her father being Harrison Chidester of a pioneer family of the same. Mr. and Mrs. Feather lived about eighteen months in Ohio, then returned to Preston county and soon after bought a farm near his old home at Lenox, where he actively and successfully engaged in farming until he sold the farm to his brother M. L. Feather in 1894 and moved to Terra Alta where he bought property and lived until the time of his death.

In 1905 he was elected a director of the Terra Alta bank and as such and a member of its finance committee, he has been ever since a most faithful and capable officer. He was also a director of the Englehart Woolen Mill company of Guseman, W. Va.

Mr. and Mrs. Feather had one daughter, **Amy L(o)uella**, who died April 9, 1881, at the age of about eleven years.

They both became members of the Lutheran church about the time of their marriage and were active in all the work of the church at Lenox until they moved from that locality. In Terra Alta he aided in the planning and financing the new Methodist church and later became an official member. Their home life was that of the ideal Christian family. A beautiful companionship always existed that helped to alleviate the suffering to which they have been subjected in later years. Every laudable enterprise received his attention and support. As a member of the board of education he was a strong influence to obtain a high standard of public education. He was a member of the GAR, Knights of the Golden Eagle, Knights of Pythias, DOKK (side lodge) and the Odd Fellows, and took great interest in these social orders, being often an officer and for years a member of the Rank and Knight team in the Knights of Pythias.

He lived the life urged by these orders, and was a most pleasant and sociable man whose hospitality was genuine and friendship quiet and sincere. Few men had a larger circle of friends, and it is probably true that "Uncle Dan" did not have a single enemy in the world.

As a man Mr. Feather towered in his true properties. His principles were such that no one ever questioned his perfect honesty and sterling integrity. Of him it was true that his word was as good as his bond. . . . He coveted no man's property and suffered loss himself rather than perform any act that might have even the resemblance of any but the most honorable practices. His life will long be an example and inspiration to all his host of colleagues, friends and acquaintances who appreciate and prize an upright man.

A bit of Feather trivia: While music was common in the log cabins and homes of West Virginia's early settlers, that did not seem to be the case with many of the Feather family members. D.C. Feather may have been a notable exception.

A notice in *The Preston County Journal* of April 15, 1897, stated that D. C. and Professor S. C. Smith of Oakland drove over to Cranesville to visit and stay with "his parents" for a few days. Afterwards, the professor went to Bruceton, where he gave instruction to the Crescent band. In the same newspaper, it was noted that J.W. Feather had purchased a Whiting piano from a Cumberland dealer.

David O. Feather
August 9, 1841–March 15, 1906
Lineage: John S. & Mary (Irvin), Jacob & Mary
Row North J / 3

David O. Feather was one of Crab Orchard's most prominent citizens. He and his wife, **Amanda Jane Albright Feather** (1849–1912), had one son, Clinton Daniel Feather (April 8, 1870–May 12, 1932).

On October 11, 1869, David O. Feather became one of the jurors who would decide the fate of Elihu Gregg, charged with setting fire to the Preston County Courthouse on March 7, 1869. The fire destroyed all of the country

David O. Feather, continued

courthouse records from the time of its formation in 1818. The trial was for his second indictment; Gregg slipped out of a prior guilty verdict and death sentence via a successful filing of errors with the Court of Appeals. The jurors of the second trial again found Gregg guilty and sentenced him to death. Gregg slipped out of his jail cell overnight and escaped to Canada and the West. He sent a letter to the editor of *The Preston County Journal* expressing regret that he was unable to keep his date with execution on January 28, 1870, as other business would detain him.

Obituary for David O. Feather:

> He was born August 9, 1841, and died March 15, 1906, aged 64 years, 7 months and 6 days. He leaves a widow, a son and wife, and two grand-children, of whom he was very fond. In his home he was very clever and lively. Everybody enjoyed his company. He was a member of a family of fifteen children, of which there are but four left, namely, Mrs. L. J. Forman, Jacob E. and James C. of the Craborchard and J. M. of Kearney, Neb.
>
> He joined the Lutheran church early in life and lived a faithful member. He was married to Amanda, eldest daughter of the late Daniel Albright. He was a man of very good judgment and kept himself well informed and was always ready to give good advice to any one willing to accept it. He had many friends far and near who will greatly miss him.
>
> He was married January 14, 1869, and leaves a companion to mourn the loss of a good husband after 37 years of domestic happiness. In 1865 he joined the church, making forty years' service in the army of the Lord. He acquired considerable property, leaving his wife and only son well provided for.
>
> In politics Mr. Feather was a staunch Democrat, and was the nominee of his party several times for various offices of trust and honor. His death was sudden and unexpected, as he had been in his usual health day of his death and was stricken down with apoplexy late that evening and lived but a few hours. The funeral was held Saturday, March 17, at the Lutheran church in the Craborchard and the burial in the cemetery nearby.

Clinton Daniel Feather, the only child born to this couple, in 1892 married Eglon resident Annie Dial Mherling Hayden (1876–1964). Her paternal ancestors were John Alden Sr. and Priscilla Mullins, the famous Mayflower passengers whose love story became embedded in American folklore. John Alden was a cooper, purchaser, and undertaker for the Plymouth Colony. His alleged rivalry with Miles Standish for the hand of Priscilla became the basis of Henry Wadsworth Longfellow's narrative poem, "The Courtship of Miles Standish."

Clinton Daniel and Annie had two children, Karl Ward Feather (1893–1964) and Helen Mabel Feather (1896–1973). They lived at Crab Orchard, where they worked a large farm—285 acres with a total assessed value of nearly $5,000. According to Morton's 1914 *History of Preston County*, Clinton D. lived on the farm that John Solomon, his grandfather, owned "midway between Albright and Lenox, and consists of 285 acres of the best farming land in this part of the state." Morton further stated that the "farm has been in the family from the time of its exemption," a confusing statement as land records indicate that at that point in history, the Rev. Joseph B. Feather, Adam's son, was living on the homestead farm. Prior to circa 1845, John Solomon did live on his father's and mother's homestead property, but he purchased the Reckart farm about that time, and Adam moved back to Preston County from Pennsylvania to work the homestead farm. Morton's *History* states that the old house on that property is where John and his family also lived. And, in 1914, it is where Clinton Daniel lived. "The house now standing there was built by him (John Solomon) over eighty years ago," Morton wrote.

One of the most tragic events to shake both the Crab Orchard community and Feather family occurred the night of May 12, 1932, when Clinton Daniel was shot by a group of unknown men outside his home during an attempted robbery. Clinton was taken to Kingwood for treatment and lingered there for nearly two days before succumbing to his wounds at the age of 62. He was buried in Kingwood's Maplewood Cemetery.

The assailants were never captured, no arrests were made. The incident became a dark blot on county and state law enforcement. *The Preston County Journal* of May 19, 1932, noted that, "The untimely murder of Clint Feather last week brings to the people of the county the realization of what a crime of this order means. Mr. Feather, a good citizen who possibly never harmed a soul in his life, was fatally shot on the night of the elections by a band of thugs possibly looking for what money they might obtain. If there is such a thing as a hot corner of hell, criminals of this sort will certainly be shoveled in that end. The law cannot be (too) severe, and is possibly too weak."

Clinton Daniel's wife, Annie, moved to Los Angeles, where Helen Mable lived. Annie died at the age of 87. She is buried in Roosevelt Memorial Park, next to her daughter, who died October 9, 1973.

Karl Ward Feather followed in his mother's footsteps and became a teacher. He also owned an automobile dealership in Pennsylvania and, during World War II, worked as an airplane mechanical engineer for Glenn L. Martin. He wrote a book, *Statistical Concepts*, that became a best seller in its field. He always had a passion for antique cars and their restoration. Karl Ward and his wife, Emma Sybil Castle Feather, are buried in Maplewood Cemetery, Kingwood.

Although virtually forgotten nearly a century later, the shooting death of Clinton Daniel Feather remains one of Preston County's most contemptible and unsolved murders.

Deborah Ann Chidester Feather
May 13, 1848–April 18, 1927
Row North Q / 6

Deborah A. Chidester Feather was the wife of **Daniel C.** She was the firstborn child of Harrison (1826–1897) and Sabina Falkenstine Chidester (1828–1906). Savana's great grandfather was Peter Stuck (1752–1832), who was born in Germany in 1717. Peter's son, John B., was born in Lancaster County, Pennsylvania, and died in Addison, Somerset County, Pennsylvania.

Her parents, died in Hocking County, Ohio. They had seven children, Deborah being the oldest.

Deborah and Daniel C. Feather are buried next to their only child, **Amy Louella Feather,** May 15, 1870–April 3, 1881.

Dora Ellen White Feather
1909–1987
Row South C / 11

Dora Ellen White Feather married **Hoy Jackson Feather** at Oakland, Maryland, on January 15, 1927. She was a daughter of Alva James White (1871–1949) and Virginia Mary "Jennie" Hauger White (1873–1948). Her parents are buried in Pleasant Grove Cemetery, Herring, Preston County.

Jennie's maternal grandfather was **William Joseph Hauger,** who lived in Lenox and died at the age of 48 on March 11, 1897. A member of Zion Lutheran, he was described in his obituary as a "noble, industrious, business man highly esteemed by all who knew him." His death came as the result of a tree falling on his limb three weeks prior. Physicians Scott and Frey determined that his only chance of living was to amputate the limb, but "he was not able to withstand the shock and died within a hour afterwards," according to a newspaper brief. "His last words were, 'I am resting good now. All is well.' He raised his eyes and fell asleep, calm and peaceful."

A month later, his wife, **Tresia Lucretia Welch Hauger,** died of pneumonia (April 10, 1897). Six of their 11 children were underage and became orphans that day. (Dora's mother was 24 at the time her father died.)

Wendy Feather McLaughlin shares her memories of this couple in the Hoy Jackson Feather entry.

Obituary:

> Dora W. Feather, 77, of Kingwood, died Monday, Feb. 9, 1997, at Preston Memorial Hospital.
>
> She was born Sept. 7, (1909) at Albright, a daughter of the late Alva and Mary Hauger White. She was a member of Wesley United Methodist Church and the Kingwood Women's Club.
>
> She is survived by two sisters, Maude Hyre of Kingwood and Agnes Davis of Masontown.
>
> She was preceded in death by her husband, Hoy Jackson Feather in 1960, and by three brothers and one sister.
>
> Friends may call at the Browning Funeral Home ...

Effie Estella Livengood Feather
June 7, 1879–March 16, 1968
Row North E / 13

Effie Estella Livengood married **Benjamin C. Feather**. She was a daughter of David Samuel (1849–1929) and Virginia Crane Livengood (1855–1935), who are buried at the Centennary Cemetery, Preston County. Effie died in Macob County, Michigan.

Effie and Benjamin had one child, Paul Dana Feather (1909–1981), who is buried in the Terra Alta Cemetery.

Livengoods in America were established with the immigration of Johann Peter Livengood (Liebengut) Sr. (1733–1814) from Bas-Rhin, France, to Pennsylvania in the 1700s. Daniel Samuel Livengood's parents were Samuel Sherman (1822–1896) and Mary Jane Herring Livengood (1827–1906). Samuel Sherman was born in Somerset County, Pennsylvania, which is to the northeast of Preston County. Somerset County fostered many Palatine immigrants prior to their migration into Virginia.

The topography and climate of the Alleghenies were similar to what these Palatinate immigrants knew in the Rhineland and Bavaria and explains their gravitation toward this rugged landscape. Jacob and Mary Feather spent at least a decade in Bedford/Somerst counties before moving deeper into the Alleghenies. Jacob Feather's parents are buried in Somerset County, as well as his sister, who married a Somerset County German immigrant, Dewalt Schneider. By moving into Preston County, the families were following the same line of mountains to a slightly higher altitude. This strong push into what were Virginia's western lands came only after the Revolutionary War and signing of Indian treaties that made the land somewhat safer for this group of hardy, first-generation immigrants.

George Washington Herring (1791–1872), the maternal grandmother of Samuel Sherman Livengood, was among those residents of Bedford County, Pennsylvania (parent of Somerset county). who pushed southwest to Hazelton, Preston County.

Elina "Ella" Deal Feather
January 13, 1886–June 10, 1949
Row North E / 13

Elina Deal Feather was a daughter of John Henry Deal and Lucy Ann Deberry. In 1906, she married **Winfield Scott Feather** (1881–1951); they had two children, **Lena Alfreda Feather** (1909) and **Fred Lynn Feather** (1923–2000).

Her father was born April 19, 1843, and died April 11, 1911. He is buried in Shady Grove Cemetery, Brandonville. His ancestor, Henry Deahl, immigrated from Germany in 1776. His son, Henry Jr., migrated to Preston County from Cambria County, Pennsylvania, 1823. Their homestead was near Hazelton.

Lucy Ann Deberry was John Henry Deal's second wife. His first, Martha Jane Hileman, died three months after they were married in 1876.

Martin (1822–1902) and Nancy Guthrie (1821–1891) DeBerry, were Lucy Ann's parents. They are buried at Shady Grove Union Cemetery, Brandonville. While Martin and Nancy Deberry had eight children, only three lived to adulthood: Archibald J., Lucy Ann, and Susannah Ella. Archibald J. (1850–1895), had 10 children with Rebecca Graham, who died in 1892. Those children plus one other whom Archibald had by another wife were orphaned in 1895, when Archibald J. died in a coal mine explosion in Perry County, Ohio.

Martin's paternal grandfather was John Ray DeBerry (1745–1832) who immigrated from France and died in Preston County. He married Catharina Elisabetha Schrupp (1778–1830). The DeBerry family, of French origin, has a strong presence throughout Preston County and within the Feather family.

Elizabeth "Betsy" Ervin Feather
August 6, 1815–January 26, 1898
Row North R /5

The daughter of **Isaac** (1767–1824) and **Eve (Smith) Ervin** (1774–1860), **Elizabeth Ervin** married **Zaccheus "Zack" Feather** December 14, 1831, at Lenox. Elizabeth bore 13 children during her lifetime: **Clarissa Jane Welch, Isaac B., Jacob F., Mary Ann Conner, Daniel C., Nancy Maria**

Stokes, John Solomon (1847–1929), **Eva Catharine, Amanda Jane Peaslee, Luther Martin,** Sara Elizabeth Kelly, (b. 1856), **Minerva Bell Feather,** and an **unnamed female infant.**

Elizabeth was a sister of **Mary Ervin,** who married **John Solomon Feather.** A brother, Jacob (1807–1892) married Catherine Cress and Mary Menear; his burial location is undetermined. Another brother, **John** (1805–1865) is buried at Lenox Memorial.

Isaac Ervin was born in Pennsylvania and married Eve Smith in April 1800. They were living in Somerset County, and it is very likely that the couple were acquainted with Jacob and Mary Feather before they migrated to Monongalia County, Virginia, where Elizabeth was born.

Elizabeth Ervin Feather's obituary:

> Elizabeth Feather, nee Ervin, consort of the late Zaccheus Feather, died at her home at Lenox, Preston county, W.Va., January 26, 1898, in her 84th year. She was the mother of twelve children, all of whom are living, and all were permitted to see her frequently and assist in caring for her in her last affliction. All of her children except John, and many of her grandchildren and relatives and friends, were allowed to participate in the memorial services which were held on the 7th in the old Lutheran church and at the grave beside her sainted husband, which were conducted by the Rev. H. E. Friend and a well selected choir.
>
> Too much cannot be said in praise of this saintly woman. She gave her heart to God and united with the Evangelical Lutheran church more than sixty years ago, and during all the years that followed she was noted for her attention and care for the sick and needy, and for her regular attendance upon all the public and private means of grace. Her presence always brought life and sunshine into the homes she visited. And no wonder that in her last long and severe affliction her patience and resignation triumphed over all. No wonder that as the frail tenement was dissolving she only thought and talked of "going home." She was a model woman and has left a large legacy, in her example and peaceful death to a large circle of admiring and mourning friends. May we all meet her in that bright world where parting words are never spoken.

Elizabeth Reckart Feather
May 9, 1834–October 9, 1917
Row North E / 11

Elizabeth Reckart Feather was the wife of **Isaac B. Feather**; they were married in 1864. Her parents were **George Ludwig Lewis Reckart** (1799–1871) and **Ann Elizabeth Lewis Reckart** (1810–1885).

The Reckart surname is widely dispersed through the Feather line. Of German extraction, **Earnest August Reckart** (1755–1843) and **Maria Elizabeth "Mary" Standle Reckart** (1760–1853), were George Ludwig's parents and lived to the north of the Jacob and Mary Feather farm. Earnest was allegedly a Revolutionary War soldier who came to the colonies with General von Steuben and assisted him in transforming the Continental Army into a serious fighting force during the encampment at Valley Forge. If that legend, which cannot be documented, is true, Jacob Feather and Earnest Reckart probably became acquainted with each other during the winter and spring of 1778. Further discussion of this Feather/Reckart legend can be found in the author's book, *My Fathers' Land*.

Earnest Reckart and his wife are buried at Lenox Memorial Cemetery, but their graves are unmarked.

Tradition states that the Reckarts donated the land for the cemetery, which was adjacent to the Reckart Farm.

Eliza V. Feather
1867–1888
Lineage: John Summers & Sarah M. Harvey, Adam & Mary (Summers),
Jacob & Mary
Row North J / 1

Eliza V. Feather died as a young adult. She shares her parents' grave marker. Her siblings were Solomon B. (1850–1944), Margaret Jane Forman (1853–?), and Orpha Christine Feather Cramer (1874–1945), none of whom is buried in Lenox Memorial.

Elmer B. Feather
May 28, 1862–January 17, 1940
Lineage: Joseph B. & Mary (Atkinson), Adam & Mary (Summers),
Jacob & Mary
North section, family headstone with smaller individual stones

Elmer B. Feather was a son of the **Rev. Joseph B. Feather** (1833–1920) and **Mary Atkinson Feather** (1833–1881). He was the fourth generation to live on the homestead property on Lutheran Church Road. Elmer married **Minerva Bell Feather** (1862–1950); the couple had one child, **Brantson Claude.**

Elmer was a farmer, working the land his grandparents and great-grandparents once owned. According to the Preston County Land Book of 1939, Elmer and Minerva Feather owned three parcels in Portland District: 120, 96, and 7 acres.

The Preston County Journal of November 22, 1894, reported that on November 14th of that year, Elmer's barn was destroyed by a fire, the cause of which was undetermined. "The barn contained considerable grain and feed, wagons, harnesses, four head of hogs and two good horses all of which were consumed. The loss as reported to *The Journal* is about $500 with no insurance. Mr. Feather is not sure as to the how the fire originated. The burning of barns and buildings so mysteriously throughout the county is becoming so frequent to appear the work of an organized gang of incenduaries. [sic]" A news brief from Lenox that was published October 13, 1892, in *The Preston County Journal* stated "Mr. Elmer Feather has made quite an improvement to his dwelling by putting up two porticoes." The same newspaper of January 31, 1895, noted that Elmer had completed a new barn.

Elmer's name appears quite often in the pages of the newspaper as having visited Kingwood, often with his wife, on business matters. The newspaper never explained what type of business Elmer was conducting, but it is a safe assumption that it involved farming.

Elmer's grave is part of a family plot in the north section that includes his wife, son, daughter-in-law, and their only, beloved son, "Willie." A large, red stone inscribed "Feather" marks the plot, with ground-level stones to the north of it. The names do not appear on register or map, where there is an opening between Rows N Q, R and S.

Emma Belle Feather Haun
December 26, 1868–April 25, 1918
Lineage: Isaac B. & Elizabeth (Reckart), Zaccheus & Elizabeth (Irvin),
Jacob & Mary
Row North E / 16

Emma Belle Feather married **George Calder Haun** (1873–1942) on October 24, 1895, at Lenox. The couple had one child, Bertha Loe Haun Shaw (1896–1955), who married John Clarence Shaw in 1917. He died the following year and is buried at Mount Calvary Cemetery, Morgantown.

George was a son of Norval Paul and Margaret Jane Haun. He came from a large family—12 siblings—and his parents selected interesting names for the children, including "Quitman Worth," "Bat," and "Nerva."

The 1900 U.S Census shows George and Emma Belle living in the Winfield District of Marion County with Bertha, age 3. George was employed in the coal mines. After Emma Belle died, George married **Odessee "Dessie" Kelly**, a daughter of John W. and Margaret Malinda Kelly.

In the 1930 U.S. Census, George was living in Morgantown and married to Dessie. Bertha L. Shaw, his daughter, and Opal M. Shaw, granddaugher were living with the couple. George was working in construction, and his daughter was a stenographer for the university.

George died August 28, 1942, and is buried adjacent to his two wives.

Eve (Eva) Catharine Feather Lewis
January 1, 1798–December 17, 1854
Lineage: Jacob & Mary
Unknown grave for both

One of four daughters born to **Jacob** and **Mary Feather, Eve Catharine Feather** married **John Lewis** (1794–1870). They lived in Terra Alta and had nine children, seven of them girls. Only the last child born to them, **Lydia Lewis** (1845–1864) is buried in Lenox. It is possible that their first two children, Margaret (1824) and Mary (1828), both of whom died in infancy, were interred in Lenox.

The couple's children chose spouses outside of their community. A daughter, Catharine Eva Lewis (1830–?), married Thomas Patrick Spencer, a farmer, in 1868 and lived in St. George, Tucker County. She and Thomas are buried in the Fairview Cemetery. Rebecca (1836–?), their seventh child, married Joshua Messenger; both are buried in the City Cemetery, Parsons, W.Va. Firstborn son, James A. (1833–1908), is buried in Oak Grove Cemetery, Portland District. Their other son, Christian F. (1836–?), married Lecretia Warthen; both are buried in Taylor County, W.Va.

John Lewis' parents are unknown. He remarried in 1857 to Jane Dodge Stemple (1828–1911), who is buried in Oak Grove Cemetery, Terra Alta. Three children were born to them.

Eva Catherine Feather
July 4, 1849–July 11, 1927
Lineage: Zaccheus & Elizabeth (Irvin), Jacob & Mary
Row North R / 7

Zaccheus and Elizabeth had 13 children; of them, **Eva Catherine** was the only one who survived to adulthood and did not marry. According to her death certificate, her employment had been "housework." The 1920 U.S. Census places her in the Pleasant District home of Amanda Peaslee, Eva's sister, as a "lodger" with no occupation.

She enjoyed a great social life. *The Preston County Journal* of July 12, 1917, printed a story about her birthday celebration held at Lenox:

A surprise birthday party was given Miss Eve Feather at the home of her sister, Mrs. Amanda Peaslee, at Lenox, on Sunday, July 8th, 1917, in honor of her 68th birthday. Early in the forenoon relatives began to arrive from all directions and before the noon hour had arrived, the crowd had grown to 85 in number. In the crowd was the oldest, youngest, fattest and leanest Feather in the county. About 1 o'clock a table constructed of tables and lumber about 30 feet long was groaning under its weight of good things to eat, the dinner was served in courses, that is one continuous course lasting about one hour, after which the lean were fat and the fat were almost past going. W.A. Whitehair looked like John Cramer when he finished his dinner. Soon after dinner a foot race was arranged for, and C.F. Welch and Mrs. Joseph R. Ringer were the first to have a try out. They ran a distance of about two hundred feet in something less

Eve Catherine Feather continued

than one hour, and no doubt would have done better had it not been for the fact that the new state road law provides a severe penalty for running any sort of a vehicle either human or otherwise at a greater rate of speed than 35 miles per hour over any public highway.

Some of the married ladies and old maids had a coffee race which was (v)ery much enjoyed by all present. About 5 o'clock the people began leaving for their homes and while it is supposed that the state is bone dry there was not one in the crowd, even Carlo, the old dog, that was not full.

Those present were Jacob Feather and wife and son Grant, Walter Bishoff and wife, Claude Feather wife and children Pauline and Mary, Mary Ann Conner and daughter Grace, Claud Cramer and wife and son Derrill, George Englehart and wife and son Wilfred, Jos. R. Ringer and wife and daughter Vernie, Carl Gibson and wife and son Hugh, F. W. Crane and wife and daughter Virginia, W. S. Kelley and wife, C. F. Welch and wife and sons Thomas and Herman, Howard Peaslee and wife and son Roy, H. Foster Hartman and wife and children, Ruby, Donald and Harlan, W. A. Whitehair and wife and son Hugh, Bert Feather and wife and children, Dailey, Paul and Virginia, Pearl Freeland, Elma Martin, Myrtle Crane and sons, Smith and Stanley, Andrew Feather and wife, Mrs. Sarah Hileman, Mrs. B. Z. Peaslee and children, Mabel, Cora and Ray, C. F. Jenkins and wife and daughter Cora and son Frank; Fay Oneal, Bruce Awman and wife and daughter Elva, Jane Miller, Jerry Stokes of Parsons, Mrs. Charles Stokes and children, Floyd Herbert and Blaine of Parsons, and Nancy Stokes of Parsons.

Fred "Freddy" Lynn Feather
March 23, 1923–February 25, 2000
Lineage: Winfield Scott & Elina (Deal), Jacob Emory & Mariah Ann (Welch), John S. & Mary (Ervin), Jacob & Mary
Row South C / 17

Fred Lynn Feather's grave is marked with a military service plaque; he served in the U.S. Navy during World War II. Fred worked for Monongalia Power for 32 years.

He married **Mary Rebecca Keener** (1925–2010), who lived on Coal Lick Road and died August 18, 2010, at her home. The daughter of Floyd E. and Bessie Cole Keener, Mary was a Marion County native.

Fred and Mary Rebecca had a son, Mark Lee Feather, of Wheeling, and a daughter, Kathy Dobrowolski, and six grandchildren.

His sister, **Lena Alfreda**, died as an infant.

Georgia Etta "George" Jackson Feather
November 10, 1864–August 23, 1924
Row North C / 22

Georgia Etta "George" Jackson was the wife of **Harvey Arlington Feather**. Their children included a daughter of the same name, also buried in Lenox Memorial. **Georgia Etta,** the daughter, married Harry Jesse McGinnis in Kingwood, January 9, 1933. The children of Harry Jesse and Georgia Etta were Larry Keith Sr. McGinnis (1933–2016) and **Terry Lynn McGinnis** (1943–2019).

Larry Keith Sr. came to own the former John H. and F. Madeline Feather farm on Coal Lick Road in Portland District. For many years, the property was marked with a "Feather Farm" sign in the front yard. In 2023,

Kary Keith McGinnis Jr. and John Harvey McGinnis, heirs to the Larry Keith McGinnis Sr., estate, sold the farm to James J. Miller, Sara Ann W. Miller, and Enos Miller. The Millers are Amish. Their purchase established a beachhead for other Amish families in Portland District.

Gwendolyn Hyre Feather
December 14, 1929–August 8, 2010
Row South C / 20

She was the wife of **William Lloyd Feather** (1929–2013).
Obituary

Gwendolyn H. Feather, 80, of Albright, died Sunday, August 8, 2010, in Ruby Memorial Hospital with family by her side.

She was born December 14, 1929 in Masontown, a daughter of the late Loren and Maude White Hyre. Gwendolyn was a loving wife, sister, mother and grandmother; she was a Member of the Wesley Chapel United Methodist Church, a member of the Lenox Homemakers, the Preston County Historical Society and the Preston County Association of retired School Employees.

She is survived by her loving husband of 60 years, William L. Feather, a son and spouse, William Larry Feather and Julie of Albright; a daughter and spouse, Wendy McLaughlin and Robert of Arthurdale; a brother and spouse, William Hyre and Wilma of St. Marys; four grandchildren, Stephen McLaughlin and spouse, Sarah, Kyle McLaughlin, Matthew Feather and spouse, Casey and Alyssa Feather.

Harrison Feather
January 17, 1823–May 22, 1903
Lineage: John Solomon & Mary (Ervin), Jacob & Mary
Row North L / 14

Harrison Feather acquired the 100-acre **Earnest Reckart** farm, which was between the Lutheran Church Cemetery and the Feather homestead.

He was a man of many talents, often involved in the settlement of estates and surveying land, according to brief mentions in *The Preston County Journal*. He acquired a portion of the homestead farm from his son, **Jared**.

Catharine Jane Welch (1829–1884) was his first wife. They married in 1848 and had five children: **Samantha Jane Feather Rodeheaver** (1851–1934), **Ruth Annie Feather Kelly** (1853–1919), **Jared "Jurd" Allen** (1856–1941), Mary Caroline (1st, Rodeheaver, 2nd Godley) (1857–1922), and **Levi Hess** (1858–1920).

His second wife, Abigail "Abbie" Kelly, is buried in Cranesville Cemetery. Abigail's first husband was Samuel D. Crane, (1822–1883) and they had eight children.

From *The Preston County Journal* of May 28, 1903:

> Harrison Feather was born Jan. 17, 1823, and died May 22, 1903, aged 80 years, 4 month and 5 days. He was one of the oldest and best known residents of the Crab Orchard settlement and was known to be a good neighbor. Early in life he united with the Methodist Episcopal church and remained a member of the same until "God took him" and made him a member of the Church Triumphant. The berieved [sic] family have the sympathy and prayers of the entire community.
>
> Funeral services were conducted by the Rev. W. M. Shultz assisted by the Rev. J.B. Feather, at the Lutheran church, after which his remains were laid to rest.

Harvey Arlington Feather
(February 1, 1864–August 18, 1939)
Lineage: James Connery and Martha Virginia (Rodeheaver),
John Solomon & Mary (Ervin), Jacob & Mary
Row North C / 21

Harvey Arlington Feather married **Georg(ia) Etta Jackson** (1864–1924) on June 15, 1887. The Rev. T. R. Faulkner officiated. A brief in *The Preston County Journal* of March 10, 1887, noted "Harvey Feather, Esq., of Portland District, came over to Kingwood, Saturday and stayed till Sunday. It is a very plain case, he came over to see his best girl."

The esquire title may have been in jest. Harvey was in his early 20s at the time, and it is doubtful he would have already earned his law degree.

Another brief, from May 1, 1890, does not mention him being a lawyer. Rather, Harvey needed one.

> On Tuesday the case of M. L. Crane against Harvey Feather was decided in favor of Mr. Crane, who brought suit to recover $20 paid Mr. Feather on a horse. Feather sold the horse to Crane for $130, of which $20 was paid in cash and $110 in a due-bill. Feather guaranteed the horse to be a good worker in the lead. Crane averred that the horse wouldn't work; and Feather, that it would, and that it balked on Crane because it was worked with a balky horse. There was a number of witnesses, and the case lasted all afternoon. Crogan for plaintiff, Forney for defendant.

On a happier note, the newspaper reported on May 30, 1895, that a daughter (Annie Evelyn) had been born to Mr. and Mrs. Harvey Feather of Crab Orchard.

Harvey owned 52 acres in the Crab Orchard (1924). His death certificate listed his occupation as farmer.

The obituary for Georgia uses the plural version of Feather throughout, unusual for the Feather family members who resided in Crab Orchard. The marker uses the singular version but refers to Georgia as "George."

The couple had 10 children, and all of them were given the plural version of the surname in her obituary that appeared in *The Preston County Journal* of August 28, 1924. That same obituary notes that the family had difficulty in locating Cliff Feathers, Harvey's brother of Uniontown, Pennsylvania, when contacting the family's next-of-kin about Georgia's death. Cliff was away on an automobile trip, "but not being able to locate him, a description of his (vehicle?) was broadcasted by radio from Clarksburg with the result he was located at Frostburg, Md. He immediately started for his brother's home, arriving about half an hour before the funeral."

The children of Harvey and Georgia were: Josephine Fay Seal Feather Wolfe (1888–1975), **Paul Harold** (1890–1975), Hugh Clifton (1892–1945), Annie Evelyn Feather Armstrong (1894–1949), **Mary Henrietta Feather Johns** (1896–1951), Martha Elizabeth Haigh (1898–1951), **Hoy Jackson** (1904–1960), **Georgia Etta Feather McGinnis** (1906–1949), and John Harvey (1908–1965). Mary Henrietta's husband, **Burgett Parker Johns** (1898–1971), was part of an ensemble that entertained at Feather reunions, and Josephine Fay served as its secretary.

Hoy Jackson Feather
February 22, 1904–November 3, 1960
Lineage: Harvey & Georgia (Jackson), James Connery and Martha Virginia (Rodeheaver), John Solomon & Mary
Row South C / 12

Hoy Jackson Feather married **Dora Ellen White** (1909–1987) in Oakland, Maryland, January 15, 1927. The couple had no children.

Like his father, Hoy was a farmer. He and Dora owned 64 ½ acres on Roaring Creek in Portland District (1950).

Wendy Feather McLaughlin has many warm memories of Hoy and Dora Ellen, who was her maternal grandmother's sister.

"Aunt Dora and Uncle Jack were like grandparents to Larry (her brother) and me," she recalled. "They did not have any children, but helped raise my mother, **Gwen(dolyn) Hyre Feather**. Uncle Jack worked in a steel mill in Gary, Indiana when my mother was in high school. She lived with them and graduated there. When I was young, Aunt Dora and Uncle Jack owned a dairy farm on Coal Lick Road across from (Feather Lane). We lived in an old farm house on the property Marvin Morgan now owns (gas well area). Marvin also owns the farm that belonged to Aunt Dora and Uncle Jack. The barn is still there, but the house has been gone for years. After Uncle Jack passed away, Aunt Dora moved to Frederick, Maryland, where she worked in an office. Upon retirement, she returned to Preston County and purchased a house in Kingwood. She always considered Preston County her home."

Obituary:

Hoy Jackson Feather of Route 2, Albright, died yesterday morning at his home. He was 56.

A native of the community, he was born Feb. 22, 1904, a son of the late Harvey and Etta Jackson Feather.

He was a former steelworker and a member of the Methodist Church.

Survivors include his wife, Mrs. Dora W. Feather; two brothers, Paul and John, both of Albright; three sisters, Mrs. Josephine Wolfe of Valley Point, Mrs. Mary Johns of Grafton and Mrs. Hazel Tichnell of Bruceton Mills; and several nieces and nephews.

He was predeceased by a brother and three sisters.

Huldah Catharine Ringer Feather
April 20, 1869–October 15, 1961
Row North M / 13

Huldah Catharine Ringer Feather was the wife of **Levi Hess Feather** and daughter of George W. Ringer Jr. (1865–1947) and Augusta Florence Heare Ringer (1864–1962). Both G. W. Ringer Jr. and his father were Methodist ministers. Born in Kingwood, George Jr. died in Somerset County, Pennsylvania, where he had retired after 50 years of ministerial service in West Virginia and Pennsylvania.

George Ringer Sr. was born in Somerset County and died in Preston County. His father was Jacob Ringer (1803–1884), who is buried in the Ringer (A. C. Ringer Farm) Family Cemetery, Irish Meadow Lane, a couple of miles north of Lenox on the Brandonville Pike. His father, Joseph Ringer (1775–1863), lived in Mercer County, Pennsylvania.

It appears that Huldah moved off the farm after her husband died.

From *The Preston County Journal* of July 3, 1924, we have this obituary of Mary Ringer, Huldah's mother:

Mary Ringer, widow of G. W. Ringer, was born October 28, 1833, near Sugar Valley, and died June 24, 1924, at the home of her grandson Ashel Fortney, with whom she had been living for several years. She was the daughter of John and Elizabeth Gross, and was the last of the family.

In 1850 she was married to G W Ringer and to this union seven children, four sons and three daughters, Mrs. Rachel Fortney of Valley Point, Marshal at home, Noah of Centenary, Mrs. M. T. Cale of Terra Alta, William who died in 1907, Rev. G W Ringer of Armagh, Pa., and Mrs. Hulda Feather of Morgantown, W.Va.

Grandma Ringer was a very kindly woman and was loved by all who knew her. She spent her entire life in the neighborhood in which she was born. She always had a smile and a cheery word for all whom she met and in cases of sickness would go many miles to do anything she could to relieve the suffering of those she knew and loved. In early married life she joined the Evangelical church and had lived a Christian life and believed in her Savior until the last. For the last 10 years she has borne all her suffering with a smile and was always kind and patient.

She leaves besides her children, 19 grandchildren and 22 great grandchildren and many friends and relatives ... She was laid to rest beside her husband who proceeded her to the Great Beyond 22 years ago to await the great day.

Infant and child burials

Two of the stones in the cemetery mark the graves of what were most likely stillborn infants. One of them was a son born to **J. A. & S. J. Feather,** the other a daughter of **Z. & E. Feather** (born and died July 25, 1860).

There are numerous children who were taken from the arms of their parents and given rest in Lenox Memorial. This list is only for those with the surname of "Feather."

Infant and child burials

Amy Louella Feather, May 15, 1870–April 9, 1881, daughter of **Daniel C.** and **Deborah Ann Chidester Feather.**

Ar(i)zona E. Feather (1884–1891), daughter of **Jacob F. & Nancy Wilhelm Feather.**

Charles B., 1892–October 7, 1897. Son of **Obediah** and **Nettie Florence Reckart Feathers.** He died of croup.

David R., died January 19, 1844, aged 2 years, 8 months, 2 days, a son of **Adam** and **Sabra Feather.** He was born in Somerset County, Pennsylvania and died there, but his little body was carried back to Lenox Memorial for burial.

Edith A. Feather, August 6, 1888–July 17, 1903, daughter of Isaac Emerson (1857–1946) and Sarah Jane Doyle Feather (1865–1939). She had one sibling, Molly Letitia Feather Molisee, who lived to be 92 (April 25, 1898-February 7, 1992) and is buried at Masontown Cemetery. Edith's passing was noted by the newspaper but no cause was attributed.

Ellis, died February 8, 1881, aged 9 years, 2 months, 14 days, son of **Jacob F. & Nancy Wilhelm Feather.** Row North R / 10.

Gilbert Z., died February 27, 1887, aged 3 years, 5 months, 10 days, son of **J. & N.**

Icie E., 1885–1887, daughter of **Isaac Emerson** and **Sara Jane Doyle Feather** (Roger's *Genealogy*). Row North R / 9.

John Quincy Feather, June 6, 1827–October 20, 1846, son of **John Solomon** and **Mary Irvin Feather.** John and Mary honored their president at the time, John Quincy Adams, by naming their third son after him. John Quincy Adams Feather lived to be only 19 years old and had no wife or children.

Lena A., February 12, 1909–April 27, 1909, daughter of **Winfield Scott** and **Elma Feather.** She died of pneumonia. Her death notice in the newspaper stated "The pall bearers were four very small girls dressed in white. The little one held in her hand a very delicate rose bud. She was but a little rose bud here on earth but she will bloom in heaven." The funeral was held in the Lutheran Church. **Fred Lynn Feather** (1923–2000) was her brother.

Lena Blanche, January 31, 1902–April 9, 1902. The daughter of Ezra A. and Flora M. Park Feather, she died in Illinois but was brought back to Lenox for burial. Row North X / 11.

Lulu Blanche Feather, 1886–1887. A daughter of Henry L. and Naomi

Leticia Engle Feather. Lulu was their first child and only daughter. The parents are buried in Richwood.

Mary Jane Feather, November 3, 1843–1845, daughter of **Christian** and **Catharine Dunham Feather.**

Terry Alan Feather, May 18, 1966–June 28, 1966. Row North C / 30. A son of Charles E. (1914-1993) & Shirley Ann Shrout Feather (1939–2012), both buried in Sunset Memorial Gardens, Kingwood. Shirley's obituary makes note of three surviving sons and two daughters, plus two deceased sons, Terry A. and Michael E. Feather.

Virgil Gay Feather, March 19, 1898–March 21, 1898. A son of **Levi Hess** and **Huldah Catharine Ringer Feather.**

Willis B. Feather, November 16, 1913–April 24, 1914, only son of **Brantson Claude** and **Adah Blanche Ringer Feather.** His sisters, Pauline Virginia (Kelly) and Mary Waunita (Thomas) Feather, lived to adulthood. Willis's stone is in the Feather plot next to his parents' graves.

This is an incomplete list. The cemetery records indicate there are numerous "unknown" and "Feather" graves in Lenox Memorial but their names have been lost to time. Infant and child deaths were as much a fact of life as the sun and rain, blizzards and drought, that tested the spirits and stoic determination of our Feather, Reckart, Haun, Ringer, Rodeheaver, and other Palatinate ancestors.

Irena Ellen Ervin Feather
1855–1931
Row North L / 2

The wife of **James Christian Feather Jr., Irena Ellen** was the daughter of John (1805–1865) and Julia A. Smith Ervin. John was a brother to **Mary Ervin,** who married **John Solomon Feather,** and **Elizabeth Ervin,** who married **Zaccheus Feather.** John's parents were **Isaac** and **Eve Ervin.**

Irena and James Christian had nine children:

⚜William Victor, October 9, 1875–January 14, 1967. He is buried in Pleasant View Cemetery, Smithfield, Fayette County, Pennsylvania. He married Sara Ann Rankin (1880–1953). They had five children: Violet Ann (1900-1903), Mildred Irene Feathers Cooley (1905-1981), Edna Leah Feather

Irena Ellen Ervin Feather, concluded

Luman (1907-1995), Opal June Feather Funk (1st), Dick (2nd) (1914-1996); Ora Virginia Feather Stephanic (1917-).

⚜ Oakey Jarvis, December 30, 1877–January 19, 1960, buried in Mount Moriah Baptist Cemetery, Smithfield, Fayette County, Pennsylvania. He married Myrtle Mae Coffman (1883–1947). They had seven children: Eugene Jarve (1907–1990), Gerald Spencer (1909–1990), Harry Kendall (1911–1994), Gilbert Woodrow (1913–1964), James Stephen Sr. (1920–2011), Catherine Irene Merkel (1921–1988), Virginia Ruth Dils Marcinek (1929–1982); Bruce Myers, b. February 12, 1879;

⚜ Malinda Theodothia "Mollie" Feather Sypolt, April 4, 1882–February 25, 1957. She married Floyd Homer Sypolt in 1901. They had five children: Opal Mae Sypolt Peaslee (1902–1957), Pearl Virginia Sypolt Cox (1905–1965), Everett Clifton Sypolt (1910–1974), Darwin Wayne Sypolt (1912–1986), and Ralph William Sypolt (1923–1923, aged 12 days);

⚜ Osa Grace Feather Lemmon, October 13, 1883–1982. She is buried in the Cook-Walden Capital Parks Cemetery and Mausoleum, Pflugerville, Travis County, Texas. She married Caleb Dorsey Lemmon (1886–1931). Her son was **Merle C. Feather**. With Caleb Dorsey she had four more children: James Dorsey Lemmon, Georgia Lucille Lemmon Jayner, Martha Ruth Lemmon Abernathy, and Robert Warner Lemmon.

⚜ Dressie M. Feather (May 10, 1887–June 17, 1887), she died of spinal disease at one month old and is likely to be buried in Lenox Memorial. There is an "unknown" occupant in the grave next to Irena's

⚜ Jessie Flo Feathers Roby (November 19, 1889–March 17, 1926). She married Jesse Lloyd Roby (1886-1960) in 1913, and they had five children: Harold Lloyd Roby (1913–1983), Clyde G. Roby Sr. (1915–1973); Jesse Paul Roby (1918–1990); Helen Ruth Roby Funk (1920–2017); and Goldie M. Roby (d. 1917);

Verna May Feather Welch (July 17, 1894–July 9, 1975). She married Earl Welch (1892–1972) in 1916. They had four children: Dorotha Alfreda Welch Folk (1917–2009), Dr. Charles Darrel Welch (1919–2021), Willis Hugh Welch (1933–2017), and Kathryn Elaine "Kay" Welch Rose (1936–2011).

Edgar Roy, (September 13, 1892-November 16, 1892).

Isaac B. Feather
December 5, 1834–April 30, 1921
Lineage: Zaccheus & Elizabeth (Ervin), Jacob & Mary
Row North E / 10

Isaac B. Feather was the husband of **Elizabeth Reckart** (1834–1917). They were married in 1864.

Their children were **Andrew Elias** (1865–1947), Melissa Ellen Feather Bishoff (1867–1923), **Emma Belle Feather Haun** (1868–1918), Thomas Jefferson (1870–1953), Henry Clay (1874–1947), and **Benjamin Gilbert Feather** (1877–1918).

He was a Civil War veteran, serving in Company A of the 7th Infantry. The 1880 U.S. Census showed his occupation as farmer. In 1873, he owned 108 acres on Muddy Creek adjoining Joseph Miller's lands.

Isaac suffered a farm-related accident in 1909. *The Preston County Journal* of July 29, noted that "Isaac B. Feather who is seventy four years old, fell off a load of hay yesterday and broke his collar bone and right shoulder. He was standing on the hay wagon when the horse suddenly started and the jerk threw him to the ground."

Isaac Christian Feather
March 25, 1866–September 21, 1934
Lineage: Jacob Luther & Phebe Jane (Martin),
Christian & Catherine (Dunham), Jacob & Mary
Undetermined location

Isaac Christian Feather married Rosa May Wilson (1880–1964) in 1900. Their children were Hannah Catharine Feather Smouse (1st) Albright (2nd) (1896–1956), Nechie Loye Feather Titchenell (1898–1981), Phoebe Jane Feather(s) Pounds (1899–1977), **Russell Jacob Benton Feather,** (1901–1969), Remington Charles Edward Feather, b. 8/21/1914, and Curtis Earl Feather(s) (1918–1992).

Isaac C. was a farmer. In 1930, he owned 93½ acres on Morgans Run in Kingwood District. He died in Manown, Preston County, after a year of suffering from stomach cancer. Rosa, who died October 11, 1964, is buried in Maplewood Cemetery.

Rosa's obituary states she was survived by three sons—Charles and Russell Feather of Masontown and Curtis of Kingwood—and two daughters, Mrs. Nititia Titchenell of Kingwood and Mrs. Pheobe Jane Pounds of Morgantown. Curtis, who used the plural version of the surname, was a sergeant in the US Army and is buried in the West Virginia National Cemetery at Pruntytown, W.Va.

Isabelle Rodeheaver Feather
August 2, 1857–November 18, 1948
Row North D / 9

The wife of **Josiah Feather, Isabelle Rodeheaver** was born in McHenry, Garrett County, Maryland. She was a daughter of Samuel Patrick and Mary Anne Sisler Rodeheaver. The Rodeheavers were from Virginia; Isabelle's grandfather, Christopher (Christian) Columbus Rodeheaver, was born in Virginia in 1796 and died in Garrett County, Maryland. He is buried in the Parnell Cemetery at Cuzzart. Samuel Patrick Rodeheaver (1822–1883), Christopher's son, is buried in the Rodeheaver Cemetery, Oakland, Maryland. Josiah and Isabelle did not have children.

Jacob & Mary (Connoly) Feather
September 10, 1759–May 22, 1832
Lineage: Joseph Christian Vätter & Ann Marie Wismanns Vätter
Row North O / 8

Jacob Feather, patriarch of the Feather (Vätter) family in Preston County, was born in Frankenthal, the Palatinate region of Germany, to Joseph Christian (1733–1799) and Marie (Maria) Wismanns Vätter (1737–1800). He came to the Pennsylvania colony aboard the *King of Prussia* ship with his parents and sister in the fall 1775.

Jacob served as a private in the American Revolutionary War and was with Washington's army when it crossed the Delaware River in a near blizzard

Jacob & Mary Connoly Feather, continued

Hallowed ground for Feather descendants; the burial spot of Jacob and Mary Feather.

December 25–26, 1776, to make a surprise attack upon the Hessian soldiers at Trenton, New Jersey. He encamped at Valley Forge and was present at the surrender of Cornwallis at Yorktown, 1781.

Jacob came as a redemptioner. He had to pay for his passage, and possibly that of his sister, by working for his benefactor or master. That person could have been a relative or a Philadelphia-area resident to whom Jacob became indentured. Unfortunately, indenture documentation for that period of Philadelphia history has been lost, so we do not know who redeemed Jacob.

By 1790, Jacob, his parents and sister had migrated to Bedford County, Pennsylvania. He married Mary Connoly (Connery) May 24, 1791, in Milford Township, now Somerset county. Mary is a mystery. Her birthplace has traditionally been reported as Bedford County, but the region was sparsely populated in 1769. No adults by that surname could be located in historical and tax records for that time in Bedford County. And no Connoly family members were at the wedding. The author proposes several scenarios in *My Fathers' Land*, which delves more deeply into this "Mystery of Mary."

Following the deaths of his mother and father, the family pushed into Preston County, circa 1803, and established their first home at Guseman, where Jacob owned 75 acres.

Jacob & Mary Connoly Feather, continued

The children of Mary and Jacob Feather were:

✤ **Mary Ann Feather**, October 28, 1792–December 12, 1794. She is buried in the Schneider Family Cemetery on private property at Casselman, Pennsylvania, where her grandparents, aunt, and uncle are buried.

✤ **John Solomon Feather**, February 8, 1794–March 25, 1870. Born in Bedford County, Pennsylvania. Married **Mary Ervin.**

✤ Jacob Feather Jr., March 2, 1796–December 24, 1847, born in Bedford County. His first wife was Mary Sisler, who bore one child, Jacob Adam. Next was Susan Mah Wolfe, who gave him two children, Daniel Wolfe (b. 1821), and Susan F. Feather Nugent (b. 1825). His third wife was Mary Silgens (Siggens) (1805–1890). Their children were Mary Feather Core (b. 1829), Ezekiel Clarence (b. 1831), James (1836–1903), Narcissus Amelia Feather Fawcett (b.1838), Sara Elizabeth (1842–1917), and Sophia (1845–1848).

Some Feather trivia: James moved to Aledo, Warren County, Illinois, where he became a very successful businessman, "accumulating an estate of $100,000," according to his obituary. In 2024 purchasing power, that would be more than $3 million!

Jacob Jr. obtained a patent for land along Green's Run near Kingwood circa the late 1820s, which marked the exodus of a second-generation Feather from Crab Orchard. Because two of his wives had the same first name as his mother, references to "Jacob and Mary" can be vexing for researchers. By the third generation, there are even more "Jacob Feathers" to contend with—at least five Jacob Feathers are buried in Lenox Memorial.

✤ **Eve Catharine Feather,** January 16, 1798–December 17, 1854, Somerset County, Pennsylvania. She married **John Lewis.** They had nine children, six of them survived to adulthood.

✤ **Adam Feather,** April 25, 1800–July 30, 1884, Somerset County, Pennsylvania. His wives were **Mary Summers, Sabra Eusebia Summers.**

✤ **Christian Feather,** August 15, 1802–January 1, 1883, Somerset County, Pennsylvania. Married **Catharine Dunham.**

✤ **Zaccheus Feather,** July 14, 1805–March 1, 1891, Monongalia County, Virginia. His wife was **Elizabeth Ervin.**

✤ Sarah Feather, June 24, 1807–May 24, 1893, Monongalia County, Virginia. Married James Beatty and they had nine children, all born in Preston County: Robert (1829-1862), Jacob (1830–1897), May C. (b. 1832), Elizabeth Beatty Snyder (1834-1892), John T. (1835–1920), Louisa (b.

1839), Martha Ann Beatty Blicksenderfer (1841–1888), Hulda Sarah Beatty Taylor (1844–1911), and Lucy A. Beatty Charlton (1846–1905). There are some discrepancies between the Findagrave dates and Rogers' book. Sarah and James headed west to Iowa sometime after the birth of their last child. Sarah died in Grace Hill, Washington County, Iowa, and is buried at Keota Cemetery, Keota, Iowa, where her husband also was interred, but not together. The cemetery is Moravian; in that faith, men are buried in one section, women in another.

⁂ **James Feather,** June 4, 1809–May 29, 1886, Monongalia County, Virginia. Married **Catharine Jane Lewis; Christeen Summers**.

⁂ Jane Virginia Feather, October 14, 1810–October 2, 1876, Crab Orchard, Virginia. She married Israel Shaffer (Shaffaer) and they worked a portion of the former William Morgan farm. Both are buried in Kingwood. They had eight children: Zaccheas Allen (b. 1836), Mary Elizabeth Schaeffer Trowbridge (1837–1869), Susanna Katherine Shaffer Wilson (1839–1922), Nancy Maria Schaeffer Shaw (1840–1929), Jacob F. (1842–1866), Rev. Gustavus Cresap (1844–1927), William Morgan (1847–1924), and Sarah Jane Shaffer Wilson (1849–1899).

Zaccheas Allen, according to a newspaper article, "left home in early life and (was) never heard from." Jacob F. was a soldier in Company A, 7th West Virginia Infantry. He contracted tuberculosis and died a few months after the war ended. All of the children are buried in the Kingwood area except Gustavus, who is in Center Grove Cemetery, Warren County, Illinois.

⁂ Joseph B. Feather, July 14, 1816–June 29, 1896, Crab Orchard, Virginia. He married Lydia Hartman and they had six children: Mary Jane Feather Falkenstein (1838–1926), Sara Elizabeth Feather Cale (1840–1882), John Hartman (1842–1894), Margaret Catharine Feather Michael (1844–1932), Jacob Wesley (1845–1930), and Michael E. (1849–1889). Joseph and Lydia are buried Bruceton Mills.

Joseph B. was a very successful businessman and highly regarded in the community. Jacob Welsey served in Company K, 17th West Virginia Infantry.

My Fathers' Land goes into greater detail about Jacob's life, military service, farms that he owned, the German-farmer traditions practiced in America, and life in Crab Orchard. It also provides much more information on Christian and his son, **Adam H.**, and Adam's son, Walter James Feather, and grandson, Russel Feather.

Jacob Adam Feather
March 29, 1819–January 23, 1856
Lineage: Jacob Feather Jr. & Mary (Sisler), Jacob & Mary
(Likely) Row M / 15 (Mary Feather)

Jacob Adam Feather was the only child born to Jacob Jr. and his first wife, Mary Sisler, who possibly died in childbirth. Jacob Adam married **Mary Ann Kelly** (1824–1901). She was a daughter of Joseph and Dorcas Browning Kelly.

Jacob Adam and Mary Ann Feather had one son, **Josiah Feather**, who survived to adulthood.

The headstone is for Mary A. Feather. Evidently, Jacob Adam's marker did not survive or never existed. The location is based on the assumption that Mary A. is in 15 and the "unknown" occupant of grave 16 is her husband.

Jacob Emery Feather
January 10, 1835–January 7, 1925
Lineage: John Solomon & Mary (Evin), Jacob & Mary
Row North G / 6

Jacob Emery married **Mariah "Annie" Welch Feather** (1837–1920). Their children were Thalbert Clairnton (1862–1897), Theodore Samuel (1864–1947), Lilly Catharine Harned (unknown), **John Mark** (1875–1940), and **Winfield Scott** (1880–1951).

From the *Preston Republican* of Terra Alta, January 15, 1925:

> Mr. Jacob E. Feather died suddenly in the depot at Albright on Wednesday evening, January 7, 1925. His death was due to heart failure and old age. He was ninety years old. His wife preceded him to the grave about five years ago. Four children survive, three sons who live near Albright and a daughter in Ohio. Funeral services were conducted by Rev. McCarty at the Lutheran Church near Lenox. Mr. Feather had reached the oldest age ever attained by a Feather in this section and had been a resident of Preston County all his life.

He lived in Portland District and, in 1910, owned 36 ¾ acres on Muddy Creek off Coal Lick Road. From *The Preston County Journal* of January 2,

1896, we know he raised turkeys, delivering to J. A. Lenhart a lot of dressed turkeys, the largest of which weighed 22 pounds. The bird earned him $2.20.

As with many Preston County land owners, Jacob E. and his wife sold their mineral rights in the early 20th century. In 1902 they sold rights to 110 7/8 acres of coal situated on the waters of Coal Lick Run in Portland District.

By 1884, their son, Thalbert, was living in Kansas. Tragedy followed both sons of Thalbert Clairnton and his wife, Anna Felton. Private Carl T. Feather, died November 1, 1918, at Camp Cody in Deming New Mexico. He was 28. Carl's brother, Sargent Roy Leeland, died at Camp Zachary Taylor, Louisville, Kentucky. Roy was killed while riding hurdles on a horse. The horse fell and crushed Roy, 31, who had gone through World War I as a regular soldier in Europe without any injury. The brothers are buried side-by-side in the Odd Fellows Cemetery, Jefferson County, Kentucky.

Thalbert moved to Kansas in 1884 and died at New Ponca, Oklahoma, January 8, 1897. "Just before he died he called his wife and two little boys to his side and bid them good-bye and said: "Tell father, mother and my brothers and sisters not to weep for me, for I am ready and the Savior is waiting for me to come." (*The Preston County Journal*, April 15, 1897). Thalbert C. is buried in the Odd Fellows Cemetery, Ponca City, Oklahoma.

Jacob F. Feather
January 4, 1837–June 15, 1919
Lineage: Zaccheus & Elizabeth (Irvin), Jacob and Mary
Row North Q / 3

Jacob F. Feather married **Nancy Wilhelm** (1840–1921). Their children were Henry L. (b. 1864), Ezra A. (1865–1914), Ulysses Simpson Grant (b. 1868), Flora B. (b. 1869), **Rhuea J. Kelly** (1870–1892), **Ellis** (1871–1881), **Marth**a (1874–1881), **Gilbert S.** (1877–1881), and **Arzona S.** (1884–1891).

Feather trivia: By the third generation, there were so many Jacob Feathers in Preston County, residents distinguished them by their traits. There was Lying Jacob, Horse-Stealing Jacob, and Drinking Jacob, for example. We don't know what traits Jacob F. possessed. He seemed to have lived a very obscure life, and no published obituary could be located. Considering that none of his children survived him, he was a man well acquainted with grief and loss.

Jacob Luther Feather
July 18, 1846–May 1, 1935
Lineage: Christian & Catherine (Dunham), Jacob & Mary
Row North P / 5

Jacob Luther married **Phebe Jane Martin.** Eleven children were born to the couple: **Isaac Christian** (1866–1934), Sarah Catherine Feather Bishop (1867–1958), Minerva Jane Feather Shears (1874–1904), **Joseph Wesley Feather** (1875–1878), Laura Rebecca Feather Tichnell (1878–1955), Benton Luther (1880–1953), Harriet "Hattie" Belle Feather Metheny (1881–1968), Nora Ella Feather Metheny (1890–1978), Myrtle Allie Feather Davis (b. 1891), Curtis Jesse Feather (1896–1971).

The 1880 U.S. Census recorded Jacob L. as a laborer. In 1930, he owned 36 ¾ acres on Muddy Creek.

James Feather
June 26, 1810–May 29, 1886
Lineage: Jacob & Mary
Row North W / 3

James Feather was a farmer and owned 145 acres on Crab Orchard Run. He died at the home of his son, Samuel E. Feather, near Cuzzart. His obituary stated that he probably died of heart disease and "died very suddenly, having complained of feeling badly only a short time before his death." He was a member of the M.E. Church and recalled as "a very kind man, and loved by all who knew him," according to his obituary.

He and his first wife, **Catharine Jane Lewis Feather** (1809–1839) had three children: Jacob (1832–1889), Malinda Jane White (1834) and Joseph Czalmon (1837–1920).

Malinda married John Nelson White (1827–1864) on December 23, 1855. He was a corporal in Company C of the 3rd Infantry of Virginia. He died from dysentery October 13, 1864, in Andersonville Prison, leaving her to care for her four children. She died at the age 54.

With his second wife, **Christeen Summers Feather,** James had 11 children (see her listing for names).

James Christian Feather, Jr.
March 9, 1848–July 27, 1937
Lineage: Christian & Catherine (Dunham), Jacob & Mary
Row North L / 1

James C. Feather Jr. married **Irena Ellen Ervin** in 1874. Their children are listed under Irena's entry.

Their daughter, Osa Grace Feather Lemmon (1875–1982), who is buried in Cook-Walden Capital Parks Cemetery and Mausoleum, Pflugerville, Texas, bore a son, **Merle C.**, before she married Caleb Dorsey Lemmon (1886–1931). Rogers' *Genealogy* identifies Osa's first husband and Merle C.'s father as "J.A. Feather." Merle C. married **Wanda Ellen Hillery** (1907–1998), a Cranesville native.

Wanda recalled those early days of marriage and living on the farm in a memoir, contributed to this work by her granddaughter, Wendy Feather McLaughlin. The following excerpt draws a detailed picture of what life was like on a Feather farm in the late-1920s and early 1930s.

> Merle was busy planting corn. Grandpa Feather (James C.) helped. He was in his late seventies, but in real good health for his age. Grandma (Irena) had arthritis and asthma, at times almost helpless. Other times she did real well. Grandpa had been helping with the housework. Merle helped when he wasn't with the outside work. ...
>
> Grandma was a good teacher. I enjoyed being outside. I helped in the garden, hoed corn and learned to milk. I'd hurry to finish the dishes so I could help with the milking. We milked four cows, separated (the milk and cream), fed the milk to the pigs and churned the cream into butter. ...
>
> When hay season came we all helped. Merle mowed and when the hay was cured, I raked with old Fanny. Using a dump rake, Merle pitched the hay onto the wagon with a pitchfork. Grandpa would load it. Old Jenny and Norm pulled the wagon. When the raking was done, I would get on the wagon and help tramp the fluffy hay. Grandma would have dinner and supper ready for us. It sure tasted

good. In the barn they pulled the hay up with a hay fork. This was pulled with a horse and tripped by pulling a rope.

We canned green beans and corn from the truck patch. This was done by placing a board in the clothes boiler and putting the jars in and covering them with water. They were brought to a boil and boiled ninety minutes. We never had any food poisoning. We canned cherries, peaches, pears, apples, applesauce and made lots of jams and jellies.

We peeled a tub of apples one day and the next day we built a fire very early and hung a fifteen gallon copper kettle over it. Into this was poured fresh apple cider and the apple snits as they were called. One person stirred, the others peeled and cored more apples to fill in with until the kettle was full of applesauce. This was cooked for hours until it had a reddish color. Sugar and spices were added. This was Grandma's job. She was good at it. The apple butter was divided. Some was put into jars and sealed for the next summer's use. The rest was put into crocks. This was used during the winter months. They were stored in the milk house until the very cold weather. They were then moved upstairs.

We also made our soap for laundry, washing dishes and scrubbing. We did a soft soap for the scrubbing. This was made in an iron kettle outside. We used cracklings left over from rendering lard, fats from frying sausage, bacon, and other meats. Along with lye, this was boiled together. It was stored in large crocks.

This was also used to wash the carpet. The carpet was woven from rags torn into strips, sewed together, and rolled into balls. A few homes had looms on which to weave the carpet, but you could send the rags away to a factory to be woven. The strips of carpet were sewed together at home and tacked to the floor with carpet tacks. Sometimes this was taken up and washed by scrubbing with a brush outside on a table. Other times it was scrubbed on the floor. We didn't have a sweeper, only a broom.

Late November, we butchered three or four large hogs. Neighbors helped one another. They built a fire, heated a large barrel of water and put the killed and bled hog into it, half at a time. They then scraped the hair off. They hung them by putting a wooden peg

James Christian Feather, Jr., continued

through at the ankle and hanging them on a scaffold. The insides were then taken out and the carcass was washed down. They hung over night. If the weather was very cold, they were hung in the barn floor.

The next day they were cut into hams, shoulders and bacons. These were salted or sugar cured, then hung in the smokehouse until March and then smoked. Hickory wood was used. They were put into cotton bags. These were rehung in the smokehouse until they were sold at the store or used at home.

The head was cut up and cooked for mincemeat. The tongue was skinned and cooked to eat or added to the feet shanks for souse. Sometimes liverwurst was made by adding the liver. These were put into crocks and stored in the milk house. The trimmings were ground for sausage. Some of it was put into crocks after frying first. Hot lard was poured over to seal. This was eaten during the winter. For summer use, the sausage was cold packed. The ribs and backbone were cooked, sealed with lard, and stored for winter use.

The fat was rendered for lard. This was put into jars, sealed while very hot. We used lard in cookies, for pies, and frying. We didn't know anything about cholesterol. With all the work and walking we did we didn't worry about being overweight.

Grandpa Feather wanted meat on the table at every meal. It was depression time, but we ate very well. In fact, better than I ever had. . . .

Irena died March 13, 1931, a little over a year after her great-grandson, William Lloyd "Bill,",was born to Wanda and Merle C. Wanda's memoir includes her recollections of the relationship between Bill and her grandfather, James C.

> Grandpa grew even closer to Bill after her death. Family visited often, but he seemed happier just sitting with Bill, reading to him, or taking long walks.
> I would try to relieve Grandpa, but neither would have it. Bill even slept with him. When Bill started to school, Grandpa would

James Christian Feather, Jr., continued

walk with him to the end of the lane. He would meet him in the evenings.

(James C.) had trouble with his eyes. He had cataracts on both eyes. Something burst in one eye. They took him to a doctor in Morgantown. They removed his eye. He was blind after that and didn't seem to get his strength back. His mind had been slipping for some time. He thought the Albright National Bank had cheated him out of some money. No amount of reasoning could change his mind.

Most of the time he seemed to function very well. We were milking eleven cows, separating and feeding the skimmed milk to the calves. This was what we were doing when he fell and broke his hip. Bill would lead him around. He was real good at it. (One) morning he led him to the chair. Grandpa sat down but missed the chair. The doctor didn't set his hip. He wanted to wait. Within ten days (James C.) had developed pneumonia. He only lasted a few days. He was 89 years old. We missed him so much. Aunt Molly and Aunt May helped care for him.

The family still thought of the farm as home. They loved visiting us or coming home. The children still came to spend their vacations with us. Grandpa's sister, Aunt Sarah, came for visits. We enjoyed them all very much. We had bought the stone house farm from the Morgan heirs. This was before Grandpa died. He gave us some money on the down payment. He didn't want to leave his home, so we rented the house to Lias Kelly's family.

Merle farmed both farms and the way Grandpa was, I wasn't much help. We had a real hard year. The next fall we moved to the stone house. The house was in need of repair. Several families had lived in it. Nobody did anything to improve it. We did a lot of painting and papering.

Wanda Hillery Feather

James C.'s brother, **Adam H.**, died in 1888, leaving several children as orphans (his wife died the prior year). James C. and Irena took on the responsibility of raising the children and settling the estate.

They eventually acquired Adam's land, which is part of the "Feather Lane" property that Merle C. and his son, William L. Feather, farmed.

William's son, Larry, and his wife, Julie, own and the land in 2024, and they live in the stone house that dates to 1821 (built by the Cress family).

James Connery Feather
June 9, 1837–August 13, 1927
Lineage: John Solomon & Mary (Ervin), Jacob & Mary

James Connery Feather married **Martha Virginia "Mattie" Rodeheaver Feather.** Their children were **Alva Clifton** (1863–1933), **Harvey Arlington** (1864–1920), Alitia May "Allie" Feather Crane (1866–1944), and Bessie Ada Feather Hayden (1872–1957).

Although all of his children were born in Albright, which encompasses the lower end of Coal Lick Road, James died in Red Stone Township, Fayette County, Pennsylvania. He was one of the longest lived male Feathers, attaining the age of 90 before succumbing to paralysis.

James Connery's name is of particular interest, for it suggests that the surname of Mary Feather was not Connoly, but Connery; several 19th century documents support this theory, including the Feather family Bible and reunion minutes.

Tracing James Connery's story through the pages of *The Preston County Journal* is treacherous because James C. Feather (prior entry) also lived during the same time and in the same area. For example, a "Crab Orchard Culling" from *The Preston County Journal* of September 30, 1886, states that "James C. Feather and Uncle Mike Albright have gone to Hagerstown with a car-load of cattle." In that same column, it was noted that "James C. Feather talks of moving to Terra Alta this fall. Jim is one of our best citizens; would be sorry to lose him from our midst." This is most likely a reference to James C. Jr.; the 1870 and 1880 U.S. Censuses place him in Terra Alta; the 1900 U.S. Census places him in Portland District.

From U.S. Census records, it is clear that James Connery was content to stay in Portland District, where he was a farmer—even at the age of 82, when the 1920 U.S. Census was taken.

Jared Allen Feather
(December 22, 1856–June 23, 1941)
Lineage: Harrison & Catherine (Welch), John Solomon & Mary (Ervin),
Jacob & Mary
Row North K / 2

Jared "Jurd" Feather briefly owned a portion of the original Jacob and Mary homestead farm on Lutheran Church Road. Jared married Sarah J. Hartman (1860–1949), the daughter of **Joseph** and **"Annie" Susanna (Miller) Hartman**, in 1881. They had an unnamed male child, born and died January 13, 1888, and buried in Lenox Memorial. No grave markers could be found for the child or parents.

A brief mention in *The Preston County Journal* of 1884 places his home in Willey. Jared owned 170 acres in Crab Orchard, Pleasant District, in 1915. His death certificate states his occupation was farmer, but during the school term of 1881–82 in Pleasant District, Jared served as a teacher (as did J.H. Feather).

Jerad's siblings were **Samantha Jane Feather Rodeheaver** (1851–1934), Mary Caroline Feather Rodeheaver-Godly (1855-1924, buried in Tennessee), and **Levi Hess Feather** (1858–1920).

John Harvey Feather
February 5, 1908–October 3, 1965
Lineage: Harvey Arlington and Georgia Etta (Jackson), James Connery and Martha Virginia (Rodeheaver), John Solomon & Mary (Ervin), Jacob & Mary
Row South C / 10

John Harvey Feather married **Madeline Florence Shaffer** (1910–1998) on July 14, 1928 in Oakland, Maryland.

They had no children. The 1950 Preston County land book shows them owning approximately 90 acres in Crab Orchard. His death certificate shows his occupation was farmer.

John M. Feather
1875–1940
Lineage: Jacob Emery & Mariah Ann (Welch),
John Solomon & Mary (Evin), Jacob & Mary
Row North S / 14

If a stone carver were to fill in the date of death on the headstone for **John Mark Feather**, it would read "1940." Perhaps because his wife had died 10 years before him, that detail was not attended to after his passing on February 7, 1940. A marriage license was issued to John M. (22) and **Annie R. Kelly** (28) in September 1897. Rogers' *Genealogy* gives her middle name as "Sirissi." They had one son, **Earl Smith Feathers**.

John Mark's World War I draft card showed his occupation as a self-employed farmer living in Albright. He was medium height, slender build, had blue eyes and brown hair.

John Solomon Feather
February 11, 1794–March 25, 1870
Lineage: Jacob & Mary
Row North M / 16

Born in Bedford County, Pennsylvania, **John Solomon Feather** would have been a teenager at the time Jacob and Mary migrated to Preston County. It is likely much of the hard work of breaking the land fell upon his shoulders and back.

John Solomon, Jacob's and Mary's firstborn son, was a farmer. He most likely inherited and continued to farm Jacob's land after his father died, but according to the "Reckart Saga," John Solomon purchased the Reckart farm and Adam took over the homestead farm circa 1845. This is conjecture as the courthouse records from that period were lost to fire. We do know that John and Mary sold 145 ½ acres to James C. Feather for $1,500 in April 1868..

John Solomon, following in his father's tradition as a soldier in the Revolutionary War, enlisted in the Virginia Militia September 19, 1812, and was discharged April 10, 1813 (War of 1812).

He married **Mary Ervin**, who was born February 19, 1800, in Monongalia

John Solomon Feather, continued

John Solomon's and Mary Feathers' stones have retained much of their lettering. Row North M, Nos. 15 and 16. The cemetery register has John's grave as "unknown."

County, and died September 30, 1878. She had a very productive life and bore 15 children:

🙵 Abraham, February 16, 1818–March 29, 1905. He married Elizabeth Boylan (1818–1907) in 1837. At the age of 16, he was considered a proficient team master and drove a six-horse team from Wheeling, W.Va., to Baltimore. He served in the 212th Regiment 6th Heavy Artillery of Pennsylvania for nine months of the Civil War. A Lutheran from the time he was eight days old, he joined the Methodist camp at the age of 20 and served as both a class leader and song leader in the congregation. His obituary noted that Abraham's home was always open to ministers of all denominations. "He believed and taught, that religion was the highest aim of man, peace and unity the source of happiness. He sided with the poor and oppressed and willingly gave alms."

His funeral service was conducted at the Baptist Church in Albrightsville, and Abraham was laid to rest in the Albright Cemetery.

At the time of his death, Abraham 13 children, 31 grandchildren, and 28 great-grandchildren in his line!

⚜ Lydia, June 19, 1839–February 25, 1905. She married David D. Bishoff (1840–1903). They had three children. Like Adam, Lydia was committed to the Methodist Episcopal Church and was described as an example of sincerity in her faith. She is buried in Maplewood Cemetery, Kingwood;

⚜ **Harrison,** 1823–1903;

⚜ **Rebecca Feather Kelly,** October 6, 1825–October 15, 1900;

⚜ **John Quincy Feather,** June 6, 1827–October 29, 1846 (**Infants and Children**);

⚜ **Rachel Virginia Feather Scott,** September 27, 1828–October 29, 1846;

⚜ **Levi Feather,** June 17, 1830–November 21, 1861;

⚜ **Louisa Jane Feather Forman,** May 30, 1832–March 4, 1917;

⚜ **Isaac,** November 18, 1833–April 16, 1865;

⚜ **Jacob Emery,** January 10, 1835–January 7, 1925;

⚜ **James Connery,** June 9, 1837–August 13, 1927.;

⚜ Joseph Marcellus Feather, April 3, 1839–April 3, 1918. He was a private in Company F, 17th W.Va. Infantry, serving from June 1864 to June 1865. He married Malinda Ellen Hartman. Joseph is buried in the Kearney Cemetery, Buffalo County, Nebraska. They had a son, Artimus Milroy Feather, born in Wheeling August 3, 1865, and died January 19, 1930, also buried in Nebraska;

⚜ **David O. Feather,** August 9, 1841–March 15, 1906;

⚜ Samuel E. Feather, January 25, 1843–May 30, 1876. He married Alcesta Jane Brownfield (1847–1909). They had two children: Etta B. Feather McDonald (1870–1952) and Guy Allen (1876–1958), both buried in the Mount Moriah Baptist Cemetery, Smithfield, Fayette County, Pennsylvania.

John Summers Feather
January 7, 1827–February 13, 1909
Lineage: Adam & Mary (Summers), Jacob & Mary
Row North J / 1

John Summers Feather married **Sarah M. Harvey** in 1850, and they had eight children: Solomon Bell (1850–1944); Margaret Jane Feather Forman (1853–?); Joseph W. (1856–?); Melissa May (1862–1880); Mary Catharine Guseman (1864–1946); **Eliza V.** (1867–1888), who shares the gravestone with

John Summers and Mary Catharine Feather, Guseman/Feather wedding

her parents; Cora Belle Feather Cramer, (1872–1944); and Orpha Christine Feather Cramer (1874–1845).

John Summers died February 13, 1909, at the home of his son, Solomon, in Terra Alta.

A brief article in *The Preston County Journal* of April 6, 1893, makes note of a tragedy that fell upon the family:

> John S. Feather, who purchased the Cramer farm near Preston Tannery last spring and moved his family onto it from Craborchard, had his dwelling house and all its contents destroyed by fire recently. The loss falls heavily upon him and his neighbors are lending a helping hand.

A Gathering of Feathers: 1888 wedding

A wedding was an occasion for eating and celebrating in the Crab Orchard community. *The Preston County Journal* of March 1, 1888, provides a glimpse into the festivities involving Mary Catharine Feather, daughter of John Summers and Sarah Harvey Feather. She was born September 16, 1864, and was a granddaughter of Adam Feather. Her groom, Theodore Jacob Guseman, was born April 5, 1867.

> Our quiet neighborhood was shaken from centre to circumference by the announcement that a wedding was to take place on Wednesday, Feb. 22, '88, the contracting parties being Mr. Theodore Guseman and Miss Catharine, daughter of John S. Feather, of the Crab orchard. The ceremony was performed at Brandonville by the Rev. L.W. Roberts, after which the happy couple drove back to the residence of the bride's parents, where a large number of guests were awaiting their arrival. After congratulations, the party repaired to the dining room, ample justice was done to an excellent supper. An old fashioned serenade was given them. It was late when the pleasant party dispersed.
>
> The following is a partial list of the presents: Olive Feather, butter dish; Lilly Feather, fruit dish and salt shaker; Hess Feather, set table spoons; Maxie Forman, pickle dish; Mrs. L. J. Forman, parlor lamp; H. M. Martin and C. D. Feather, $1; Mrs. J. A. Feather,

meat dish and pickle dish; Orlena Childs, spoon holder; Mr. and Mrs. J. F. Rodeheaver, pair towels, large lamp and jelly cake; May Welch, pickle dish; Mr. and Mrs. Jos. Welch, pair towels; U.S. Welch, Turkish towel; Mr. and Mrs. Josiah Feather, cream pitcher an desert dish; J. W. Childs, pickle dish; Mrs. E. Forman, jelly dish; Mack Hartman, cream pitcher; Jud. Childs, butter dish; Belle Forman, cake stand; Clay Crane, pepper box; Smith Crane, large fruit dish; Scott Crane, glass set; Mr. and Mrs. J. C. Feather, bread plate and large cake; Mollie and Bessie Feather, pair glass dishes; Frank Hartman, pickle dish; Mrs. and Mrs. Elmer Feather, large pitcher; Alice Feather, cake stand; Mollie Forman, counter pin; Mr. and Mrs. Harry Feather, cream pitcher and molasses mug; Willie Forman, glass pitcher.

Despite this warm reception in Crab Orchard, the couple did not remain in the community. Their first child, Clara Phelicia Guseman, was born in Missouri on January 21, 1891, and died July 31, 1892. Their second child, Italia May Guseman, born March 29, 1890, died June 20, 1891, also in Missouri. Their third child, John Willie Jacob Guseman, lived to be only 14. Their next five children were born in Missouri, lived to adulthood and married, but tragedy struck again in 1900 with Lovina Guseman, who lived for only 54 days. Their last child, Elmer Theodore Guseman, lived to be 72.

Both Mary Catharine and Theodore Jacob Guesman are buried in Inglewood Park Cemetery, Los Angeles County, California. One has to wonder if all those pickle dishes went west with them.

(The Rev.) Joseph B. Feather
November 3, 1833–August 15, 1920
Lineage: Adam & Sabra Eusebia (Summers), Jacob & Mary
Row North M / 10

Joseph B. Feather was born in Pennsylvania and moved to Preston County with his parents as a teenager. Although raised Lutheran, Joseph B. followed the path of Methodism as a teenager and therein found his calling as a pastor who served in Methodist Episcopal churches throughout West Virginia.

There is courthouse documentation that suggests Joseph B. owned the

Joseph B. Feather, continued

The Rev. Joseph B. Feather is buried with his first wife.

portion of the farm that included the home and barn (both long gone, see *My Fathers' Land* for further information). His circuit ministry took him away from the homestead as he served two-year pastoral terms across West Virginia. While virtually all of his ancestors had spent their adult lives toiling on the soil, Joseph B.'s primary interest was in cultivating hearts for the Gospel.

He was married twice. His first wife was **Mary Atkinson** (1833–1881). They met through his ministry in the Charleston area and had four children. Firstborn Jennie Virginia Feather (1858–?) married her cousin, Solomon Bell Feather. Firstborn son Elmer B. (1862–1940) married his cousin Minerva Bell Feather. Mattie E. Feather (1868–1919) married Elias B. Woodruff of

Green County, Pennsylvania. Frank Atkinson Feather (1876–1933) married Nellie B. Smith of Arnettsville (Yukon), Monongalia County.

Mary Atkinson Feather died in 1881, and three years later, Joseph B. married **Mary Lou Mercer** (1856–1919). Their only child, **Dana Wilbur Mercer Feather** (1886–1914) followed in his father's footsteps as a pastor.

Joseph B. gained the respect of the layperson and fellow clergy during his decades of service to Christianity. His obituary in *The Preston County Journal* of August 26, 1920, states that, "Many were the beautiful eulogies pronounced by the ministers in charge of his funeral regarding his unceasing labors of the long passed and the hardships and privatations [sic] he endured in the service of his Master in the earlier days of his beautiful Christian life and the wonderful work that has been accomplished under his kind and directing hand. The spirit of Rev. Joseph B. Feather has passed out of this world into life eternal but his long, useful and beautiful life will cling to our memories as long as life shall last."

The *West Virginia Pulpit of the Methodist Episcopal Church, Sermons From Living Ministers,* a book by George Wesley Atkinston, published in 1883, provides a personal sketch of Joseph B. Feather:

> In the good, old county of Preston, West Virginia, where the Allegheny mountains lift their summits toward the skies, on November 3, 1833, Rev. Joseph B, Feather was born. His parents, Adam and Sabra Feather, were of German extraction, and were well to do citizens of Northwestern Virginia. They were members of the Evangelical Lutheran Church, and in it, Joseph, the subject of this sketch, was baptized and brought up. When he was about seventeen years of age, he attended a revival meeting, carried on by the Methodists, near his home, and was converted. Shortly afterwards, he was licensed as an exhorter—having connected himself with the Methodist denomination—and at once took a leading part in Sunday School and other public religious services.
>
> In those days, schools were scarce, but Bro. Feather pursued his studies closely; and by the time he was eighteen years of age, he was himself prepared to teach, and began the business of teaching the young in the public schools—if such they could be called. He taught for two years, but (all) the while was preparing himself for

Joseph B. Feather, continued

the ministry, as he had satisfied himself fully that he had received the divine call to that great work.

January 1st, 1853, at the age of twenty, full of energy, life and hope, he was licensed to preach the unsearchable riches of Christ. This authority was received from the hands of the well-known Rev. H. Z. Adams, who has preached in almost every portion of what now comprises the territory of West Virginia.

Brother F.'s first Circuit was Barbour county, which he traveled as a "supply," with Rev. R. L. Brooks as preacher in charge. Having served his two years "on trial," he was admitted to the Conference in June, 1854, and sent to Glenville Circuit, with W. L. Hindman, as senior preacher. The two years following, he traveled Fork Lick and Charleston Circuits respectively, and his efforts on both of them were crowned with abundant success.

In April 1857, he and Miss Mary Atkinson, of Kanawha county, were united in marriage. Their union was a happy one, as they were devoted to each other, and bore the burdens of life as one. His kind and affectionate wife died June 11, 1881, in the triumphs of a living faith. Brother Feather in writing to me concerning the death of his companion, among other things said, "She was a great comfort to me, and was a valuable assistant in bearing the burdens of a ministerial life."

In addition to those already given, Bro. Feather filled the following appointments: Buffalo Circuit, one year; Monticello Mission, one year; Winfield Circuit, two years; Blacksville Circuit, two years; Monongalia Circuit, two years; Grantsville Circuit, two years; Brandonville Circuit, two years; Marshall Circuit, two years; Hartford City Station, two years; Evansville Circuit, one year. On account of feeble health, he took a super-anuated relation; but in the middle of the year, he was sent to Wesley Chapel, Wheeling, by Rev. Franklin Ball, D.D., the Presiding Elder of the Wheeling District. During the time of his pastorate there, he had a grand revival, which about doubled the membership of the station.

Owing to the failing health of his wife, and at his own request, he was sent to Palatine, a small Circuit in the interior of the Conference, where he remained three years. From there he went to

Pruntytown, where he served one year. Next, he went to Marion Circuit, and remained one year. His last appointment is Pleasant Hill Circuit, where he has been for two years, doing an earnest work for the Master.

Bro. Feather is a plain, earnest, faithful Gospel preacher. He is unassuming—bashful. He never sought a good appointment, nor would he allow any one to do anything looking to his advancement, if in his power to prevent. His rule has always been to go wherever sent, accept the situation, and do his best to spread the Truth among the people. Strange as it may seem, yet it is true, because the writer knows the man, he always preferred circuit to station work. He enjoyed the work of moving among the people and encouraging them to holy and upright lives. His has not been a brilliant life, but like the deep river, his course has been silent, steady, onward.

In the same book is published one of Joseph B.'s sermons, "The Half Has Not Been Told." The volume can be accessed at archive.org and through the download link at https://mds.marshall.edu/feather_josephb/1/.

Joseph B. suffered many hardships in his work and personal life. Those long distances between his home and conference assignments were often traversed on horseback. He had the sorrow of losing both of his wives to the grave, as well as his only son with Mary Lou Mercer, who was 23 years younger than Joseph B.

His course, as the biographer stated, was "silent, steady, onward."

Josiah Feather
June 8, 1853–August 8, 1928
Lineage: Jacob Adam & Mary Ann Kelly,
Jacob Feather Jr. & Mary (Sisler), Jacob & Mary
Row North D / 8

Josiah Feather married **Isabelle Rodeheaver** in 1877. They did not have children.

Josiah and Isabella owned 23 acres on Muddy Creek in Pleasant District and 76 acres on Cheat Hill. He was involved in local politics and served as Pleasant District justice of the peace. He narrowly defeated David S.

Josiah Feather, continued

Feather for that job in 1924. A Lutheran, he was a member of the church at Crab Orchard and served as superintendent of the Sunday school in 1901.

Josiah, identified as a merchant on his death certificate, was involved in several business ventures. A notice in the April 3, 1902, *Preston County Journal* announced that "Josiah Feather and Ezra Feather, are building a blacksmith shop one half mile north of Lenox and will fulfill the requirements of the people." Several years later, he was running a store at Lenox, which was the target of a robbery in 1904.

John Metheny and Jess Davis
Lodges in Jail Charged with Robbing a Store at Lenox

Yesterday John Metheny and Jess Davis were brought here and lodged in jail charged with robbing the store of Josiah Feather of Lenox. On Tuesday, Feather came to town and asked for a search warrant as he had information that his goods were in the possession of Metheny. The warrant was issued by Squire Morris and a posse went to that section to make investigation, and yesterday morning between four and five o'clock Metheny was met in the road. He had in his buggy a trunk and a good sized cracker box. When questioned he stated that he was going to Terra Alta. He was then placed under arrest and the box and trunk searched and found to contain clothing. He with the box and trunk were loaded into a wagon under the charge of Bruce Carroll and sent on to Kingwood. S.H. McClain, Arthur Miller and W. L. Addy had gone along to assist in the searching, but as they found the goods with Metheny, also returned, but D. R. Jackson went on to Terra Alta, hoping the intercept one of the Davis boys.

On Wednesday afternoon it was telephoned to town from Albright that Jesse Davis had just been there and had gone on toward Terra Alta. The sheriff telephoned there for them to catch him and sent Major Fields down to bring him up. John Elliott and Mart Mayfield caught Jesse Davis about two miles from there and brought him back from Albright, where they turned him over to D. R. Jackson and Minor Fields, and he was lodged in jail yesterday evening. Sim Davis another of the gang made his escape.

The two Davis boys are not natives of Preston county, having come here from Elkins, Randolph county. There were three brothers of them and all three served a term in the Reform School and one was hanged a few years ago at the penitentiary for the killing of the policeman at Elkins. Sim and Jesse have been here for about four years, while they did not make this there permanent home they were here (a) considerable (amount) of their time.

The Preston County Journal
December 29, 1904

That same newspaper of June 27, 1907, announced that "Josiah Feather and M. W. Hauger each got a carload of fertilizer for the farmers of this (Lenox) community." In another announcement, March 21, 1907, the newspaper stated, "Our (Crab Orchard) merchants C. W. Forman and Josiah Feather are doing a very nice business."

Josiah's store also housed the Lenox telephone switchboard, which in 1907 was moved from Englehart Woolen Mill.

In a notice published in the May 13, 1909, *Preston County Journal,* Josiah offered a $5 reward for information about "a young man by the name of Foster Hann" who had left Josiah's home on the 8th. The person was 14 years old, about 5 feet in height and 140 pounds with a dark complexion.

Josiah's will stipulated that Hillery W. Rodaheaver, his half-brother, would receive $5; Dayton Welch, Joseph Brice Welch and Goldie Welch (heirs of Olive Welch, his half-sister), each receive $1. The balance went to his wife, and after her death, whatever remained of the estate would go to Ezra and Emma E. Ringer.

Levi S. Feather
June 17, 1830–November 21, 1861
Lineage: John Solomon & Mary (Ervin), Jacob & Mary
Location unknown

Levi S. Feather married Emily Jefferys (Jefferies) of Brandonville at the bride's home (Edmund Jefferys) on December 17, 1859. They had one child, Margaret Ella Feather, born April 1, 1861. She married Albert Miller.

When the call went out for volunteers to fill Union ranks in the Civil War, Levi enlisted in Company A, 7th Infantry West Virginia, which conducted operations in the Potomac region in November 1861. Four Feathers were in the company: Levi, Issac B, and Josiah Feather, and Jacob Shaffer, son of Israel and Jane Feather Shaffer.

While on picket duty the morning of December 4, 1861, Levi was accidentally shot by Jacob H. Welch, a Company A corporal. Levi's commander, Samuel W. Snider, gave this account of the incident that occurred at Romney:

> While Levi Feather was going over a bank, his companion J. (Jacob) Welch pushed him with the muzzle of his gun and in doing so the lock caught on some brush causing the gun to go off, and the wound received caused his death November 21, 1861, he being at the time in the service and in the line of duty.

Emily died October 19, 1867, at the age of 36. Her burial location is possibly the Jeffers Cemetery in Hazelton. Her death rendered Margaret Ella a 6-year-old orphan, and John Feather was appointed guardian. U.S. Census records place Margaret in Fayette County, Pennsylvania, as early as 1870.

Margaret Ella married Albert Cameron Miller in Preston County on December 24, 1877; they had 11 children. She died July 7, 1923, and is buried in the Mount Moriah Baptist Cemetery, Smithfield, Fayette County, Pennsylvania.

Jacob Harrison Welch (1836-1906), the corporal who shot Levi, was related to Levi through Jacob's marriage to Rebecca Katherine Martin, the daughter of Lydia N. Feather, a daughter of **John S.** and **Mary Ervin Feather.** According to Jacob's obituary, he "saw more than two years of hard service" in Company A.

Levi Hess Feather
October 23, 1858–August 29, 1920
Lineage: Harrison & Catherine Jane (Welch), John S. & Mary (Ervin), Jacob & Mary
Row North M / 12

Levi Hess Feather was likely named for his uncle, **Levi Feather**, a son of **John Solomon**. Levi Hess married **Hulda Catharine Ringer** (1869–1951) on April 4, 1893. The had five children: Noral Faye Feather Fox (1894–1979), Mary Pearl Feather (1896–1947), **Virgil Gay Feather** (1898–1898), Jane Blanche Feather Nethamer (1905–1971), and Wanda Ameta Feather Allen (1908–1992). Only the infant is buried in Lenox Memorial.

It appears that Levi was known by his middle name, perhaps out of respect for his uncle. His death certificate lists his occupation as a farmer in Lenox. A Hess Feather owned 56 ½ acres at Crab Orchard in 1919. There are numerous references to Hess Feather in *The Preston County Journal*, as well. Some of those references place his residence as "Hayden," which was south of Crab Orchard.

⚜ Hess Feather has returned from the West. He says that Kansas is the best State he ever was in, and produces the most grain. April 2, 1885. (Note: H. S. Whetsell of Kingwood served as an agent for Kansas land and touted its wonders in Preston County newspapers. The rich, sub-irrigated soil was being offered at $12.50 to $35 per acre in 1907.)

⚜ Hess Feather will move on the Ballion farm this spring to crop for them. March 7, 1895

⚜ Hess Feather the genial farmer of the Crab Orchard was trading in town (Terra Alta) Tuesday. January 31, 1907

⚜ Mr. Hess Feather improved his dwelling house, by the addition of a new Kitchen. Hess is a hustler. March 7, 1907

⚜ Hess Feather is working for the Riley Lumber Co. Hess is a hustler. July 18, 1907

⚜ Hess Feather was exonerated from the payment of $1.00 road tax erroneously assessed to him, he being more than 50 years old. April 8, 1915

Louisa Jane Feather Forman
May 30, 1832–March 4, 1917
Lineage: John Solomon & Mary (Ervin), Jacob & Mary
Row North N / 13

Louisa Jane Feather married **John Forman** (1830–1880) on November 19, 1857. They had four children: Amanda Virginia Forman Nedrow (1859–1937), Rhuea Belle Forman Hartman (1864–1950), Mary Ellen Forman Hayes (1866–1940), and Willey McGrew Forman (1869–1945).

The Formans were Quaker English immigrants who came to William Penn's colony in 1682 and settled in the area of Philadelphia. In the early 1780s, Robert Forman and his wife, Mary Naylor Forman, departed Buck's County, Pennsylvania, and settled on property in Brandonville. They had 10 children; a son, Samuel (b. 1792), married Rachel Jeffreys. John, husband of Louisa Jane, was one of Samuel's and Rachel's children.

There have been numerous Forman/Feather marriages, perhaps most notable that of **Mahala "Hallie" I. Smith** (1854–1924) to **Charles Waitman (C. W.) Forman,** (1857–1925), a son of **Calvin Crane Forman,** John Forman's brother. Mahala was a daughter of Catharine Feather (1821–1891), who was a daughter of **John Solomon** and **Mary (Ervin) Feather.** Catharine married **Jacob Smith** (1818–1904).

Charles Waitman (C. W.) Forman and Hallie had one child, **Worley Klet Forman** (1887–1962). C. W. Forman opened a general store one mile north of Willey, the community often mentioned as the location of the Feather homestead. That places Forman's store in Lenox, where the Bolinger family maintains the continuum of shopkeeping that C. W. established. Klet eventually took the reins of this family business, which was likely in competition with the store operated nearby by Josiah Feather.

W. Klet Forman married Nina Crane (1892–1974). They lived with C. W. and Hallie; indeed, W. Klet was born and died in the same house.

He was industrious and enterprising, always ready to learn about the latest labor-saving, transportation, or entertainment option and market it to his neighbors. He had a Ford car garage, wired homes and installed lighting plants, sold Atwater-Kent radios, farmed, operated a sawmill with a partner, and ran the Lenox Funeral Home, which occupied one side of the store (thus, the wide doors on that side). They had two children, Wade and June.

Louisa Jane Feather's husband, John Forman, was a Preston County assessor for the east side of the Cheat River.

From *The Preston County Journal* of April 8, 1880:

> Every one about Kingwood was much surprised on Saturday to learn of the death of Mr. John Foreman [sic], of Willey, the Assessor on the East Side. Mr. Foreman came home on the Saturday night previous about 11 o'clock, having been away all the week assessing, and his family saw at once that he was out of his head. A physician was called, who pronounced his disease typhoid fever. In a day or two other physicians were summoned, as Mr. Forman gradually got worse and became frantic. On Friday night about 10 o'clock he breathed his last. John Forman was one of the most substantial citizens of this county. He has been merchandising at Willey for many years, and was widely known. He was industrious, frugal, honest and upright. He was elected Assessor on the Republican ticket for the East Side in 1876, and was a candidate for the nomination again, and had developed much strength. His death will be a cause of surprise and sorrow to very many. The funeral sermon was preached over the remains at Mr. Forman's house, on Sunday morning at 11 o'clock, by the Rev. L. H. Jordan, pastor of the Kingwood M. E. Church. After the sermon the remains were taken to the churchyard of the old Lutheran Church, where they were interred. The funeral procession was large, there being present about 400 persons. Mr. Forman's family consisted of his wife, three daughters, and a little son.

From the Virginia *Argus* (Kingwood), of April 10, 1880:

> Died, on Friday night at 10 o'clock, at his residence at Willey, Mr. John Forman.

Louisa Jane Feather Forman, continued

> Mr. Forman was buried in the Lutheran grave yard near Willey, on Sunday afternoon at 1 o'clock. The funeral sermon was preached by Rev. Jordan at the residence of the deceased in the forenoon. About four hundred persons followed his remains to the grave and it was the largest funeral procession ever witnessed in that neighborhood. Deceased was about 45 years of age, and at the time of his death held the office of Assessor for the East side of the river. He leaves a wife and three children—two daughters and one son—to mourn his loss who have the sympathy of the entire community in this their sad bereavement. Mr. Forman was a gentleman possessed of many noble traits of character, and was beloved and esteemed by all who knew him. His demise is a great loss to his community.

Louisa Jane lived another 37 years after losing her husband to typhoid fever. Her obituary, *The Preston County Journal*, March 15, 1917:

> Mrs. Louisa Jane Forman, nee Feather, departed this life at the home of her daughter, Mrs. McClelland Hartman, at Valley Point, with whom she had made her home the past ten years, Sunday, March 4th, 1917, aged 84 years, 9 months and 1 day. She was married November 19th, 1857, to John Forman, by Rev. Spencer King. Her husband preceded her to the great beyond 37 years ago the 2nd of April 1917. To this union four children were born, Mrs. J.S. Nedrow and Mrs. Mollie Hayes, of Clarksburg, Mrs. McClellan Hartman of Valley Point, and Willey M. Forman, of Morgantown, who were all present with her during her serious illness, and all was done that loving hands could do to ease and soothe mother's aches and pains. She had been in poor health for the past two years, but was able to go about a part of the time until within the last six months she was confined to her room. She bore her suffering patiently. She was endowed with unusual alertness of mind and was always cheerful in her conversation with both young and old, and affectionately called "Aunt Lide" or "Grandma Forman." She will be sadly missed by the immediate family and a large circle of friends and acquaintances

[sic]. She devoted her life to her children after she was left alone, and was a loving mother.

At an early age she united with the Methodist Episcopal church at the chapel in the Carborchard near her old home, where she held her membership until she was called from the church militant to the church triumphant. She loved to read her Bible as long as she was able, afterwards asking some one to read it for her, and passed away fully trusting in a loving Savior ... She also leaves three aged brothers to mourn their loss: James C. Feather, Jacob E. Feather of Albright, and (Joseph) Marcellus Feather of Kearny, Neb.

Rhuea Belle Forman Hartman the only one of the Forman children buried in Lenox Memorial, married **McClellan George Hartman** in 1890. They had four children: **Nina Mildred Hartman Hartman** (1891–1942), Verna Louise Hartman (1893–1992), Villetta Willard Hartman Powell (1906–2003), and Marguerite Helen Hartman Collison (1909–1978).

Madeline Florence Shaffer Feather
April 4, 1910–January 20, 1998
Row South C / 9

The wife of **John Harvey Feather, Madeline Florence Shaffer** was a daughter of Jacob Thomas "Jake" (1876–1948) and Martha Arminta Nice Shaffer (1881–1950). Florence and John Harvey had no children.

Madeline's great-grandfather was Jacob Rhodes Shaffer Sr., a pioneer of Methodism in the Aurora community. His parents were Adam Johann (1770-1834) and Catherine Elizabeth Wotring Shaffer (1772-1850). Adam Johann were from Saxony, Germany. He was born in Schaefferstown, Lebanon County, Pennsylvania. He settled at Brookside (Aurora) in 1789. His wife was the daughter of Abraham Wotring and Margaret Troxell, also Aurora pioneers. Adam and Margaret had 13 children.

Mahala Catherine Feather Reckart
October 3, 1846–January 19, 1911
Lineage: Adam & Sabra Eusebia (Summers), Jacob and Mary

Mahala Catherine Feather married **Henry Lewis Reckart** (1839–1912). Mahala was born in Preston County; all prior births to **Adam** and **Sabra Eusebia** were in Somerset County, Pennsylvania. The couple moved back to Preston County circa 1845 after John Solomon purchased the Reckart farm.

Henry Lewis was a son of George Ludwig "Lewis" Reckart (1799–1871) and Ann Elizabeth Lewis Reckart (1810–1885). Henry's grandfather was **Earnest August Reckart** (1755–1843), a German immigrant who allegedly served under General de Steuben and made connections with Jacob Feather during encampment at Valley Forge. A Reckart plot is in Lenox Memorial.

Henry and Mahala had three children: **Belle Nora Reckart Miller** (1888–1961), **Abraham Reckart** (d. 1865), and **John F. Reckart** (d. 1874).

Mariah Ann Welch Feather
July 7, 1837–February 14, 1920
Row North G / 7

Mariah Ann Welch was the wife of **Jacob Emery Feather.** Her parents were John F. (1802–1861) and Barbara Hazelett Welch (1802–1880). From *The Preston County Journal* of April 1, 1920, we have Mariah's obituary:

> Mrs. Mariah Feather nee Welch wife of Jacob E. Feather, daughter of John and Barbara Welch, was born July 7, 1837. Died. Feb. 14, 1920, aged 81 years, 7 months, 7 days after an illness of short duration. She leaves a husband and four children as follows: Mrs. L. E. Harned of Geneva, O. , T. S. Feather, John M. Feather, W. Scott Feather, all of Albright. Also one brother Jos. J. Welch together with a host of distant relatives and friends to mourn their loss.
>
> She was united in marriage July 25, 1861 to Jacob E. Feather. She was a living wife and mother. She joined the M. E. church early in life and was a great reader of the Bible, having read it through several times. Funeral services were conducted at the

Lutheran church near Lenox by Rev. Sallaz of Albright after which her remains were laid to rest in the nearby cemetery.

The family extends their thanks to the people for their kindness in time of trouble. . . .

Martha Virginia "Mattie" Rodeheaver Feather
October 11, 1841–September 30, 1920

The wife of **James Connery Feather,** Martha Virginia "Mattie" Rodeheaver was a daughter of **Roamma Jenkins Rodeheaver** (1818–1875) and Col. John F. Rodeheaver (1813–1891). He is buried at Crab Orchard, in the John Rodeheaver Cemetery behind the Wesley Chapel. His obituary appeared in *The Preston County Journal* of December 31, 1891.

> Col. John Rodeheaver, one of the prominent men of the county, died at his home in Craborchard on Wednesday morning, Dec. 23. He was a Colonel in the militia before the war, an honorable businessman and enjoyed the confidence and respect of a large following of friends and acquaintances. He was a leading Democrat. The funeral took place Christmas day, the Rev. Joseph B. Feather, of the M.E. church, preaching the funeral discourse, and his remains were interred in the family burying ground.
>
> Col. Rodeheaver was born in 1813. He leaves several children, among whom are Messrs. Jared A. Rodeheaver of Terra Alta, and J. Frank Rodeheaver and Mrs. James C. Feather of Craborchard.

Martin Luther (M.L.) Feather
December 14, 1853–December 14, 1913
Lineage: Zaccheus & Elizabeth (Ervin), Jacob & Mary
Row North R / 1

There is no published record of **M.L. Feather** going by his given name, which, based upon the birth date and marriage to Amanda Ringer in Rogers' *Genealogy,* was "Luther Martin Feather," a son of Zaccheus and Elizabeth Ervin Feather. The order of the first and middle names appears to have reversed by the researcher. This **Martin Luther Feather** probably wanted

Martin Luther (M.L.) Feather, continued

to distinguish himself from **Martin Luther Feathers** (1865–1939), son of Christian and Catherine, who is buried at Terra Alta.

M. L. Feather married **Amanda Ringer** (1860–1937) on September 14, 1882. From *The Preston County Journal* of September 28, 1882, we have this account of their wedding.

> Wedding Bells—Still another wedding chronicle—that of M. L. Feather and Miss Amanda Ringer, the daughter of John Ringer. The ceremony was performed by the Rev. Joseph Feather, Thursday evening, September 14, at 8 o'clock at the residence of the bride's father. A number of friends and relatives gathered to see the knot tied. The guests numbered fifty. The bride looked lovely in her cashmere dress and white-flowers and trimming. Immediately after the ceremony and congratulations, all passed to the dining room, where there were luxuries of four seasons in lavish profusion. Mrs. Ringer is noted for her skill it this respect. It makes one hungry to see her table. There was not only a brides' cake, but a "grooms" cake also—but we won't attempt to particularize. The couple remained here, a fact which is very pleasing to all their friends. They have our warm wishes for a happy life. No girl in our community would be more missed here, and we are glad to have her made a happy home for our friend M.L. Feather.

The Preston County Journal of November 30, 1882, published a notice that the couple had moved into "our village" in Portland District the prior week. The new residence was the house most recently occupied by Charlie Forman, who had moved into a house he built.

The 1910 U.S. Census includes a M. L. Feather and wife Amanda, with a 21-year-old, "Lessie." Both were farmers. This is the only occurrence of the M. L./Amanda Feather combination in Census records.

The Preston County Journal of April 11, 1912, notes that "M.L. Feather had a bad accident a few weeks ago. His team ran off and hurt one of the horses badly, and he was on the sick list (balance illegible.) The tidbit comes from "Center Knob."

Two obituaries were published by the newspaper. The first used his initials:

M.L. Feather Dead

M.L. Feather died at his home in the Crab Orchard last Sunday morning just as he was getting out of bed. He had gotten up and was sitting on the side of the bed when he coughed a few times and fell back on the bed lifeless.

The deceased was sixty years old on the day of death, Dec. 14, and was one of the prominent, respected and well to do farmers of that section.

He is survived by his wife, Amanda Ringer Feather. His only child, a daughter, had proceeded him to the grave several years ago.

...

The obituary published December 25, 1913, used a different name, "Martin Luther" and sheds more light on his life:

It was with a sense of deep sadness that we received the news of the death of Martin Luther Feather, which occurred at his home at Lenox, on last Sunday morning, the 14th inst. His death was sudden and unexpected, being seized with apoplexy and expiring before rising from his bed. He leaves behind to mourn the loss, a grief-stricken wife and a host of friends and relatives. He was married September 4, 1882 to Miss Amanda J. Ringer. To this union was born one child, Bertha Blanche, August 14, 1883, who married Harvey C. Moss, July 15, 1908, and died May 7, 1909.

Mr. Feather was one of the representative farmers of the Lenox settlement and an exemplary citizen, quietly disposed, energetic, hopeful, pleasant, generous and kind. He had the warm affection of all. He the faculty of the wisely busy man, of always having plenty of time, and that he shared with his friends in that hearty and healthful companionship which has made his name of blessed memory throughout the community in which he was born and reared. Was full of kindness and human sympathy, and loyal to his friends. Thirty-two years ago he proclaimed himself a Christian, and he began, so he continued until his death, a consistent child of the church. In his views he was broad and recognized that the paths of others lead to the same heaven.

Funeral services were conducted from the old, historic Lutheran church at Lenox, of which he was a member, by Rev. W. H. Berry, of Morgantown, a close friend of the family, and who was the deceased's pastor from 1891 to '98. The order of Knights of Pythias of Terra Alta, of which he was a member of long standing, were present and performed the solemn obsequies of that order at the grave. The services were largely attended, all available space in the church being occupied, Mr. Feather was born December 14, 1853, his age therefore being 60 years. Let the pleasant memories of his life prove a stimulant in the conduct of ours, and let us look beyond to the great fact of immortality and be comforted with the thought that after life's fitful fever, he sleeps well.

Mary Ann Feather Conner
May 10, 1839–January 23, 1919
Lineage: Zaccheus & Elizabeth (Ervin), Jacob & Mary
Row North F / 12

Mary Ann Feather married **Benjamin A. Conner** (1833–1915). The couple had 10 children: Clara (1861-1862); **Elma Ophelia Martin** (1862-1933); Jane R. Conner Greaser (1st), Miller (2nd) (1865-1936); Emma Mary Conner Wilson (1st), Kelly (2nd) (1867–1932); Lulu Bell Louisa Conner Lenhart (1869–1945); Aretta M. Conner Crane (1871–1949); William Zaccheus Conner (1873–1961); Frances C. Conner Wolf (1875–1959); Ida Arizona Conner Falkenstein (1877–1970); and Gra(y)ce Blanche Conner Layman (1879–1953). That makes nine girls and one boy!

Greatly outnumbered, William Zaccheus went West to Williamstow, Missouri. His younger sister, Frances Wolf(e), went to Watongo, Oklahoma, and his older sister, Arreta, went to Stockton, California. The rest remained in the vicinity of Preston County.

Mary Ann, Benjamin, Elma and an **Emma M. Conner** (1884-1935) are the only Conner burials in Lutheran Memorial, although it is likely little 2-year-old Clara was laid to rest there, as well.

Benjamin Conner (1933–1915) was the great grandson of Irish immigrant John M. Conner (1721–1796). He was born in Ulster and came to the Pennsylvania colony from Troy. John M. married Mary Forman (1725–1796) in

Philadelphia on January 17, 1746. He died December 2, 1796, in Monongalia County. He worshiped with the Grant District Quaker Colony, one of the earliest religious groups in what became Preston County.

Benjamin's parents were William Conner Jr. (1799–1868) and Mary Glover (1808–1892); his grandparents were William (1765–1839) and Elizabeth Forman Conner (1769–1845), who were married August 28, 1790, at Bruceton Mills.

In the 1900 U.S. Census, Benjamin, 67, was listed as a farmer in the Portland District, Terra Alta. Daughters Grace B., 20, and Ida A., 23, were still in the household.

Mary Ann Kelly Feather (Rodeheaver)
August 16, 1825–January 30, 1901

Mary Ann Kelly was the wife of **Jacob Adam Feather,** who died in 1856 at the age of 36. After Jacob's death, she married James B. Rodeheaver (1838–1897), who is buried in the Parnell Cemetery, Cuzzart.

Mary Ann was a daughter of Joseph M. (1794–1873) and Dorcas Browning Kelley (1800–1880). They are buried in the Kelly Cemetery at Afton, Preston County.

Mary Ann's mother was born at Great Glades, Garrett County, Maryland. She was the oldest daughter of Mary Polly McMullen (1781–1839) and Meshach Browning (1781–1859), legendary backwoodsman, hunter and explorer of the watersheds of the North Branch Potomac and Youghiogheny rivers. He wrote a memoir, *Forty-Four Years of the Life of a Hunter,* that was published in 1859, the year he succumbed to pneumonia.

Meshach was born in Damascus, Montgomery County, Maryland; his father was an English soldier who had escaped from Braddock's massacre. He deserted the British and settled in Western Maryland's highlands, where Meshach learned the skills that enabled him to life off the land, except for the gunpowder he used to harvest the forest animals. Meshach claimed to have killed 2,000 deer and 500 bears during his 40 years of subsistence living in western Maryland.

Mary Ann's second marriage was to another legendary pioneer family, the Rodeheavers of Crab Orchard. John F. Rodeheaver, a saddler, was peddling his harnesses in western Virginia when he took note of the Crab

Orchard area in 1796. He returned in 1808 and settled his family on 191 acres on Crab Orchard Run. John "Sadler John" Rodeheaver (September 12, 1773–November 6, 1838) and his wife, Mary Magdalen "Polly" (1778–1838), are buried in the obscure John Rodeheaver Cemetery on private property behind Wesley Chapel Church (off Coal Lick Road).

Mary Ann had two daughters by her second husband. **Missouri Olive Rodeheaver Welch** (1859–1912) and Hillery W. Rodeheaver (1859–1925), buried at Parnell Cemetery, Cuzzart.

Mary Anna Feather Teets
December 23, 1843–November 18, 1919
Lineage: James & Cristena, Jacob & Mary
Row North X / 1 & 2

Mary Anna Teets was the wife of **Albert Teets** (1841-1918). The couple had son, Walter A. who was living with them when the 1880 U.S. Census was taken. Rogers does not list this child. Albert was a farmer in Pleasant District, owning 16 acres in the Cranesville area of Portland District. in 1910.

Albert's obituary, from the August 22, 1918, *Preston County Journal:*

> Albert Teets . . . was born near Brandonville, Prest county, Va., in the year 1841, and died August 3rd, 1918, in the 78th year of his age.
>
> At about 20 years of age, being a strong stalwart young man at th the beginning of the great rebellion in 1861, he joined Company C, Third regiment, West Virginia cavalry, which was organized at Brandonville October 12, 1861.
>
> At the close of the Civil war he married Miss Mary Ann Feather and lived many happy years on the farm, which he purchased at that time of Alfred Kelly, now owned by Roy Kelley, on the waters of Beaver creek in Pleasant district. Selling his farm he and his beloved wife bought property in Cranesville and lived there quite a while, selling out their property at Cranesville they moved to Terra Alta, owning town property there which they sold to Mr. Frazee, and afterwards returned to Cranesville where he ended his days and peacefully fell asleep in Jesus, whom he trusted for nearly 50 years of his life.

Mary Ervin Feather
February 19, 1800–September 30, 1878
Row North M / 15

The wife of **John Solomon Feather**, **Mary Ervin** was a daughter of **Isaac** and **Eva Ervin**. Her sister, **Elizabeth Ervin Feather**, married **Zaccheus Feather**, John Solomon's younger brother.

Mary, who died eight years after her husband, has her own headstone of a different design from that of John Solomon. She is identified on the cemetery register, but her husband is listed as "unknown."

Her father was the first burial (1814) in Lenox Memorial; he is buried between John D. Feather and infant Welch in Row N O/ 10. Mysteriously, there is no John D. or any John Feather with a middle name that begins with "D" listed in Rogers' *Genealogy*.

Mary and John S. had 15 children. The list is under the John Solomon Feather entry.

Mary Henrietta Feather Johns
November 24, 1896 or 1900–March 6, 1971

A daughter of **Harvey Arlington** and **Georgia Jackson Feather**, **Mary Henrietta Feather** married **Burgett Parker Johns** (1898–1971). They had one child, Rosemary Johns Stephenson (1936–2021).

> Obituary:
> Mary Henrietta Johns, 70, of Grafton, died Wednesday night in the Broaddus Hospital in Philipp.
> She was born Nov. 24, 1900, in Lenox, a daughter of the late Harvey A. and Georgetta Jackson Feather.
> Survivors include her husband, Burgett Johns; a son, Thomas P. Johns of Grafton; one daughter, Mrs. Rosemary Stephenson of Aliquippa, Pa.; one brother, Paul H. Feather of Albright; two sisters, Mrs. Kenneth (Hazel) Tichnell of Bruceton Mills and Mrs. Josephine Wolfe of Valley Point; and three grandchildren. Three brothers and three sisters preceded her in death.
> She was a member of the Daughters of America of Albright . . .

Mary Jane "Mollie" Welch Feather
November 8, 1886–1980
Row North F / 4

The wife of the **Rev. Dana W.M. Feather**, **Mary Jane Welch** was the daughter of **Jacob Wesley** (1856–1924) and **Matilda Jane Dunn Welch** (1859–1946).

Dana was the son of the **Rev. Joseph B. Feather**, who officiated at the marriage of Dana and Mollie on August 11, 1909. They had one child, Beatrice Lucille Feather Flynn. Although only four years younger than Dana, who died at the age of 28, Mary lived 66 years beyond her husband. She did not remarry, which raises the question of how she survived financially all those years.

Mary Jane's three siblings also are buried in Lenox Memorial: **Frank Elmer Welch** (1880–1957), **Ida Mae Welch Jackson** (1882–1969), and **Idessie Blanche Welch Hartman** (1885–1961).

Mary Jane Broomhall Feather
February 1850–1887
Row North Q / 9

Mary Jane Broomhall, the wife of **Adam H. Feather**, was the daughter of Quaker parents Mahlon and **Elizabeth Welch Broomhall**. Mary Jane was eight years younger than Adam H. Their children were William C. (1867–1869), Oliver Andrew Allen (1869–1950), Lona May (Hiles) (1872–1940), James Walter (1874–1959), Letitia Olive (Blamble) (1877–1950), Troy A. (1880–1885). It is possible Troy and William are buried at Lenox in unmarked graves.

Mary Jane died June 16, 1887, of consumption, an illness most likely responsible for the deaths of her mother, husband, and a child in a span of less than four years. From *The Preston County Journal* of July 31, 1884, we have the death notice of Mary Jane's mother, whose ancestors are unknown:

> BROOMHALL—On July 28, 1884, at the residence of her son-in-law, Isaac Fleighle (Feather), in the Crab Orchard, Elizabeth Broomhall. Her remains were buried in the Lutheran Church Cemetery on Sunday in the presence of a large concourse

of friends. She was an affectionate mother; a faithful christian; and will be sadly missed in the community, but our loss is her gain.

Mary Louisa "Lou" Mercer Feather
September 9, 1855–August 13, 1919
Row North F / 5

Mary Louisa Mercer was the second wife of the **Rev. Joseph B. Feather;** his first wife was **Mary Atkinson.** Mary Louisa was from Charleston and 23 years younger than Joseph B.. She and Joseph had one child, **Dana Wilbur Mercer,** who was born December 27, 1886, and married **Mary Jane Welch** on August 11, 1909, at the bride's residence.

Mary Louisa's obituary from From *The Preston County Journal* of August 21, 1919:

Mary Lou, wife of Rev. Jos B. Feather and daughter of the late Robert and Jane Mercer, departed this life August 13th at her home near Lenox, aged 63 years 11 months and 5 days.

Early in life she was converted and joined the M.E. church and ever remained a true and faithful Christian woman.

In 1884 she was united in marriage to Rev. Jos. B. Feather, a well known minister of the M. E. church. To this union was born one son Rev Dana W. M. Feather, who preceded her to the great beyond over five years ago. Her parents and brother Rev. B. L. Mercer died several years ago.

She has left behind her to mourn their loss her aged husband, one brother, Prof. F. F. Mercer of Fairmont, one sister Mrs. (Susan) Effie Donaldson of Cumberland, her daughter-in-law Mollie, and granddaughter Beatrice. Three step children, Jennie, Elmer and Frank Feather, and a host of friends.

Impressive services were held in the Lutheran church Friday conducted by her pastor Rev. Flanagan, assisted by Dist. Supt. Moore and Rev. W. M. Shultz and body was laid to rest by the side of her son, Dana.

Mary Rebecca Keener Feather
October 22, 1925–August 18, 2010
Row South C / 18

Mary Rebecca Keener was born in Marion County and married **Fred Lynn Feather.**

Excerpt from her obituary from the (Morgantown) *Dominion Post:*

> Mary Rebecca Keener Feather, 84, of Coal Lick Road, Albright, died Aug. 18, 2010, at her home.
> She was born Oct. 22, 1925, in Marion Co., a daughter of the late Floyd E. and Bessie Cole Keener. She is survived by one son, Mark Lee Feather, of Wheeling; one daughter and spouse, Kathy and Paul Dobrowolski of Bridgeport; six grandchildren. In addition to her parents, she was preceded in death by her husband of 49 years, Freddy Lynn feather, on Feb. 25, 2000; two brothers, Archie Keener and Oliver Keener; two sisters, Edna Gardner and Lucy Keener. Interment will be in the Lenox Memorial Cemetery.

Mary Sisler Feather

Mary Sisler was the first wife of **Jacob Feather Jr.** (1796–1847), son of Jacob and **Mary Feather.** It is assumed she died in 1819. Mary's grave site is unknown, as are her parents' information and birth date.

Mary Summers Feather
May 19, 1804–January 19, 1827

The first wife of **Adam Feather, Mary Summers** was born in Pennsylvania to John and Mary Frankhouser Summers and died in Maryland at the age of 22. She bore two children for Adam: Sarah Feather White (1825–1894) and **John Summers Feather** (1827–1909). Sarah was buried in the White Family Cemetery on the White farm in Pleasantdale. **John** was born in St. Mary's County, Maryland, which suggests that Adam tried his luck at a venture beyond the Preston County farm of his parents, Jacob and Mary.

Following the death of Sarah, Adam married her sister, **Sabra Eusebia**

Summers, born in 1807. Their first children—Joseph B., William G., Mary Feather Parnell, **David R.**, and Lydia A. Feather (1st Trembly, 2nd Goff, 3rd Park)—were born in Pennsylvania. Their last child, Sabra Jane Feather Rodeheaver (1851–1921), was born in Preston County November 16, 1851. By that time the couple had moved onto the homestead farm of Jacob and Mary Feather. Prior to Adam taking over the farm, John Solomon and his family lived on the land and farmed it for his widowed mother.

Maxine Alice Elliott Feather
April 27, 1922–June 29, 2008
Row North H / 5

The wife of **Wilmeth Bill Feather, Maxine Alice Elliott** was a daughter of Isaac Forman Elliott (1922–2008) and Mary Ann Ridenour Elliott (1897–1947), buried in the Terra Alta Cemetery.

She and Bill had one child, **Robert Lynn "Bob" Feather,** 1945–2022.

Her second great-grandfather was John Elliott, who was born 1801 in Virginia and died in Preston County in 1870. He is buried in the Shay and Elliott Cemetery, Pleasantdale, Preston County.

Merle Clifton Feather
July 7, 1905–June 1987
Lineage: ? and Osa Grace, James C. & Irena (Ervin), Christian & Catherine (Dunham), Jacob & Mary
Row South D / 16

Merle C. Feather and his wife, **Wanda E. Hillery Feather,** farmed a portion of the James C. Feather Jr. and Adam H. Feather farm on Feather Lane (Coal Lick Road access). See the **James C. Feather** entry for a detailed look at life on that farm.

Merle's granddaughter, Wendy Feather McLaughlin, recalls her grandfather as a checkers champion who helped her work the Sunday paper crossword puzzles. Wanda enjoyed playing Chinese checkers and Scrabble. In their latter years, the couple lived in an apartment in Kingwood, where Wanda enjoyed volunteering at the library. In 1975, Wendy's parents moved

Merle C. Feather, continued

to the farm, and her grandparents moved from their Kingwood apartment to a mobile home on the family land.

"Grandpa helped with the farming as long as he was able and Grandma enjoyed growing a garden each summer," Wendy wrote in her commentary on Wanda's memoir. "She always had something for you to take home, garden produce, canned goods, flowers, etc. She loved animals and took great delight in feeding and watching the birds.

"Grandma and Grandpa were married for more than sixty years. Grandpa passed away June 19, 1987. Grandma lived to be ninety-one years old She was a special person who left behind this wonderful story for those of us who knew and loved her, and for future generations."

Merle's and Wanda's son, William L. Feather, wrote this tribute to his father and the farm in the *1979 Preston County History* book:

> Merle C., my father, lived with his grandfather and grandmother, working the family farm, raising sheep, hogs, cattle and grain. He married Wanda Hillery, a Cranesville native, in 1927. I was born on November 27, 1929. My father and mother purchased the former William Loyd Feather Farm, where they still live, in 1936.
>
> I attended Forman Gate, a one-room school, where the building was heated by a Burnside stove. Water was carried from a spring in the woods. We played games, studied reading, writing, math, and many other subjects. Here I met my future wife, but after she moved from the community, I did not see her for fourteen years.
>
> I was married in Albright in 1950 to Gwendolyn Hyre. We moved to a farm adjoining the property where we now live. The next four years were spent in the United States Air Force, with our daughter being born in Mississippi in 1955. Shortly after our son was born in 1957, we moved to Arthurdale, where we lived for sixteen years. Moving back to the family farm in 1975, we live in a farmhouse built of natural stone and clay mortar. The house was built in 1821 by J. C. Cress.
>
> I was employed by Sterling Faucet and worked at the Pittsburgh Valve Plant in Reedsville for twenty-two years. I am now employed by the Preston County Board of Education in the maintenance

department. My wife is an instructional aide at the Albright Elementary School.

Our daughter, Wendy Lanette, married to Robert F. McLaughlin, Jr., lives in Arthurdale and teaches first grade. Our son, William Larry, lives on the farm and is employed by the Department of Highways in Kingwood.

Beef cattle now graze on the pasture, and hay is harvested for winter feeding. We enjoy the farm for its beauty and privacy. Taking walks over the farm with our Norwegian elk hound gives the whole family a proud feeling.

Merle's obituary:

Merle C. Feather, 81, of Route 2, Albright, died Friday, June 19, at Preston Memorial Hospital in Kingwood.

He was born July 7, 1905, in Crab Orchard, Albright, a son of the late Osie Feather Lemmon.

He was a member of the Wesley Chapel United Methodist Church.

He is survived by his wife, Wanda Ellen Feather; one son, William (Bill) Feather of Albright; one half-brother, Robert Lemmon of Bagdad, FL; two half-sisters, Georgia Joyner of Foster, VA and Martha Abernathy of Winston-Salem, NC; two grandchildren and three great-grandchildren.

He was preceded in death by one half-brother.

Friends were received at the Browning Funeral Home in Kingwood. A service was held Sunday at the funeral home with the Rev. Jonas Johnson officiating. Interment was in the Lutheran Cemetery in Lenox.

Minerva Bell Feather Feather
June 17, 1862–April 14, 1950
Lineage: Zaccheus & Elizabeth (Ervin), Jacob & Mary

Minerva Bell Feather married **Elmer B. Feather**, son of the **Rev. Joseph B.** and Mary Atkinson Feather. Elmer was from the line of Adam Feather, Minerva from Zaccheus.

Nancy Wilhelm Feather
1840–1921
Row North Q / 4

Nancy Wilhelm was the wife of **Jacob F. Feather** and one of 10 children born to Jacob and Catharine Sines Wilhelm. Catharine died at the age of 56, and Jacob remarried in 1872 to Lorata McKabe (1827–1874). Jacob Wilhelm's father was Solomon Wilhelm Sr., 1790–1885, who was born in McHenry, Garrett County, Maryland and died on Christmas Day, 1885 in Cranesville. Peter Wilhelm was pre-1800 settler in the Cranesville area and a brother of Solomon Sr.

The Wilhelm line is intertwined with the Feather line, and Wilhelm/Feather descendants own the homestead property on Coal Lick Road (Kelly Wilhelm Andrews and her brother, Jeff).

Nancy Maria Feather Stokes
June 12, 1844–May 6, 1920
Lineage: Zaccheus & Elizabeth (Ervin), Jacob & Mary

Nancy Maria Feather married Jacob C. Stokes (1841–1907) on October 4, 1868.

They had five children: Cyrena E. Davis (1869–1935), Charles Edward (1871–1959), **John E.** (1872–1874), Etta M. (b. 1875), and Benjamin Frank (1878–1881).

Jacob was born in New Hampshire and came to Lenox as a child. In the 1880 U. S. Census, Jacob is listed as a farmer living in Pleasant District with two sons and two daughters. By the early 1900s, Jacob and Nancy were living in Tucker County, where he died.

Ora F. Stanton Feather
April 2, 1896–February 13, 1979
Row South B / 17

The wife of **Clarence T. Feather, Ora F. Stanton** was born at Albright to James Thomas Stanton/Staunton (1874–1900) and Laura Effie "Laurie" Casteel Stanton (1871–1942). Clarence was her second husband; her first, Boyd Christian Wolfe (1885–1913), died August 27, 1913, at the age of 28. He was buried in the Sisler Cemetery at Mount Carmel (Terra Alta). Their daughter, Edith Virginia, was born January 13, 1914, after her father's death.

Laura Effie's father was **Solomon Wesley "Sol" Casteel** (1839–1920). He is buried in Lenox Memorial, as is his wife, **Sarah Ann Sypolt Casteel** (1839–1927). Solomon Wesley was a Civil War veteran, serving in Co. H of the 6th W.Va. and Co. A of the 7th W.Va. His father, Nathaniel Casteel, was born in St. Mary's County, Maryland and is buried in the Albright Cemetery.

Paul Harold Feather
March 12, 1890–July 15, 1972
Lineage: Harvey Arlington & Georgia Etta (Jackson), James Connery and Martha Virginia (Rodeheaver), John Solomon & Mary (Ervin), Jacob & Mary
Row South C / 14

Paul Harold Feather married **Anna May Lee** (1896–1985) in 1915. She was from Davis, Tucker County, and the daughter of Samuel Ellsworth (1863–1950) and Elma Jane Nedrow Lee (1871–1934). Paul Harold worked as a mail carrier. From *The Preston County Journal* of November 11, 1915:

Craborchard: A couple of our young people, Paul Feather and Miss Annie Lee, surprised many of their friends by slipping off to Oakland last Saturday where they were quietly married.

The couple's one child, Dorothy Lee Feather Elliott, was born December 16, 1916, and died October 2, 2002. She married Paul B. Elliott (1909–1984) and is buried in the Maplewood Cemetery, Kingwood.

Phebe Jane Martin Feather
July 20, 1849–August 7, 1917
Row North P / 6

Phebe Jane Martin was the wife of **Jacob Luther Feather.** The couple had 11 children, listed under Jacob Luther's entry.

She was a daughter of Isaac W. (1825–1910) and Sara Matheny Martin (1793–1887). Phebe's father, Jacob B. Martin (1793–1850), was born in Fayette County, Pennsylvania. Daniel Martin, Jr, was Jacob B.'s father. Daniel was born in 1748 and died at the age of 102 (!) October 30, 1850.

Testimony given by neighbors for the purpose of Mary Feather, widow of Jacob, receiving a widow's pension for her husband's military service stated that Daniel and Jacob became acquainted through their Revolutionary War experiences. Daniel testified to being with Jacob at Valley Forge. This military service and testimony is discussed in greater detail in *My Fathers' Land*.

Daniel Martin was from Woodbridge Township, New Jersey, as were his father, Daniel Martin, and paternal grandfather, Gersom Martin. The family was probably of English origin.

After the Revolutionary War, Daniel settled near Valley Point, Monongalia County, Virginia. There are several references pointing to him and Jacob continuing their friendship in Preston County. Inevitably, Martin and Feather offspring married—Daniel had eight children. He donated the land for Mount Moriah Cemetery at Valley Point, where more than 50 Martin descendants are buried. Daniel was laid to rest in a obscure family plot near Valley Point on land that was strip mined.

Rachel Virginia Feather Scott
September 27, 1828–September 2, 1903
Lineage: John Solomon & Mary (Ervin), Jacob & Mary
Location undetermined

Rachel Virginia Feather married **John Wesley Scott** and they had one daughter, Flora B. Scott Sisler (1864–1949) buried in the Terra Alta Cemetery, and two sons, Willie John Scott (b. 1862) and Equatious V. Scott (1867–1954), who married Luella Burkhalter in 1892 and Zuella DeWitt in 1899.

John Wesley (February 1, 1838–February 10, 1907), was a highly respected citizen. He was born near Kingwood and died at Elkins, W.Va., following an "attack of dropsy, the culmination of a case of Bright's disease."

The Preston County Journal of February 14, 1907, reported that, "The body of J.W. Scott was taken through town Monday to the Lutheran Cemetery in the Crab Orchard, where the funeral services were held. Mr. Scott was an old and respected citizen of Preston county, and leaves two sons J. W. Scott of Aurora and Nathan Scott of Rowlesburg and a daughter of Mrs. Flora Sisler of Elkins to mourn their loss." The information regarding the sons is inconsistent with Rogers' *Genealogy*.

Rebecca Feather Kelly
October 6, 1825–October 15, 1900.
Lineage: John Solomon & Mary (Ervin), Jacob & Mary
Location undetermined

Rebecca Feather married **Joseph Kelly** (1822–1902) on December 27, 1853. They had eight children, six of them girls.

Their children were Mary Catharine "Kate" Kelly Walker (1854–1907), **Rachel B. Kelly Ringer** (1856–1930), Sarah Adaline Kelly Miller (1858–1937), Virginia Lenhamina "Jennie" Kelly DeBerry (1860–1946), Amanda Hyde Kelly Matthews (1863–1909), **John Solomon Kelly,** (1864-1942), **Carrie E. Kelly VanHoesen** (1866–1920), and **Willie Kelly** (1869–1877). Mary

Catharine and her husband, Joel Walker, went to Kansas and are buried there; the others are in Preston County.

Joseph Kelly's grandfather was John Kelly (1755–1853). He was born in Fairfax County, Virginia, and died in Union City, Darke County, Ohio.

According to Rebecca's death notice, she died in Cuzzart after years of suffering with "a cancer of the face."

Robert Lynn "Bob" Feather
December 17, 1945–May 21, 2022
Lineage: Wilmeth Scott & Maxine (Elliott), Winfield Scott & Ella (Deal), Jacob Emery & Mariah Ann (Welch), Solomon & Mary (Evin), Jacob & Mary
Row South H / 7

Obituary:

Robert "Bob" Lynn Feather, 76, of Spotsylvania, Virginia, went home to be with the Lord on Saturday, May 21, 2022, at home with family.

Robert was born December 17, 1945, in Cranesville, WV, a son of the late **Maxine** and **Wilmeth Feather.**

He was the owner and operator of Feather Construction. He loved fishing, hunting, golfing, and spending time with loved ones. In his spare time, he enjoyed showing, training, and riding horses. He is survived by his wife of 32 years, Linda Feather; daughters and spouses, Jocelynn Feather, Syndee and Shawn Payne, Lisa and Mike Perrin, Sherri Mullins, Robbie and Russell Fitzgerald, Wendy and Glen Griffin, Beverly and Shawn McNabb, Michelle and Gary Everett, Robin and Boyd Pape; 26 grandchildren; several great-grandchildren; sisters and spouses, Linda and Max Elliott, Ella Livengood, Maryann McCabe; many nieces and nephews he dearly loved.

In addition to his parents, he was preceded in death by his daughter, **Season Feather.**

Russell Benton Jacob Feather
May 28, 1901–February 5, 1969
Lineage: Isaac Christian & Rosie Mae (Wilson), Jacob Luther
& Phebe Jane (Martin), Christine & Catherine (Dunham), Jacob & Mary
Location undetermined

Russel Benton Jacob Feather was born at Valley Point and died in Cleveland Heights, Cuyahoga County, Ohio.

He married Verdia Blanche Anderson (1911–1986), a Clarksburg native, in 1929. According to her obituary, her sons were Russell, Teddy E., and Howard Feather of Lutz, Florida, and Phillip Feather of Tampa. She also had six daughters: Mrs. Mary Smith, Mrs. Allie Eddy, Mrs. Gathel Watkins, (Mrs.) Ethel Bigler, Mrs. Viola Strickland, Mrs. Dorothy Hughes.

She was survived by her second husband, Theodore Jennings Cottrill (1911–1992) and evidently had moved to Florida after Russell Benton died.

Verdia Blanche is buried at Rose Hill Memorial Park, Tampa, Florida. An Earl T. Feathers (1947–2001) is buried next to her. Findagrave identifies this person as her child.

Russel Benton also had a son, Curtis Christopher Feathers, born January 22, 1921, at Fairchance, Pennsylvania. Assigned to the 377th Field Artillery, 101st Airborne Division, Curtis Christopher died during the Allied invasion of Normandy, June 6, 1944. He is buried in the Normandy American Cemetery, France, Plot C Row 4 Grave 34. Since Verdia Blanche would have been only 9 years old when Curtis Christopher was born, Russel Benton must have had this son with a different woman. The Findagrave site identifies that woman as Edith Hughes Feather.

Ruth Annie Feather Kelly
February 18, 1853–April 18, 1919
Lineage: Harrison & Catharine Jane (Welch),
John Solomon & Mary (Ervin), Jacob & Mary
Row North L / 15

A daughter of **Harrison** and **Catharine Jane Welch Feather,** Ruth married George Allen Kelly (1850-1930) on August 2, 1877. The couple had two children: Clyde Forrest (1878–1945) and Faye Evelyn Kelly Windell

(1888–1971). Ruth Annie's headstone says "Mother . . . wife of George M. Kelly. George is buried in the Centenary Cemetery but is listed on the Lenox Memorial register as being in grave 16, Row North L.

George was a farmer in Pleasant District, owning 100 acres on Muddy Creek in 1917. Annie was a housewife. Her passing went unrecorded by the county's newspaper.

Sabra Eusebia Summers Feather
January 20, 1808–December 20, 1858
Unmarked grave

The second wife of **Adam Feather, Sabra Eusebia Summers** was most likely the sister of his first wife, **Mary Summers** (1804–1827). Her parents were John Peter Summers and Mary Anna Maria Frankhouser. The "Summers" surname appears to have been derived from a German surname, "Zook" or "Zug." John Summers was born in Lancaster, Pennsylvania, although his birth year of 1788 is suspect as it means he would have fathered Mary at the age of 16. John Peter Summers died in Holmes County, Ohio, an enclave of the Amish.

Seven children were born to Adam and Sabra: (Rev.) **Joseph B.** (1833–1920); **William G.**, (1836–1868); Mary (Parnell) (1838–1906) buried in Johnson Chapel Cemetery, Fayette County; **David R.** (1841–1844); **Lydia A.** (Trembly/Goff/Park) (1844–1924),buried in Hope Town Cemetery, Lostant, Illnois; **Mahala Catherine (Reckart)** (1846–1911), and Sabra Jane (Rodeheaver), (1851–1921), buried Parnell Cemetery, Cuzart.

Sabra's sister, Christeen (1818-1885), married James Feather. Another sister, Matilda, married Jesse A. Childs.

Sarah M. Harvey Feather
April 10, 1835–March 28, 1919
Row North J / 2

Wife of **John Summers Feather** and mother of his eight children (see his listing for names). Sarah was born in Maryland, but her parents are not named by either Rogers or Findagrave.

Season Lynn Feather
August 10, 1984–July 28, 2018
Lineage: Robert Lynn & Linda, Wilmeth Scott & Maxine (Elliott), Winfield Scott & Elina "Ella" (Deal), Jacob Emery & Mariah Ann (Welch), Solomon & Mary (Evin), Jacob & Mary
Row North H / 6

Obituary:

Season Lynn Feather, 33, of Partlow, VA, died on Saturday, July 28, 2018, at the VCU Medical Center, in Richmond, VA.

Season was born August 10, 1984, in Beckley, WV, a daughter of Robert Lynn and Linda Feather of Spotsylvania, VA.

She was a manager for Shoresite. Season began showing horses in Western Pleasure at a young age, in which she won two VQHA Championships in the youth Western Pleasure division. She also qualified for the Youth World Show in Fort Worth, Texas at the Will Rogers Coliseum. Season loved her time with her dogs, King and Goliath.

In addition to her parents, she is survived by her fiancée, Brian Lewis of Spotsylvania, VA; sisters and spouses, Jocelynn Carter and Joshua of Spotsylvania, VA, Syndee Payne and Shawn of Fredericksburg, VA, Lissa Perrin and Michael of Howell, MI, Michell Everett and Gary of Spotsylvania, VA, Sheri Mullins and Eric English of Fredericksburg, VA, Beverly McNabb and Shawn of Fredericksburg, VA, Robbie Fitzgerald and Russell of Pensacola, FL, Robin Pape and Boyd of Craig, CO, Wendy Griffin and Glen of Mannington, WV; several nieces and nephews, several aunts, uncles and cousins.

Friends will be received at the Rotruck-Lobb Kingwood Chapel,

295 South Price on Wednesday, August 1, 2018, from 5–8 p.m.; on Thursday, August 2, 2018, from 10:00 a.m. until the time of the funeral in the funeral home chapel at 11:00 a.m. with Reverend Michael Argabrite officiating. Interment will follow at the Lenox Memorial Cemetery, Lenox, WV.

Wanda Ellen Hillery Feather
1907–1998
Row South D / 17

A daughter of Judson Gilbert and Flora Bell Ringer Hillery of Cranesville, **Wanda Ellen Hillery** was the wife of **Merle C. Feather.**

When she was 3 years old, Wanda's parents moved to Oklahoma so her father could pursue construction jobs there. Her mother died from a thyroid condition and her father remarried. The family followed construction jobs across the western states. When she was in the fourth grade, the family returned to West Virginia, where Judson found work in the Morgan Mines of Valley District and ran a boarding house. When in fifth grade at Reedsville, Wanda had to make buckwheat cakes for six to 12 boarders and wash the dishes before leaving for school.

Once again following work, her father moved them to Morgantown, where she got a job at a glass factory during the summer. She later found work caring for her grandfather and grandmother Ringer and serving as a caretaker to the children of a businessman.

She and Merle C. Feather were married May 14, 1927, at the Albright parsonage. They moved to the **James C. Feather** farm, where, two weeks after they were married, their neighbors along the mail route serviced by Stanley Crane, put together a reception for them with candy bars, cookies and coffee for refreshments.

The couple had one child, **William Lloyd Feather** (1929–2013).

Wanda wrote a memoir about her childhood and early years of

married life spent on the farm of her grandparents, James C. and **Irena Feather**. See the James C. Feather entry for an excerpt.

Obituary

Wanda Elien Hillery Feather, age 91 of Albright, died Monday, August 17, 1998, at Heartland of Preston County.

She was born on January 23, 1907 in Cranesville, WV, the daughter of the late Judson Gilbert and Flora Bell Ringer Hillery. She was a homemaker and former member of the Lenox Extension Homemakers. She attended Wesley Chapel United Methodist Church on Coal Lick Road.

She is survived by a son and daughter-in-law, William "Bill" and Gwendolyn Feather of Albright; two brothers, George Hillery of Mentor, OH and Floyd Hillery of Kingwood; two grandchildren and spouses, Wendy and Robert McLaughlin of Arthurdale and William Larry and Julie Ann Feather of Albright; and four great-grandchildren: Stephen and Kyle McLaughlin of Arthurdale and Matthew and Alysa Feather of Albright.

She was preceded in death by her husband, Merle C. Feather, on June 19, 1987; her step-mother, Effie Hillery; two brothers, Dailey Hillery and an infant; two sisters, Pauline Casseday and Wilma Hillery. . . .

William G. Feather
June 17, 1836–February 13, 1868
Lineage: Adam & Sabra Eusebia (Summers), Jacob & Mary
Location undetermined

William G. Feather was born in Pennsylvania and died in Preston County at the age of 31. No documentation of marriage could be located.

William Lloyd Feather
November 27, 1929–August 17, 2013
Row South C / 19

The son of **Merle C.** and **Wanda Hillery Feather, William Lloyd Feather** lived and worked on the Coal Lick Road farm. His reflections on working and living at that farm are under Merle C. Feather's entry.

Obituary:

William Lloyd Feather, 83, of Albright, went to be with the Lord, Saturday, August 17, 2013, at Preston Memorial Hospital with family by his side.

He was born November 27, 1929, in Albright, a son of the late Merle and Wanda Hillery Feather.

He was a loving father and grandfather. He served in the US Air Force during the Korean Conflict, was stationed in Iceland and Keesler Air Force Base in Biloxi, Missouri. He was an electrician and worked for Sterling Rockwell International and the Preston County Board of Education. William was a member of the American Legion Post # 56 of Kingwood, the Preston County Historical Society and the Preston County Association of Retired School Employees. He also was a member of the Wesley Chapel United Methodist Church.

William is survived by his son and wife, William L. Feather and Julie of Albright, his daughter and husband, Wendy McLaughlin and Robert of Arthurdale; four grandchildren, Stephen McLaughlin and wife, Sarah; Kyle McLaughlin, Matthew Feather and wife, Casey and Alyssa Feather and one great granddaughter, Addyson Fearer.

He was also preceded in death by his loving wife of 60 years, Gwendolyn H. Feather.

Family and friends will be received at Browning Funeral Home in Kingwood on Wednesday August 21 from 4-8 pm where funeral services will be held Thursday 22, 2013 at 11 a.m. with Pastor Jerry Paris officiation. Interment will follow in the Lenox Memorial Cemetery where military graveside rites will be conducted by the Preston County VFW Posts, Preston County Chapter 977, Vietnam Veterans of America and the US Air Porce Homor Garden. . . .

Wilmeth Scott "Bill" Feather
June 24, 1919–May 3, 1986
Lineage: Winfield Scott & Ella (Deal), Jacob Emery & Mariah Ann (Welch),
Solomon & Mary (Evin), Jacob & Mary
Row North H / 19

Wilmeth Scott "Bill" Feather married **Maxine Alice Elliott** in 1945. They had four children: **Robert Lynn** (1945–2022), Mary Ann McCabe (b. 1947), Ella Lee Feather (b. 1949), and Linda Joy Feather (b. 1951).

Stanley Ward Livengood (1945–2020), who married Ella Lee, is buried at Lenox Memorial and his grave is marked with a bench memorial. The Livengoods were from Somerset County, Pennsylvania, as were Jacob and Mary Feather.

Wilmeth Scott was a World War II veteran, having served in the Army. At the time of his registration for the draft, he was living in Edgemere, Baltimore, Maryland, and working at Bethlehem Steel.

Winfield Scott Feather
December 9, 1881–August 20, 1951
Lineage: Jacob Emery & Mariah Ann (Welch),
John Solomon & Mary (Evin), Jacob & Mary
Row North G / 3

Winfield married Ella Deal (1887–1848). They had six children: Nellie Pauline Wiles (1908–1982), **Lena Alfreda** (1909–1909), Virginia "Virgie" Leda Shirley (1910–2000?), Rosalie Francine Henry (1916–1993), **Wilmeth Scott** (1919–1986), and **Fred Lynn** (1923–2000). Rosalie Francine was a sergeant in the U.S. Air Force and is buried in the Los Angeles National Cemetery.

Z

Zaccheus "Zack" "Ezekiel" Feather
July 14, 1805–March 4, 1891
Lineage: Jacob & Mary
Row North R / 6

The first of Jacob's and Mary's children to be born in what became Preston County, **Zaccheus Feather** is also referred to as Zachial, Ezekiel, and Ezecual in records. His family is well represented in Lenox Memorial.

He married **Elizabeth Ervin,** a sister of **John Solomon Feather**'s wife, **Mary**. Their children, all buried in Lenox Memorial except where noted otherwise, were:

Clarissa Jane Feather Welch (1832–1901), **Isaac B.** (1834–1921), **Jacob F. Feather** (1837–1919), **Mary Ann Feather Conner** (1839–1919), **Daniel C. Feather** (1842–1922), **Nancy Maria Feather Stokes** (1844–1920), **John Solomon Feather** (1847–1929), **Eve (Eva) Catherine Feather** (1849–1927), **Amanda E. Feather Peaslee** (1852–1930), **Martin Luther (M.L.) Feather,** (1853–1913), Sara Elizabeth Feather Kelly (1856–1934, buried Terra Alta); **Unnamed female infant,** born/died July 25, 1860; **Minerva Bell Feather,** (1862-1950, married Elmer B. Feather).

Ezekiel's farm, according to S. T. Wiley's *History of Preston County,* Ezekiel's farm was a mile from Wiley and was originally settled upon by the legendary hunter and frontiersman Jacob Wolfe.

Zaccheus's obituary from the March 12, 1891 *Preston County Journa*l:

> FEATHER—Though it was generally known that Ezekiel Feather was and had been seriously ill for several weeks, yet the announcement of his death was a painful surprise to the neighborhood of Lenox where he lived and to the church of which he was a member, faithful and consistent. He died March 4, 1891, in his 86th year. He was the last but two of the old Feather family; Joseph of Bruceton, and Mrs. James Beatty, of Washington, Iowa, being now the only survivors. He was much loved and esteemed by all

who knew him, which was manifest on the day of his burial, which took place from the Lutheran church at the Crab Orchard (Lenox).

Notwithstanding the day was stormy, relatives and friends gathered from far and near, until the church was filled almost to capacity. He had been a faithful and consistent member of St. Marks' Ev. Lutheran church of (Bruceton Mills) for many years. Never in our knowing was there a service held in the church but that Bro. Feather was present if at home and health permitted. Nor did the demands of the church make a call but that it received a liberal response from him.

He was the father of a large family of children, twelve, all of which survive him. D.C., president of the board of education of Pleasant district, and the wife of B.A. Conner, commissioner of Pleasant district, being two of the older. As the results largely of his example he lived to see his whole family active members of the church and walking in the truth. Thus we see that blessed are the dead that die in the Lord, in that they not only rest from their labors, but their works do follow them.

The Feathers—plural

The vast majority of the Feather clan who lived in Crab Orchard did not use the plural version of the surname. One family historian suggested that the "Feathers" variant was used by descendants who wanted to distinguish themselves from the rest of the family, especially when relocating to a new community.

Even the local press had a difficult time of keeping the surname singular. An example of this appears under the "Lenox Items" column of *The Preston County Journal* of January 31, 1895. It reported that "Uncle Harry Feathers . . . has handed his business over to his son J. A. Feathers," that Theodore Feathers was still on the list of bachelors, and "Mrs. and Mrs. Clinton D. Feathers were visiting Mr. and Mrs. L. H. Feathers one day last week." At least the writer consistently applied the error!

Earl Smith Feathers
January 12, 1902–June 4, 1961
Lineage: John Mark & Anna Sirissi (Kelly), Jacob Emery & Mariah Ann (Welch), John Solomon & Mary (Evin), Jacob & Mary
South Row A / 5

Earl Smith Feathers's use of his name's plural version is haphazard, with his Social Security identification and draft card bearing the singular version. His "Feathers" moniker may have been the result of relocating to an area where attaching the "S" was standard practice.

He married Iretta Marie Feathers, daughter of John Scott and Lillian Maude Rodeheaver Feather, August 3, 1928, at Morgantown. (She was descended from James). Iretta Marie (1910–1996) is buried at New Salem Church Cemetery, Nortonville, Kentucky. Her headstone has the plural spelling.

Earl was self-employed and living at 396 Baird St., Morgantown, when he registered for the World War II draft in 1942. He was 5-foot-9-inches tall, had gray eyes, brown hair and weighed 190 pounds.

He died in Ashtabula, Ohio, June 4, 1961. Many men from Appalachia found industrial job opportunities in Ashtabula after the war (see the author's *Mountain People in a Flat Land* book for that history). According to the death certificate, he was divorced and an autopsy was performed. The couple had four children: Elmer Stanley (1928–1999), Anna Rosa Lee Feather Chapman (1929–2006), Arthur Klett (1931–2000), and Charles Wayne (1933–1976). All are buried out of state.

Obituary, *Ashtabula Star Beacon*:

> Earl S. Feathers, 59, of New London Rd., died Sunday evening following a heart attack suffered while attending church. He was pronounced dead on arrival at Ashtabula General Hospital.
>
> Mr. Feathers had been in failing health the past year. He had been a resident of this area 10 years. He was born Jan. 12, 1902, in Morgantown, W.Va.
>
> Active in church affairs, Mr. Feathers was a familiar speaker at many area churches.
>
> Survivors include three sons, Arthur of Louisville, Ky., Charles

of Marietta and Elmer of Montana; one daughter, Mrs. Rosslee Chapman Jr. of Indianapolis, Ind., and 10 grandchildren.

Funeral services will be at 2 p.m. Wednesday at the Lutheran Church in Lenox, W.Va. Burial will follow in the church cemetery.

Obediah O. "Obe" Feathers
September 29, 1869–December 2, 1922
Nettie Florence Reckart Feathers
September 18, 1873–November 11, 1962
Lineage: David Summers & Nancy Jane (Erwin),
James & Catharine (Lewis), Mary & Jacob
North Row X / 4

Rogers' *Genealogy* does not use the plural surname in her listing for Obediah, who was born in Kingwood and, according to a death notice for his young son, Charles B. Feather, lived near Cuzzart. in 1897.

Their children were **Charles B.** (1892–1897, died of croup), Albert Franklin "Burt" (1899–1983), and Okey Cornelius (1908–1955).

Obediah's death notice from The Preston County Journal of December 7, 1922:

> Obe Feather who has made his home here for the past few years, died at his home on High street (Kingwood) last Friday morning. The funeral services were conducted last Sunday morning at Lenox church, after which his remains were laid to rest in the church cemetery there. The deceased was about 50 years old.

Nettie lived as a widow for the next 40 years. The 1950 U.S. Census places her in Terra Alta in the household of her son Burt F. Feathers.

A photograph from the collection of Sue Slimmer Dennison captures a farm wagon load of Feathers heading to the first family reunion in 1909. According to accounts of that day, some 1,500 persons attended, but only 300 of them were actually "enrolled as members of the Feather family. The annual gathering continued until at least 1972.

64 Years of Feather Reunions, 1909–1973

The following text was taken from the official Feather Family Reunion minutes as preserved in documents in the author's collection (1909–1950) and the Preston County Historical Society. Additional information about the meetings, when it supplements the minutes, was taken from *The Preston County Journal's* reporting.

Punctuation and spelling in the original documents have not been corrected or updated to modern conventions or style used elsewhere in this book. Incorrect spellings of names have been corrected in instances where the author knew the correct spelling.

August 28, 1909

The first annual reunions of the Feather family was held at Lenox, W.Va. on August 28, 1909. The members present were estimated at about 1,500, of which over 300 were enrolled as members of the Feather family. The forenoon was taken up with a general exchange of greetings, music by the Kingwood Band, and an address by Rev. Joseph B. Feather, who confined himself principally to the history of the family. In his address he brought out the following:

"Jacob Feather (or Fedder, as the name is written in the Fatherland), was the founder of the house in this state. He came from Hesse, Germany, in 1764 (correct date is 1775), when he was 14 years old, and lived for a time in Pennsylvania. Then he moved to the Craborchard and settled with his wife, who had been Miss Mary Connery, on what was later known as the Lucian Martin place. He bought the William Haugen farm and the farm now owned by the Rev. Joseph Feather and Elmer B., his son. He had served seven years in the Revolutionary War fighting for American freedom. To Jacob and his wife were born eleven children: Mary Ann, John S. Sr.,

August 28, 1909

Jacob Jr., Eve, Adam, Christian, Zachias, Sarah, James, Jane, and Joseph. It requires about four figures to number their descendants."—From *Terra Alta Republican*, of issue Sept. 2, 1909.

In the afternoon addresses were delivered by Rev. R. M. Ramsey of Kingwood, Rev. W. H. Berry of Terra Alta, and J. W. Guseman of Masontown, with the interspersion of music by the Kingwood Band, and a female quartet of Terra Alta, composed of members of the family.

On motion it was decided to effect an organization, which resulted in the following officers being elected: President, Rev. Joseph B. Feather; Vice-Pres., D.C. Feather; Sec. & Treas., Rev. W. H. Berry, with power to decide the time and place of the next meeting.

On motion, a rising vote of thanks was offered to James I. Feather of Uniontown, Pa., for the defraying in full of the expenses and service of the Kingwood Band.

Adjournment with benediction.

W. H. Berry, Secretary
Joseph B. Feather, President

The Feather Reunion
The Preston County Journal, Thursday, September 16, 1909, page 1

The first family reunion of the descendants of Jacob Feather (or Fedder according to the old German name) who came to his country from Hese, Germany, in 1764 (correct date 1775), was held Aug. 29 on the old Feather farm near Lenox, W.Va.

At least 1500 people were in attendance. The number registering were over (?) but this list is incomplete as many left the grounds because of the severe storm which prevailed at the noon hour before registration. The connection had gathered in from all parts of this state including Pennsylvania and Ohio. Early in the morning people began to pour in from all directions in a constant stream, notwithstanding the storm which interfered with the spread of a family dinner it was a time of glad hand shaking and social intercourse.

(Description of business session and election of officers omitted)

In this connection it would only be fair to say that the success of this reunion was largely due to the Rev Feather who was born and reared in this county on the old Feather farm. He is now the oldest minister in the W.Va. M. E. Conference, having been in active service for 56 years, at present however he is retired spending his latter days in his comfortable home near Lenox enshrined in the hearts of all those who know him. Jacob Feather the ancestor of the present Feather family came direct from Hesse, Germany to Somerset county, Pa., that being the home of many of the best German families of America. He was only 14 years of age at this time and later married Mary Connery of Somerset when he came to this county and settled on the farm now owned by Rev. Jos. B and his son Elmer Feather near the old Crab Orchard church, eleven children blessed their home. He volunteered his services to his adopted country when she was engaged in the struggle of Independence and served years. This sturdy son of the forest ended his stirring life near where the Rev Feather now lives and remains sleep in the old Lutheran cemetery nearby his faithful and aged companion.

Note: A *Preston County Journal* newspaper brief on page 4 of the August 19, 1909, issue, stated that the reunion would be held at the old Lutheran Church at Crab Orchard (in the cemetery). Due to the huge response to the event, it was evidently moved to the old farm.

September 2, 1910

The second annual reunion of the Feather Family was held at Morris Park[1] on September 2, 1910. The occasion was a delightful one in every respect.

Just before the noon hour all were called together at the pavilion where devotional services were conducted by Rev. Joseph Feather. After this, dinner was in order, and it is needless to say that all did full justice to the contents of well filled baskets.

At 1:30 o'clock addresses were delivered by Revs. W. H. Berry of Terra Alta, and Dana Feather of Fairmont, interspersed with singing by the audience. This was followed by a short business session. The old officers were reelected.

On motion it was decided to hold the next reunion on the first Saturday in September, at Wesley Chapel, near Lenox P.O. This is on a part of ground originally occupied by the pioneers of the Feather family, and in which community a large number reside at this time. After the singing of a hymn, the reunion closed with benediction. —W. H. Berry, Secretary

September 1, 1911

The third annual reunion of the Feather family descendants, agreeable to appointment, met in the grove at Wesley M.E. Church, near Lenox, W.Va., Sept. 1, 1911. A splendid day in every respect was very much enjoyed by the large congregation of the descendents [sic] of the Jacob Feather family of Preston County and many others that joined with them in making a day of gladness long to be remembered.

After devotional exercises conducted by the President, the principal address was delivered by the Rev. Hamrick, pastor of the M. E. Church. A basket dinner was eaten on the ground and an hour or more of greeting was enjoyed, making it a real "lovefeast."[2]

After dinner the stand was occupied for some time by the choir. The Terra Alta singing band, and the old Martin band in giving some of the inspiring songs of long ago, and the best of the present day.

The business part of the occasion was soon dispatched. The first Saturday in September, 1912, and the same grove as now were almost unanimously fixed. The same officers as last year were elected, viz. Jos. B. Feather, President; D.C. Feather, Vice-President; and W. H. Berry, Sec. and Treas.

Frank A. Feather, Acting Secretary
Joseph B. Feather, president

From the *PCJ*, page 8, of September 7, 1911:

A number of people from here attended the Feather Reunion out at the Craborchard on last Saturday, and all came back looking as if it paid them to go, some of them weighed fifteen pounds more that evening when they got back home.

September 7, 1912

The 4th annual reunion of the Feather family and descendents [sic] was held on their grounds near the Wesley M. E. Church, on September 7, 1912. After devotional services conducted by the President and Isaac B. Feather, and a song service by the Wesley M.E. Choir and Terra Alta Quartet, a very appropriate address was delivered by the Rev. D. B. Orr of Cranesville M.E. Church. After another song by the choir a regular picnic dinner was spread on the seats, and more than necessary of the good things to eat to satisfy was soon displayed to the large crowd present by the good housewives.

After dinner and hour of social entertainment, they met again at the stand. More music, more speaking by the President and others opened the way to business. It was decided to meet next year, September 6, 1913, on the same grounds, and Elmer B. Feather was elected President; Martin L. Feather, Vice President; Dana W. M. Feather, Sec. and Historian.

Almost before we knew it the pleasant day had ended and we were compelled to leave, hoping to meet again. It was estimated that between 250 and 300 had been present of the Feather relationship.

D. W. M. Feather, Secretary
Joseph B. Feather, President

September 6, 1913

The fifth annual reunion of the Feather family and descendants was held at the Wesley M. E. Church on Sept. 6, 1913. The program for the day was as follows: Opening song, "All Hail the Power of Jesus Name." Song, "Nearer My God To thee." Scripture reading by Isaac B. Feather. Prayer by J. C. Feather, Sr. Song, "God Will Take Care of You." Address by Rev. E. P. Idleman. Music by Bruceton Band. Dinner and social hour. Called to order by the president. Song by the old time choir, Thomas Bowers, leader. Address by Charles Trembly[3] of Terra Alta.

Business Session—Election of officers: Reelection of all officers except secretary. Josephine Feather elected secretary. It was also decided that the next reunion be held at Wesley Chapel on the first Saturday in September.

Solo by Hazel Englehart. Address by Rev. D. B. Orr. Closing address by Rev. J.B. Feather. The day was enjoyed by something near the same number of feather relationship as the preceding year.

Josephine Feather[4], Acting Secretary
Elmer B. Feather, President

September 5, 1914

The sixth annual reunion of the Feather family and descendants was held at Wesley Chapel in the Craborchard September 5, 1914. After an opening hymn, Rev. J.B. Feather called to mind the importance of remembering our obligations to the Creator of us all, after which he read the "Faith Chapter" and led in prayer. The names of those who had died out of the Feather family within the last 12 months were read, and a short memorial service held.

After dinner, some time was spent in social enjoyment. Rev. Albert Engle made an address in which he told of several incidents relating to the history of the Feather family. Addresses were also made by Ezra Hauger, Rev. Wilson, and Rev. J. B. Feather. A song was rendered by the choir at Wesley Chapel. The same date and same place was decided on for the next reunion. The same officers re-elected. H.A. Feather elected vice-president. Hon. W.G. Brown came just in time to make an address before closing. It was listened to and appreciated by all.

Josephine Feather, Secretary
Elmer B. Feather, President

September 4, 1915

The seventh annual reunion of the Feather family was held at Wesley Chapel in the Craborchard Saturday, Sept. 4, 1915. On account of the rainy weather, devotional services were held in the church. Services were opened by singing "All Hail The Power of Jesus Name." Rev. Morris of Bruceton read a portion of the scripture, and Rev. J.B. Feather led in prayer. A basket lunch was eaten in the grove with an hour or more of social enjoyment afterwards.

In the afternoon very fitting addresses were made by Prof. Taylor Martin of Morgantown, Rev. King of Terra Alta M. E. Church, and Rev. Morris. Prof. Martin, Prof. Groves and son, Thomas Bowers, and Rev. Morris added greatly to the music by rendering some quartets. It was decided to hold the next reunion at the same place and on the first Sat. in Sept. the next year. No change was made in the officers. Quite a number of the Feather relationship from a distance were present.

Josephine Feather, secretary
E.B. Feather, President

September 2, 1916

The eighth annual Feather reunion was held at Wesley Chapel in the Craborchard, Saturday, Sept. 2, 1916. The following is the program: Music by the Orchestra. Reading Scripture lesson by Rev. Johnson of Bruceton. St. John 14th Chapter. Song, "If Your Heart Keeps Right." Prayer by Rev. J. B. Feather. Song, "Jesus Has You on His Heart." Reading of the report of last year. Music. Dinner and Social Hour. Music by Orchestra. Recitation and song by Lillian Whitsell. Prayer by Rev. Johnson. Address by Rev. Johnson,

"What it means to meet in this family reunion, and preparation for a reunion that will never break up." Song, "Since Jesus Came Into My Heart." Address by Rev. Henderson of Cranesville on home building. "As the home is the vestibule of Heaven, so these reunions are of the great reunion."

It was voted that the next reunion be held at the same place the first Saturday in Sept. 1917. The same officers also were re-elected. Song, "The Church in the Wildwood." Benediction by Rev. Engle.

Elmer B. Feather, President
Josephine Feather Seal, Secretary.

September 1, 1917

The ninth annual reunion of the Feather family was held at Wesley Chapel in the Craborchard, Sat., Sept. 1, 1917.

Devotional exercises were held in the morning. A basket dinner was eaten and a social time after which the Orchestra favored us with music, and we had speaking by Rev. Nicolson of the Brandonville charge. His theme was the old time handshake. Also an address by Jim White. Rev. Merrells spoke, then we had a song—"Sweeter As The Years Go By."

The business session took up the next period. There was no change made in place of holding the next reunion or time of holding it. The same officers were re-elected.

Elmer B. Feather, President
Josephine Feather Seal, Secretary

September 7, 1918

The tenth annual reunion of the Feather family was held at Wesley Chapel in the Crab Orchard on Sat., Sept. 17, 1918. The morning session was called to order by the President. Song, "Dwelling in Beulah." Prayer by Rev. Engle. Song, "Brighten The Corner." Address by Rev. Shultz of Oakland, in which he told how we should reverence the men who held the country together in the sixties. He spoke of Belgium and why the boys are in France. He also told many other interesting facts concerning the War. Song, "Sail On."[5]

A basket dinner was eaten and the social hour took up the next period. Song, "America." Prayer by Rev. Howard of Kingwood. Song, "Keep the Home Fires Burning" by Mrs. Browning. Address by Rev. Engle. Address by Rev. Howard, in which he gave us many facts concerning the War. Song,

September 6, 1919

"Still Sweeter Every Day." Address by Rev. Shultz. Address by Rev. Bragg—a very interesting talk. Address by lawyer Mitchels of Terra Alta.

The business section did not take much time. Nearly everyone wanted to have the reunion the same place and the first Sat. in Sept. next year. No change was made, and the same officers were re-elected for another year.

Elmer B. Feather, President
H.A. Feather, Vice President
Josephine Feather Seal, Secretary

September 6, 1919

The 11th annual reunion of the Feather family was held at Wesley Chapel in the Craborchard Sept. 6, 1919. The weather was ideal for a picnic and by 10 A.M. one of the largest crowds that had ever assembled for a family reunion had gathered for a general exchange of greetings. The morning session was called to order by the president, E. B. Feather. Song, "In the Service of the King." Reading of Scripture lesson by James C. Feather. Song, "Sail On." Prayer by Rev. J.B. Feather. Song, "Brighten the Corner Where You Are." After this E. B. Feather read the obituary of grandmother Feather, which proved very interesting to all. Address by Joel Titchnell—a Biblical History in which he compared the names of great men of the Bible and well-known men of the Feather family. The speaker held the audience spell-bound throughout his interesting address.[6]

The meeting then adjourned for a basket dinner, which of course everyone enjoyed—until the last bit of chicken vanished. At 3 o'clock the meeting was again resumed. Music by Liston sisters. Solo by Mrs. Effie Browning. Music by Miss Hartman, Miss Hauger, and Miss Eiseman. Address by Rev. Flannigan. Song, "End of a Perfect Day" by trio. Address by E.G. Hauger of Kingwood.

The following officers were elected: President, E.B. Feather; 1st Vice President, Mrs. Effie Browning: 2nd Vice President, H.A. Feather; Secretary & Treasurer, Hugh C. Feather. Song, "God Be With You Till We Meet Again." Benediction by Rev. Flannigan.

Hugh C. Feather, Secretary

September 9, 1920

No minutes of the 1920 meeting were preserved. The numbering of the reunions suggests one was held. This was the year Joseph B. Feather died, which may account for the lapse in reporting. *The Preston County Journal* of September 9, 1920, suggests a small Feather reunion of sorts was held at Long Hollow church:

Reunion

On August 29th, a family reunion was held near Long Hollow church on the Daniel Feather farm now owned by B.T. Gibson, in honor of Wm. Feather and wife of Los Angeles, Cal., oldest son of Daniel Feather Deceased, who, after an absence of forty-one years concluded to visit his many friends and the old home of his childhood and boyhood days. Forty-two of his near relatives, and old acquaintances were represented and memories of days gone by stirred each heart.

At the noon hour a sumptuous dinner was served after which a very appropriate prayer was offered by Mrs. Feather in behalf of all present. Mr. and Mrs. Feather endeared themselves to us all during their brief stay with us, and we are sorry to say the word good by, when they leave for their far off home.

September 3, 1921

The 13th annual reunion of the Feather Family was held Sept. 3, 1921, at Wesley Chapel. The members of the Feather family began to gather in the early morning, and even though the weather was unfavorable, a song service was held in the forenoon led by Thomas Bower, with Miss Coral Whitesell and Mrs. Klet Forman as organists. Prayer and an address were given by the Rev. McCarthy of Cranesville. At noon an excellent dinner was prepared and served by the women of the family, and all partook heartily. The hour after the meal was spent in a social way.

Because of a downpour of rain, the afternoon meeting was held in the Church, where the addresses were delivered by the Rev. Bragg of Albright and the Rev. Gus C. Shaffer of Temple, Oklahoma. The latter gentleman is related to the family through his mother, Virginia Feather,[7] who was married to Israel Shaffer. He told several stories of his boyhood days in Preston County.

September 2, 1922

The Rev. Albert Engle also gave a short address, and Mrs. Effie Teets read a poem, after which a song service was held by the choir. Instrumental music was offered by Miss Lillian Whitesell and the Misses Flo and Murhl Liston. A short business meeting was held, and officers for the coming year were elected. They are: President, Andrew Feather; Vice President, Elmer B. Feather; Secretary, Mrs. McClellan Hartman; Treasurer, Miss Mary Feather; Historians, Harvey Feather and Klet Forman.

The reunion will be held next year at Wesley Chapel on the first Saturday in September, 1922.   Elmer B. Feather, President

September 2, 1922

The 14th annual reunion of the Feather family was held at Wesley Chapel in the Craborchard on Sept. 2, 1922. Many who had planned to attend were kept away by the downpour of rain in the early morning. However, by 10 o'clock the sky was clear and the day proved to be ideal for the occasion. By noon a large crowd of the members of the family and their friends had gathered for the program, which began with singing "America." The Rev. McCarthy of Cranesville read a passage of Scripture and offered a prayer. Following the singing of a hymn by the Choir, Attorney Vernon Fortney of Kingwood gave an interesting talk. The feature of the day was the musical program presented by Homer Rodeheaver, the noted choir leader. Several of his songs were his own compositions. The celebrated musician also played a group of numbers on the trombone. Later he gave a most enjoyable reading.

At noon a bountiful dinner was served by the women of the family. At 2 o'clock P.M. Elmer B. Feather, Vice President of the organization, called the meeting to order. William Layman of Fairmont, who is a member of the family, gave an interesting address. Mrs. Jesse Graham and Miss Murhl Liston played an instrumental number and Mary Elizabeth Kelly gave a recitation "Robin Red Breast."

The closed address was made by the Rev. McCarthy, after which the group sang "God Be With You Till We Meet Again." The following officers were elected for the coming year: President, Mrs. J.D. Browning; Vice President, Elmer Feather; Secretary, Mrs. McClellan Hartman. The reunion will be held next year at Brown's Park at Kingwood the first Saturday in September.

Mrs. McClellan Hartman, Secretary

September 1, 1923

Reunions were possibly moved to Brown Park to accommodate folks who lived in the big city of Kingwood.

September 1, 1923

The 15th annual reunion of the Feather family was held at Brown's Park[7] at Kingwood, W.Va., Saturday Sept. 1, 1923. Opening of the Reunion. Music by the Kingwood Band. Song service led by Prof. B. D. Ward. Prayer by G. W. Bishoff. Address of welcome by Mr. Vernin Fortney, a little poem for the Feather family.

There is a family we all know,
To their Reunion each year we go.
They feed you all you dare to eat:
Cakes, pies, salads, all kinds of meat.
They shake your hand wish you well,
Nor will they ever your faults tell.
And every reunion to which you go,
Makes you wish they were every month or so.
They come for miles and miles around,
to visit our little country town.
Say, when in the park the crowd gathers,
All claim relation to the family of Feathers.

September 1, 1924

Duet by Prof. Ward and Miss Grace Eiseman. Minutes of the meeting by Mrs. Hartman. Reading by Mrs. Geo. A. Herrney entitled "The Little Bug Will Get You By and By." At noon a basket dinner and social hour was enjoyed by all present, after which the Band favored us with music. Address by Rev. Gus Shaffer, who gave a short history of the descendants of Jacob Feather family of six generations, and of his life as a soldier. Address by Mr. Mitchell, who would enjoy an old fashioned corn shucking. A piano solo by Miss Ruby Hartman. The closing address by Mr. Layman of Fairmont, after which the group sand "West Virginia Hills" and "Old Folks at Home." This was followed by a short business session. The old officers were re-elected. It was voted that the next reunion be held at Brown's Park the first Saturday in September, 1924.

Mrs. McClelland Hartman, secretary

September 1, 1924

A large number of our members and friends of the Feather family gathered Sept. 1st for the 16th annual reunion of the Feather family, which was held at Brown's Park at Kingwood. The opening of the meeting was conducted by the President, Mrs. J.D. Browning, followed by prayer by Rev. McCarthy of Albright, after which the Highland M. E. Choir of Fairmont was introduced by J. N. Layman, who gave an interesting address. The choir sang several appropriate songs which were greatly appreciated. A duet by Misses Pauline and Mary Feather of Albright was followed by music by the Boys Band of Kingwood. Following a short period of greeting, a bountiful dinner was served during the noon hour, after which was a program of speeches and music by the choir and band. A reading was given by Mrs. Effie Feather Teets[8] of Aurora, and a short address was made by E. B. Feather of Albright, who spoke in regards to the oldest members of the Feather family who are still living, and so many near relatives that have passed away since the last reunion.

The social program was followed by a short business session, when the same officers were re-elected for the following year. It was voted that the next reunion be held at Brown's Park the first Saturday in September, 1925.

Mrs. McClellen Hartman, Secretary

September 5, 1925, September 4, 1926

September 5, 1925

The 17th annual reunion of the Feather family was held at Brown's Park, Kingwood, W.Va., Sept. 5, 1925. A large number of friends gathered for the occasion. The morning session was opened by the president, Mrs. J.D. Browning. Devotional services by Rev. McCarty of Albright. The Boys Band of Kingwood gave a concert which was enjoyed by all. A picnic dinner was served on the grounds and a social time was spent in greeting old friends. In the afternoon, the crowd was called to order by E. B. Feather in U. B. Church and a collection was taken by E. V. Fortney and W. L. Lenhart, which amounted to $9.11, which was divided equally between the minister of the U.B. Church and Boys Band. The program was as follows, directed by Mrs. B.D. Ward; Opening song, "America." Selection by orchestra. Vocal solo by Miss Pauline Englehard to Terra Alta. Piano duet by Pauline and Mary Feather of Albright, and another number by orchestra. Vocal duet by Miss Grace Eiseman and B. D. Ward. Reading by Miss DeBerry of Kingwood. Closing number by orchestra.

It was voted that the next reunion be held at Wesley Chapel the first Saturday in September, 1926. Officers elected for the year 1926 were as follows: President, Effie Browning; Vice President, E. B. Feather; Secretary, J.A. Feather.

Lou Lenhart, Acting Secretary

September 4, 1926

The 18th reunion of the Feather family was held at Wesley Chapel, Craborchard, Sept. 4, 1926. Devotional exercises were conducted by Rev. Thompson. Song by the local choir. Address by Rev. Thompson, which was greatly enjoyed by all, after which E. B. Feather gave an interesting talk on descendants of the Feather family. Recess was declared at this time for dinner. Afternoon session, song by the choir. A short talk by Mrs. Thompson, which was well received. Song by the Davis girls, Mildred and Edna of Hudson, W.Va. Reading minutes of previous reunion. Election of officers: President, E. B. Feather; Vice-president, Mrs. J.D. Browning; Secretary, J. A. Feather. Place of next reunion, Brown's Park, Kingwood, the first Saturday in September. 1927. Song by Josephine Feather Seal

Jared A. Feather, Secretary

September 3, 1927, September 2, 1931, September 3, 1932

September 3, 1927

The 19th annual reunion of the Feather family was held at Brown's Park, Kingwood, W. Va., the first Saturday in September, 1927. Meeting was called to order by the president. Morning session address by Rev. Bauman, which was well received. Song, "America," by Josephine Feather Seal. Picnic and social hour.

Afternoon session—address by Rev. Gus Shaffer of Oklahoma, which was greatly appreciated by all. Song by Josephine Seal. Song by Mrs. Annie Armstrong. Oration by Will Layman. Election of officers: President, E.B. Feather: Vice president, Mrs. J.D. Browning; Secretary, Jared A. Feather. Place of next reunion, Brown's Park, Kingwood, the first Saturday in September, 1928. Jared A. Feather, Secretary

Note: no minutes could be located for the 1928, 1929, and 1930 reunions, which were evidently held as the next entry is for the 23rd.

September 2, 1931

The 23rd annual reunion, Sept. 2, 1931, was held at Wesley Chapel. Number present, 300. Program started as follows at 1:30 P.M.: Josephine Feather Seal acted as president in the absence of Hugh Feather. Opened by song, "Home, Sweet Home" played by Charles Miller. Reading of Scripture and prayer by Josephine Feather Seal. Song by group, "Onward Christian Soldiers." Address by Mr. Landman. "Mocking Bird" whistled and played by Millard and Carney Williams. Recitation by Anna Belle Armstrong. Song by bald-headed men entitled "Sweet By and By." Song dedicated by Josephine Seal to David A. Feather, Jacob E. Feather, James C. Feather, Abraham Feather entitled "Oh, How Happy Are They." Officers present—1.

Officers elected: H. A. Feather, president; W. Scott Feather, secretary; and W. M. Lenhart, Treasurer. Place of next reunion at Wesley Chapel. Collection, $3.72. Closed by song, "God Be With You Till We Meet Again."

W. Scott Feather, Secretary

September 3, 1932

The 24th annual Feather reunion opened at 2 o'clock by singing "In The Sweet By and By," played by Charley Miller, Cornet; Pauline Feather, Piano; and Charley Manoun, violin. Second number, "Close to Thee" played by the same ones. Prayer by Rev. Somner. Piano solo by Pauline and Mary

Feather; violin, Charley Manoun. J. L. Feather and J. C. Feather were the oldest Feathers on the grounds. Talk by Hugh Feather. Reading by Anna Belle Feather. Song by Ronald Armstrong. Trio by Charley Miller, Charley Manoun, and Pauline Feather entitled "Come Ye That Love The Lord." Second number, "Marching Onward to Zion." Song by Hugh Feather and Anna Armstrong. Song by all. Election of officers: H. A. Feather, president; Frank Feather, Vice president; W. M. Lenhart, Treasurer. Closed by song "Onward Christian Soldiers." Cash on hand, $5.37. Officers present—2. (Pres. & Sec'y.)

Deaths: Rev. Charley Feather, Bruceton Mills, W. Va.; Ada Sharps Medsler; Mary R. Medsler, age 84, all descendants of Abraham Feather. C. D. Feather, Joseph W. Feather, Descendants of Jacob Feather, Masontown, W.Va.; Sarett Sue Feather, age 18 mos., daughter of Hugh Feather.

W. Scott Feather, Secretary

September 5, 1933

The 25th annual reunion of the Feather family was held at Wesley Chapel in the Crab Orchard September 5, 1933. The opening song was "Sweet By And By." Scripture reading, Matt. 8. Song by Josephine Seal and Anna Armstrong, "The Meeting In The Air." Talk by Rev. Arbogast on the home. Instrumental duet, Charles Miller and Charles Menoun. Special song by Rev. Arbogast, Mrs. Arbogast, Mrs. Klet Forman, Phil and James Jackson, and Mr. Lee. Speech by Hugh C. Feather (Joker), "Heaven is a place where you do everything you want to do and nothing you don't want to do." Song by Rev. and Mrs. Arbogast and Mr. Lee, "Follow Me." Instrumental duet, Mary Feather and Opal Shaw. Song by Hugh and boys. Violin solo, Charles Manoun. Song by Frank Welch and two daughters, Nita and Madalene, and James & Phil Jackson. Music by Mr. Laman and son with violin and harp. Quartette by Rev. Arbogast, Phil and James J. and Mr. Lee. Speech by Rev. Parson Cuppett. Song by Rev. & Mrs. Arbogast and Mr. Lee

Deaths: Frank Feather, Fairmont, W.Va., son of J.B. Feather, died Feb. 1933; J. D. Byer, Uniontown, Pa., son-in-law of J. I. Feather, died Jan. 3, 1933; D. C. Feather, son of late Wesley Feather, Bruceton Mills, died July, 1933; A. C. Feather, died March 5, 1933

Josephine F. Seal, Secretary

September 6, 1934

The 26th annual reunion of the Feather family was held at Wesley Chapel Sept. 6, 1934. Opening song, "Never Grow Old." Prayer, Rev. Myers. Song, "Rock of Ages" by Anna Armstrong and Josephine Seal. Talk by Rev. Myers—where there is sin there is suffering: a story which portrays the love of God for mankind. Reading "My First Auto Ride" by Miss Agnes Aitken. Song by Hugh and boys. Reading—Miss Agnes Aitken. Talk by Rev. Orr. He told of his first trip to Craborchard. He stopped at J. C. Feather's Sr., then went on to Cranesville, 48 years ago. He remarked that there were not so many present that were here then. Aunt Beck Welch made the statement that she would be 91 years old next Monday. Rev. Orr sang a song appropriate for a reunion.

Deaths: Mrs. Samantha Rodeheaver, July 17, 1934; Mrs Sarah Feather Kelley, June.

Josephine F. Seal, Secretary

September 7, 1935

The 27th annual reunion of the Feather family was held at Wesley Chapel Sept. 7 1935. There was no session in the morning. After a bounteous spread basket dinner the assembly was called in the church by music by Charles Miller, his friend, and Mr. & Mrs. Clet Forman, and son and daughter. Prayer by Rev. Myers. Music by Chas. Miller and others "Home Sweet Home." Talk by Rev. Meyers of Albright on "I will seek that which was lost." Music by Amato Guariglia (accordion) and Ralph Bennet (guitar) of Morgantown. Reading by June Forman. Music by Chas. Miller and others as stated. Reading by Agnes Aitken of Morgantown. Address by Prosecuting Attorney M. C. Snyder. Music by Morgantown boys. Ready by Miss Aitken. Business session: officers present—H. A. Feather, president; Wm. Lenhart, treas., & Josephine Seal, sec'y. Same officers and same place and date decided upon for next year. The program was in charge of Hugh C. Feather.

Deaths: James I. Feather, son of the late Abraham Feather; Mrs. Isa Byer died a few hours before her father, Jacob L. Feather, died; Mrs. Rebecca Welch (age 91 yrs.); J.D. Browning and Mrs. J.D. Browning; Mrs. Wesley Feather; John Scott, husband of Lyda Feather Scott; Willis Hugh Kelley, infant son of Pauline Feather Kelley; Robert Browning Haigh, son of Martha F. Haigh; Mrs. Wilber Liston; Scott Morgan.

Josephine F. Seal, Secretary

September 5, 1936, September 4, 1937, September 3, 1938

September 5, 1936

The 28th reunion of the Feather family was held the first Saturday in September 1936 at Wesley Chapel in the Craborchard. By noon quite a representation of the Feather family had gathered as well as many friends of the family from far and near. After a bountiful basket dinner was served on the grounds, the following program was rendered. Saxaphone trio by Charles Miller and friends from Cambridge, Ohio, entitled "Old Folks at Home." Hymn, "Sweet Hour of Prayer." Prayer and talk by Rev. Meyers of Albright. Music by above musicians, "Whispering Hope." Song and talk by Josephine F. Seal. In the talk she told of the home going of Rev. D. B. Orr, a friend of the Feather family for years. The title of the song was "Tell Me His Name Again." Music by above named, "Cross and Crown." Song by Junior and Marion Dewitt. Mrs. Sarah Childs was the oldest one present of the Feather family. The reunion will be held on the same day and same place next year. Same officers were re-elected.

Deaths: Jane Conner Miller died January 25; James (Little Jim) Feather died February 8.

Josephine F. Seal, Secretary

September 4, 1937

The 29th reunion of the Feather family was held at Wesley Chapel in Craborchard Sept. 4, 1937. Mrs. Whitesell of Bruceton Mills and some youngsters she brought with her favored the assembly with music. Rev. Wriston of Brandonville was the main speaker of the day. A bountiful dinner was served at noon.

Deaths: James Crane, son of Scott and Allie Feather Crane, died April 12; James C. Feather, Jr., son of the late Christian Feather; Hazel Gibson, Albright; Mrs. Annie Feather, wife of Guy Feather.

Josephine F. Seal, Secretary

September 3, 1938

The 30th annual reunion was held at Wesley Chapel the first Saturday in Sept., 1938. The program for the afternoon session was as follows: Song, "When We All Get to Heaven." Prayer by Rev. Moccia of Clarksburg. Talk by Rev. Myers of Albright. Song by Merritt Feather of Mill Creek, "If I Have Wounded Any Soul Today." Speech, Rev. Gay Feather. Talk by Rev.

Moccia—Bible stories mentioning Abraham, Joseph, Ruth and Naomi, the early church, spirit of unity. "let this mind be in you." Psalm 103. The same officers were re-elected. Sarah Childs (88) was the oldest descendant of the Feather family present. Her nephew, Merritt Feather, sang a song and dedicated it to her. It was decided to meet the same time and place next year.

Deaths: Paul H. Seal, son of C. H. and Josephine F. Seal, died Dec. 26, 1937;. Infant son of Harry Haigh and Martha Feather Haigh, died 1938.

Josephine F. Seal, Secretary

September 2, 1939

The 31st reunion of the Feather family was held Sept. 2, 1939, at Wesley Chapel. Program was led by Elmer B. Feather & Josephine Seal, as follows: Songs, "The Old Rugged Cross" and "America." Prayer by Rev. Jos. Vansickle of Albright. Reading of 19th Psalm by Rev. Vansickle followed by explanation of same and talk. Song by the 4 Sisler sisters and Mrs. Peaslee, Mrs. Freeland, Mrs. Lenhart, & Mrs. Casteel. Song by the 7 Gidley young people. Song by Josephine Seal in memory of her father, "Farther Along." Oldest member present was Jared Feather. New officers elected were: President, Walter Feather; Vice president, Josephine Seal; Secty., Frank Welch; Treas., W. L. Lenhart.

Deaths reported were Sarah Feather, wife of Isaac Feather; Harvey A. Feather, August 18, 1939; and Greeley Crane, died Sept. 17, 1938.

Josephine F. Seal, Secretary

September 7, 1940

The 32nd annual reunion of the Feather family was held at Wesley Chapel Sept. 7, 1940. The day was ideal for a gathering of this kind. A basket dinner was served at noon and a social hour followed as usual. The program of the afternoon was held in the church. Opening songs were "Love Lifted Me" and "The Church by the Side of The Road." Devotionals led by Rev. Maness. A memorial was observed to the ones who have passed away, led by Rev. Maness. Also a talk in which he spoke of his first trip here and how uncle Elmer had gone with him to visit the folks. Rev. Maness said he had a good word for every one; he was a faithful steward for over fifty years. Song by the Sisler sisters. A balloon blowing contest, for old and young, was led by the president. Charley Miller from Cambridge, Ohio, came the fartherest, over 200 miles, and hasn't missed a reunion in 20 years. No changes in officers except secretary.

Deaths: Elmer B. Feather, Jan. 15, 1940; Edna Wilhelm; Martin L. Feather, son of the late Christian Feather; Lona May Hile of Palmer, Pa. Died last of August; John Mark Feather, Jan., 1940; Karl Cramer, April 15, 1940;

Frank Welch, Secretary

September 6, 1941

The 33rd annual reunion of the Feather family was held at Wesley Chapel on Sat., Sept. 6, 1941. After a basket dinner the program was held in the church and was as follows: Song, "All Hail The Power." Devotions led by Rev. Maness. Song, "Old Rugged Cross." Talk by Rev. Maness. A place on the program was extended to the folks to tell how far and where they traveled from. Charley Miller and wife from Cambridge, O. Mrs. Lillie Harned Gray from Geneva, O. Mrs. Jenewine from Baltimore. Casteel from Winchester, Ky., 375 miles, and Bessie Hayden from Greensburg, Pa.

Song, "When We All Get To Heaven." Reading by Jessie Edaborn (Edeburn) on "Home."[10] Song by Patricia Shirley. Recitation by Reckart girls. Election of officers was held: Walter Feather, president; Klet Forman, Vice president; Josephine Seal, secretary; Will Lenhart, treasurer. Program committee: Mrs. Forman, Ada(h) Feather, and Madalene Feather. Reunion to be held same place, same time, next year. Isaac Feather was the oldest one present (86 yrs.) and James David Rembold (3 mos. today) the youngest.

Josephine F. Seal, Secretary

September 5, 1942

The 34th annual reunion was held at Wesley Chapel September 5, 1942. There was no morning session. After dinner the president led the following program: Song, "Blest Be The Tie That Binds." Scripture reading, John I, by Mr. Layman. Prayer by Mr. Layman. Song, "What a Friend We Have in Jesus." Talk by C. P. Wilhelm in which he told of historical facts concerning prominent members of the Feather family of other years, closing with an extract of the 46th Psalm. His talk was very interesting and I believe enjoyed by all present.

September 5, 1943, September 2, 1944, September 1, 1945

The same officers were re-elected for another year. Also same date and place for the next reunion.

Deaths: Mrs. Sarah Childs, age 91 yrs; (1942) George Haun; John S. Kelly; Mildred Hartman; Howard Peaslee; James F. Jackson; Martha Groves.

Josephine F. Seal, Secretary

September 5, 1943

The 35th annual reunion was held at Wesley Chapel on Sunday, September 5, 1943, in connection with the quarterly meeting. Dr. Brandt preached the sermon. There was no program due to the business meeting. Officers were elected as follows: Walter Feather, president; Clet Forman, Vice president; Will Lenhard, treasurer; and May Welch, secretary.

It was voted to have the reunion on the first Saturday of September. Deaths reported since our last reunion were: Soll Feather, Joe Feather, and Lillie Harned Grey. The oldest member present was Bess Hayden.

May Welch, Secretary
(May is not mentioned in Rogers' *Genealogy*).

September 2, 1944

The 36th annual reunion of the Feather family was held at Wesley Chapel on Saturday, Sept. 2, 1944. After a basket lunch everyone assembled in the church. The president led the following program:

Songs: "I Need Thee Every Hour." "Lord Jesus, I Love Thee." "Savior, Like a Shepherd Lead Us." A duet was sung by Roxie and Joan Peaslee entitled "I'll Be somewhere Listening." The audience was entertained by contestants who took part in the doughnut eating contest and the pop drinking contest. Prizes were given to the winners. Officers elected same as previous year. A program committee was appointed, Mrs. Lou Lenhard, Mrs. Fanny Wolfe, Mrs. Orf Cramer, Delph Deberry, Clyde Kelley, and Willie Forman.

May Welch, Secretary

September 1, 1945

The 37th Annual Reunion of the Feather family was held on Sat., Sept. 1, 1945, at Wesley Chapel. After a basket lunch those present gathered in the Chapel for the following program:

September 7, 1946, September 6, 1947

Opening song, "America The Beautiful." Minutes of previous reunion read by the secretary. Talk by Mr. Layman. Trio by Roxy and Jeane Peaslee and Mary Lou Childs, "Something Got Hold of Me." Remarks by Rev. Maness. Duet by Frances Jean Spiker and Ruth Bishoff.

A collection was taken, amounting to $4.90. The following officers were elected for the 1946 reunion: President, Walter Feather; Vice president, Clet Forman; Secretary, Mrs. Earl Welch; Treasurer, Mrs. Grace Layman. Closing song.

Deaths: Hugh Feather, Issac Feather, and Will Lenhart.

May Welch, Secretary

September 7, 1946

The 38th Annual Reunion of the Feather family was held on Saturday, September 1946, at Wesley Chapel in the Craborchard. After a basket dinner those present gathered in the church for the following program: Opening song, "Faith of Our Fathers." Second song, "The Old Rugged Cross." Prayer by Gay Feathers of Clarksburg. Song, "I Come To The Garden Alone." We enjoyed listening to a talk by Gay Feather. More songs, "Bring Them In" and "Have You Counted The Cost?" Minutes were read by sec'y. Officers were elected for 1947 as follows: President, Walter Feather; 1st Vice-president, Isaac Armstrong; 2nd Vice-president, Anna Armstrong; Sec'y, May Welch; Treas., Mrs. Clet Forman. A collection of $6.08 was taken. Program was closed by signing "God Be With You Till We Meet Again."

Deaths since our last reunion: Foster Hartman, Mrs. Lillie Welch, and Mrs. A.J. Feather.

May Welch, Secretary

September 6, 1947

The 39th Annual Reunion of the Feather family was held at Wesley Chapel on Saturday, Sept. 6, 1947. After a basket lunch everyone assembled in the church for the following program:

The president, Walter Feather, called the meeting to order by announcing we sing, "Haven of Rest: and "The Old Rugged Cross." Minutes of the last meeting were read and approved. Following was a very interesting talk given by Will Layman of Fairmont. A duet by Mae Peaslee and Myrtle Lenhart, two sisters. Following was a Bubble-blowing contest. Prizes were awarded.

September 4, 1948

Following this officers were elected for the coming year: President, Paul Feather; 1st Vice President, Thomas Welch; 2nd Vice president, Klet Forman; Secretary, May Welch; Treasurer, Nina Forman. Collection for the day was $5.87. Balance in treasury, $11.38. Total $17.25. Song, "Heavenly Sunlight." Closed by singing "God Be With You Till We Meet Again." Prayer by Mr. Layman.

Deaths since we last met were: Clay Feather, and Andrew Feather.

May Welch, Secretary

September 4, 1948

The 40th Annual gathering of the Feather family was held at the Wesley Chapel Church on Sept. 4, 1948. The day was fine, and until late dinner a good crowd had gathered and a bountiful dinner was enjoyed by all present. During the dinner hour music was furnished by Denny Feather of Tunnelton with his loud speaker.

After old friends had their back-slapping and hand-shaking a short "on the spot" program was given. Different ones of the family were called to the "mike" to say a few words informally. To show that Ike and Anna Armstrong, the program committee, had really done something, under the supervision of Paul Feather, the president, the Feather, gave the history of the meaning of the children of Harvey Feather's family. Glen Crane, followed, giving a short talk on the spiritual side of the family life. Klet Forman and Scott Feather each made a few remarks. Denny Feather, Bob Feather, Junior DeWitt, Burgett Johns, & Johnnie Feather furnished a lot of fine string music and songs. A quartet was sung by Scott Feather, Frank Welch, Klet Forman, and Guy Feather. Jack Feather played the harmonica, accompanied himself on the banjo, or vice-versa. After the program, a business meeting was held with the following officers being elected: President, Paul Feather; Vice president, Thomas G. Welch; Sec.-Treas., Nina C. Forman. Talent scouts were appointed for the 1949 program: Ike Armstrong, Anna Armstrong, Johnnie Feather, Denny Feather, and Burgett Johns.

Adjourned to meet first Saturday in September 1949. Collection for the day, $23.39. Total in treasury, $40.64.

Deaths since the year previous: McClellan Hartman, Mrs. Josiah (Belle) Feather, Mrs. Scott Feather, Mrs. Jared Feather, and Mrs. Tom Feather.

May Welch, Secretary

September 3, 1949

The 41st annual reunion of the Feather family was held at Wesley Chapel on Sept. 3, 1949. The day was fine and a fairly good crowd. A big dinner was enjoyed by all, and a meeting followed in the church under the supervision of the president, Paul Feather, with his spokesman in the person of Anna Armstrong. A lively meeting was held when Anna called for you to do something you might as well do it. Mrs. Coral Whitesell presided at the piano during the singing of several songs.

Recognition was given to different ones traveling great distances to get to the reunion. Troy Feather, brother of Coral Whitesell, from Arizona; Lester Feather, New York, brother of Mrs. Matta Trembly and son of Ike Feather; Bob Feather of Minnesota; Ray Lenhard of Los Angeles, Calif.; Charles I. Miller, Cambridge, Ohio. The program was interspersed by music from the Fairmont Creamery Duet.

The oldest member present was Mrs. Belle Feather. Officers elected for the coming year were: President, Paul Feather; Vice president, W.K. Forman; Sec'y.-Treas., Nina C. Forman. Talent scouts for the 1950 program are: Chairman, Anna Armstrong, Bobby Feather, Mollie Feather, Coral Whitesill and Edna Heffelfinger. Duet was played by Charles Miller and Bill Armstrong. Meeting was dismissed by prayer by Anna Armstrong.

Deaths since last year are Anna Armstrong, Georgia McGinnis, Will Layman, Mrs. Iretta Crane, Gay Crane, son of Clay, Mrs. E.B. Feather, and Mrs. McClellan Hartman.

Treasurer's report: No collection taken. Balance in treasury from 1948 ... $40.64. Nina Forman, Secretary-Treasurer

September 2, 1950

The 42nd Annual gathering of the Feather family was held Sept. 2, 1950 at the Wesley Chapel Church in the Craborchard. The day was cloudy and cool but no rain. Dinner was held in the grove and fairly large crowd partook. A social hour was held after dinner, and at 2:30 they gathered in the church for a short program.

Bob Feather conducted the meeting, calling for a special hymn. "Precious Memories" was sung in honor of those deceased since last year. Mrs. Coral Whitesell presided at the piano. Following this was a prayer by Mrs. Josephine F. Seal. Mrs. Whitesell presented a lovely bouquet of gladioli in

September 1, 1951

memory of Anna Armstrong, deceased. Then followed the reading of an old teacher's certificate of Mr. Hayden, signed in 1872 by John H. Feather, Superintendent of Schools. Song by Junior DeWitt, "Home, Sweet Home."

Recognition was given the folks who had traveled the greatest distance. The honor went to Jean Heffelfinger Black and husband from Iowa, 1500 miles. Jack Feather could not be present from Jacksonville, Fla., so two recordings of his songs were played and enjoyed. Denny Feather and Bill Huffman played a guitar and mandolin duet. Mrs. Anna D. Feather made a contribution to Denny and baby of $25.00 for music at the reunion. Song by Junior DeWitt, "In The Garden." Old officers were elected to hold over for another year. $2.00 was given to the janitor for his services. Special collection for Denny Feather was $14.00. Secretary's report read and approved. It was moved by Nina Forman, and seconded by Denny to buy a movie film to take pictures of the reunion. It was moved by Adah Feather and seconded by Bertha Shaw to give $15.00 of the Feather reunion funds to the Lutheran Church Cemetery Fund. Motion carried. It was also moved by Bess Hayden, seconded by Mae Peaslee, that the reunion by held at the Wesley Chapel Church in 1951. Special music by Coral Whitesill and Janett Thomas of Bruceton Mills closed the program.

Deceased since the 1950 meeting: Oliver Feather, Millcreek; Viola Feather Bradley, Millcreek; Martha Haigh, Kingwood; Will Hayden, Greensburg; Scott Feather, Albright. Balance in treasury, $40.64. Collection 9/2/50—$16.00. Less Janitor fee, $2.00. Balance of collection ($14.00) went to Denny Feather.

Nina Forman, Secretary-Treasurer

September 1, 1951

The 43rd Annual Reunion of the Feather family assembled at Wesley Chapel in the Craborchard on Sept. 1, 1951. A nice day and a little larger crowd gathered for the occasion. After a bountiful dinner, the crowd gathered in the church for a very short program. Bobby Feather, son of Hugh, presided at the meeting. All joined in singing "All Hail the Power of Jesus' Name" as the opening song. Secretary's report was read and approved. It was suggested by Bob that the new additions be recorded in the minutes instead of the passing of loved ones. Mr. and Mrs. Joseph Haigh, a new son, and Jean Black of Iowa a new baby.

A trumpet solo was played by Bill Armstrong. Piano solos by Barbara Feather. "Roseary" and "You're A Grand Old Flag." A presentation of $25.00 was made by Anna Feather to Denny Feather for special music furnished in the grove under the oak tree. Dora Feather, Annabelle Livengood, Gerald Armstrong, and Bob Feather was a special quartette assembled. After the singing of "Stand Up For Jesus" the election of officers was held by the short cut method. All officers retained for another year. They are as follows: President, Paul Feather; Vice president, Thomas G. Welch; Sec.-Treas., Nina Forman. No collection was taken, as none was needed. The meeting adjourned to meet Sept. 6, 1952.

Nina Forman, Secretary-Treasurer

September 6, 1952

The 44th Annual Reunion of the Feather family met on Sat., Sept. 6, 1952 at the Wesley Chapel Church in the Craborchard. The day was ideal and a good crowd enjoyed the day. People were slow gathering, but when they got there things moved. Everyone enjoyed the noon meal, which was abundant. Following that, music was furnished by Denny Feather and his friends from Tunnelton, which was very much appreciated. At 3:00 o'clock the crowd assembled in the church for a short business session. Bob Feather presided at the request of the president. Much discussion was made on how to get the Feathers to attend.

Much discussion was held on changing the day from Saturday to Sunday. Finally a vote was taken and it was decided to have it on Saturday. The vote was 15-14 in favor of Saturday. Jack and Dora sang "Drifting" as a special number. New officers for the coming year are: Paul Feather, president; Hazel Titchnell, Vice president; Howard Feather, Secretary-Treasurer. The meeting adjourned to meet September 5, 1953 at Wesley Chapel in the Craborchard.

Nina Forman, Secretary-Treasurer

September 5, 1953

The 45th Annual Reunion of the Feather family was held on Saturday, Sept. 5, 1953, at Wesley Chapel Church in the Craborchard. In spite of the rain, the church was well filled for the occasion. Special music was given by Charley Miller and his horn. Tommy Johns sang the "Lord's Prayer."

September 4, 1954

Special music was rendered by a quartet composed of Jack & Dora Feather, and Ruby & Gerald Armstrong. A bountiful picnic dinner was enjoyed by the group at noon.

Paul Feather, president, turned the business meeting over to Ike Armstrong. The following officers were elected for the coming year: Paul Feather, president; Claude Feather, Vice president; Howard Feather, Secretary-Treasurer. The group voted to hold next years reunion at Wesley Chapel. Motion was made by Okey Feather of Morgantown to change the meeting day to Sunday. After discussion of the matter a vote was taken. The vote was 30-15 in favor of Saturday. [9] It was decided not to appoint an entertainment comm., but to let each family be responsible for something on the program, and have the program on a competitive basis, give prizes to the 1st, 2nd, and 3rd place winners. Also to give prizes to the person coming the fartherest, the oldest, the youngest, the family with the largest number present, oldest married couple, and youngest married couple It was decided to device the present balance in the treasury ($40.64) between the Church and the 4-H Camp. Collection taken today to start a new treasury was $16.42. Meeting adjourned to meet Sept. 4, 1954. Howard A. Feather, Secretary-Treas.

September 4, 1954

The 46th Annual Reunion of the Feather Family was held in the Crab Orchard at the Wesley Chapel on Saturday, September 4, 1954. According to the register there were 165 present. The day began with the usual anticipation of who was joining our midst as the individual cars arrived. Dinner was served at noon. The grove being inaccessible the group was divided, some across the road in Mr. Richard Gidley's orchard and some in the church yard.

The weather was fine. The church was filled for the program which began with a song by the congregation, "Blessed Assurance," followed by a prayer by Mrs. Josephine Feather Seal. The Feather Family being given to song for many years sang "Blessed Be the Tie That Binds," and "Leaning on the Ever Lasting Arms." There being a succession of Feathers named David, another, and perhaps the youngest to bear the name of David sang a solo "May the Good Lord Bless and Keep You." Rose Mary Johns, matched her brothers' fine singing by a very beautiful solo, "My Friend." Our guest entertainer for the day Mr. Harry Leonard of Morgantown sang a lovely

September 3, 1955

tenor solo, "Just for Today," a song much liked by our relative and his friend the late Hugh Feather.

Prizes were awarded for the following persons:

Oldest person present:	Sarah Bell age 84
Youngest person present:	Nancy Miller age 9 months
One traveling furtherest:	Tory Feather (California)
	Anna Feather (California)
Oldest Married:	Mr. & Mrs. Walter Feather 52 years
Most recent Married couple:	Mr. & Mrs. Isaac Armstrong
Largest family present:	Mr. & Mrs. Harland Livengood 5 children

A solo by Mrs. Josephine Feather Seal "The Homecoming Week" followed the awards.

Booklets containing the minutes of all Feather Reunions since 1909 were distributed to all present.

Treasurer's report: There was some $17.86 in the treasury. This was expended in the reproduction of the reunion minutes and for prizes. This amount did not completely cover the entire costs. The deficit was contributed by Mr. Howard Feather.

In the election of new officers for 1955:

Mr. Howard Feathers:	President
Mr. Paul A. Feather:	Vice President
Mr. Robert C. Feather:	Secretary and Treasurer

Mr. Isaac Armstrong served in his usual gracious way as Master of Ceremonies. Mrs. Lydia Brand and Miss Karen Sue Jenkins were the accompanists. The Program ended with the congregation singing, "When the Roll is Called up Yonder" and "Auld Lang Syne."

September 3, 1955

The 47th Annual Reunion of the Feather Family was held in the Crab Orchard at the Wesley Chapel on Saturday, September 3, 1955. A picnic dinner was served at noon and was enjoyed by all.

The weather was fine. The church was filled for the program which began by the congregation singing "How Firm a Foundation." Prayer by Josephine Seal. Accordion duet by Darlene Crane and Mary Liston. Solo by Bob Feather. Mr. Walter Feather and Mr. Claud Feather have never missed a reunion. Mrs. Mae Peaslee has missed only one reunion. Solos "This is

My Commandment" by Harry Leonard, "You Are My Sunshine" by David Feather. Howard Feather reported that there were 1600 descendants from the Christian Feather family.

Prizes were awarded to the following persons:

Oldest married couple:	Mr. & Mrs. Frank Childs (60 yrs)
Largest family represented:	Mr. & Mrs. Walter Feather
Latest married	Mr. & Mrs. John Shiffertt
Youngest baby	2 ½ yrs, Mr. & Mrs. Keith McGinnis

Reunion to be held at Terra Alta Park first Saturday in September.

Same officers were elected to serve next year. Old officers took a stand: Walter Feather, Mr. & Mrs. Klet Forman, Josephine Seal, Paul Feather. Song: Happy Day." Robert Feather read the twelfth chapter of Romans. Violet Petso made the closing prayer followed by all singing "God Be With You."

September 5, 1956

The 48th Annual Reunion of the Feather family was held at the Terra Alta Park, September 5, 1956. Due to the Preston County Fair being held in the Park the crowd was divided. A basket dinner was enjoyed by several families in the upper corner of the Park. It was decided to hold the reunion next year at the same place the first Saturday in September.

Howard Feather died in January. John Blamble died in January.

September 7, 1957

The 49th Annual Reunion of the Feather family was held Saturday, September 7, 1957 at the Terra Alta Park. A picnic dinner was enjoyed by all. The day was spent visiting and renewing old acquaintances.

A business meeting was held, electing new officers for the following year.

President, Jack Feather; V. President, Klet Forman; Secretary & Treasurer, Mrs. Jessie Edeburn. Gifts were awarded to the following persons:

Oldest person present:	Walter Feather, age 83 years
Youngest person:	Michael Simon, age four months
Eldest married couple:	Mr. & Mrs. Walter Feather, 56 years
Youngest married couple:	Mr. & Mrs. Arnold Feather, 4 mos.
Farthest Distance:	Mr. & Mrs. Cameron Simon
	Mr. & Mrs. Marrel Biser of D.C.

It was decided to hold the reunion next year at the Wesley's Chapel on the first Saturday of September.

Treasure report = $4.86

Deaths during the year: Bessie Hayden, 84 years, Greensburg, Pennsylvania; Letecia Blamble, Gormania, West Virginia

September 6, 1958

The 50th Annual Reunion of the Feather Family was held in the Crab Orchard at the Wesley Chapel on Saturday September 6, 1950.

The weather was beautiful. The day began with the usual anticipation of who was joining our midst as the cars arrived. There were sixty-nine present. A basket lunch was served at noon, and a wonderful fellowship of eating and visiting together was enjoyed by all.

A business meeting was called by the president Jack Feather. It was decided to hold the reunion here after on the Saturday before Labor Day. At Wesley Chapel. For the election of officers Bob Feather made a motion to retain the present officers for the next year.

The minutes were read and all the following people were given awards:

Oldest person present:	Sara Bell, 88 years
Youngest person present:	Carol Lynn Januketes, 2 months
Oldest married couple:	Mr. & Mrs. Walter Feather, 57 years
Youngest married:	Mr. and Mrs. Ralph Hoty, 3 months
Largest family:	Mr. & Mrs. Bob Feather, 5 children
Farthest distance:	Mrs. Edna Kiester, 250 miles

Several left for a while in the afternoon to attend the funeral of Mr. Claud Feather, who had been killed in a tractor accident on his farm during the week.

The small children were treated with suckers.

Deaths during year: Ike Feather; Mrs. Rebecca Wilson: Carl Feather, Durbin, W.Va.; Guy Feather, Smithfield, Pa.; George Feather, Confluence, Pa.; Don Crane, Valley Point, W.Va.; Bessie McManis, Uniontown, Pa.; (B.) Claude and Ada(h) Feather

Several years of reunion minutes are missing from this point forward to 1972, the last year for which minutes could be located.

September 3, 1960

The fifty-second Annual Feather Reunion was held in the Crab Orchard at Wesley Chapel on Saturday, September 3, 1960. The reunion opened with the usual basket lunch at noon.

The program was held in the grove and Robert Feather's children entertained with several songs.

The reading of the previous year's minutes was given and the following business was transacted:

Motion made and carried to have the reunion on Sunday before Labor Day at 1:00 p.m. This idea is to be tried for a year and be voted on at the 1961 Reunion.

A motion was made to donated $25.00 toward building a restroom behind the church. Klet Forman stated he would donate the roofing for the building erected.

Election of officers for the coming year and they are as follows:

President:	John Feather
Vice President:	Robert Feather
Secretary-Treasurer:	Lucille Reckart

Prizes were awarded (to) the following:

Youngest:	Thomas Stephenson (8 months)
Oldest:	Sadie Dutton (87)
Couple married longest:	Mr. & Mrs. Bruce Morgan (55 years)
Couple married shortest:	Mr. & Mrs. Roy Wolfe (2 years)
Largest family:	Mr. & Mrs. Harlan Livengood (6 kids)

Deaths during year: Jesse Roby; Russ Trembly; Nora Shipley; Oakie Feather; Alfred Hefflefinger; Benton Rodeheaver.

A collection was taken up amounting to $12.93

Balance in treasury: $28.94 Total $41.87.

September 6, 1964

The 56th Annual Feather Reunion was held September 6th, 1964, at the Wesley Chapel Church. A large crowd enjoyed the usual basket lunch at noon.

Gifts were awarded to the following persons:

Oldest person present:	Lydia Scott, 88 years
Youngest person present:	Rebecca Anne Galloway, 6 months

September 1, 1968

Couple married longest: Mr. and Mrs. Paul Feather
Most newly married couple: Mr. and Mrs. Jim Wolfe
Traveling the farthest distance: Mr. & Mrs. Eddie Livengood, Dayton, Ohio
Largest family present: Mr. & Mrs. Harlon V. Livengood

Officers elected for the year 1965 were: President, Keith McGinnis; Vice-president, Mrs. Hazel Titchenell; Secretary/Treasurer, Jean Jenkins.

It was voted to hold the Reunion in the same place next year, the first Sunday in September.

There were 115 attending and a collection of $7.00 was received.

Deaths occurring during the past year were: Ronald Allen Armstrong, who died Dec. 30 1964, and Karl Feather who died Dec. 5, 1964.

September 1, 1968

The 60th Annual Feather Family Reunion was held Sunday, September 1st, 1968, on the Gidley Property[12] near Wesley Chapel Church.

The meal was served at noon and the blessing was asked by Mrs. R.E. Hyden.

The weather was very pleasant and everyone seemed to have a very enjoyable day. Horseshoe pitching and Football were enjoyed by the boys and men. Conversation was the main activity of the women.

The business meeting was called to order by the President, Paul Feather. The secretary read and distributed the report of last year's reunion.

Nomination of officers for the year 1969 was next in order. Edna Heffelfinger made a motion that the same officers continue in office for the next year. Mar(ga)ret Johns seconded the motion and it was voted on and carried. The following officers were declared elected for the next year. President, Paul Feather; Vice-President, Russel Feather; Secretary, Paul E. Jenkins; Treasurer, Orman Wolfe.

Gifts were presented to the following persons:
Oldest Present: Mrs. Olive Stone, 88 years
Youngest Present: Patrick Livengood, 2 years
Couple married longest: Mr. & Mrs. Paul Feather, 53 years
Couple married most recently: Tom and Margaret Johns, 2 ½ years

September 5, 1971

Family traveling farthest: Eddie & Nina Livengood & family, 320 miles
Youngest grandma present: Jean Jenkins

The Program Committee for next year was to be: Russel Feather, Chairman, and Hazel Tichenell and Paul Feather.

Collection was taken, amounting to $24.20. Balance from last year was $48.00. Gifts bought, $14.00. Mrs. Gidley for cleaning lot, $5.00. Balance after expenses, $53.20.

September 5, 1971

The 63rd Annual Feather Reunion was held Sunday, September 5, 1971, on the Gidley Property near Wesley Chapel Church.

A basket lunch was served at noon and the blessing was asked by Paul Elliott.

The business meeting was called to order by the president, Annabell Livengood. The secretary read and distributed a report of last year's reunion.

The following officers were nominated and elected for next year: President, Lucille Reckart; Secretary, Annette Thorn; Treasurer, Mary Jane Miller; Program chairman, Ike Armstrong.

Gifts were presented to the following persons:
Oldest person: Paul Feather (81)
Youngest person: Lyle Bolyard (9 months)
Couple married longest: Paul and Anna Feather (56)
Couple married most recently: Doug and Paulette Metheny
Traveled farthest: Linda Armstrong

It was agreed that next year's reunion be held at the same place on the Sunday before Labor Day.

A collection amounting to $33.15 was taken with the balance from last year of $14.65 for a total of $47.65 in the treasury.

Music was presented throughout the afternoon by Jeanette and Ike Armstrong, B.P. Johns, and Denny Feather

Secretary, Annette Thorn

September 3, 1972

The 64th Annual Feather Reunion was held Sunday, September 3, 1972, on the Gidley property near the Wesley Chapel Church.

A basket lunch was served at noon and the blessing was asked by Eddie Livengood.

The business meeting was called to the order by the president, Lucille Reckart. The secretary read and distributed a report of the minutes of last year's reunion.

The following officers were nominated and elected for the next year:

President, Joe Haigh, Secretary; Diana Kreps; Treasurer, Lucille Wolfe; Program Chairman, Ike and Jeanette Armstrong.

Gifts were presented to the following persons:

Oldest Person:	Perry Feather
Youngest Person:	Hope Livengood
Longest Married:	Effie Biser
Married Most Recently:	Paulette & Doug Matheny
Youngest Grandmother:	Lucille Reckart
Traveled Farthest:	Carl Biser

A collection amounting to $26.27 was taken, and with the balance from last year of $15.81, makes a total of $42.08 in the treasury.

It was agreed that next year's reunion be held at the same place on the Sunday before Labor Day.

Music was presented throughout the afternoon by Ike and Jeanette Armstrong.

Diana L. Kreps, Secretary

Wedding certificate for Jacob Feather and Mary Connoly.

Bibliography

Cale, Janice Sisler. *In Remembrance: Tombstone Readings of Preston County, West Virginia (Volume 1)*. 1995. Bruceton Mills, W.W.: Sisler Heritage Enterprises.

Feather, Carl E. *My Fathers' Land*. 2023. Bruceton Mills, W.Va.: Feather Cottage Media.

Maurer, B. B.& Mary Miller Strauss. *Lutherans on the Mountaintop: In West Virginia and Western Maryland*. 1992. (Available in West Virginia University downtown library).

Morton, Oren Frederic & Cole, J. R. *A History of Preston County, W.Va. (2 volumes)*. 1914. Kingwood: The Journal Publishing Co.

Reckart, Gary P. Sr., *The Saga of Ernst August Reckart*, https://reckart.net/EAReckart.html, accessed May 27, 2024.

Rogers, Edna (Davis). *Genealogy of the Jacob and Mary (Connoly) Feather Family of Preston County, West Virginia*. 1980. Morgantown, W.Va.: Feather Genealogic Company.

Sullivan, Ken, ed. *The West Virginia Encyclopedia*. 2006. West Virginia Humanities Council.

Various. *Preston County, West Virginia, History*. 1979. Kingwood: The Preston County Historical Society.

Wiley, S.T. *History of Preston County*. 1882. Parsons, W.Va.: McClain Printing (reprint).

Many of the Feather reunions were held at the Wesley Chapel, Crab Orchard, which in 2024 has a pavilion for such gatherings. The group made use of the church building for their official meeting and voting.

Reunions endnotes

1. Morris Park was on the Cheat River along the Morgantown & Kingwood. Railroad at Kingwood It hosted numerous gatherings in the early 1900s, including a Masonic Lodge gathering of more than 400 persons in 1908. The Forman family held its 150th anniversary of the settlement of the family in western Virginia at Morris Park in August 1909 (*The Preston County Journal* of August 5, 1909, page 7).

2. The use of the "lovefeast" term suggests the secretary was at least familiar with the German Baptist (Brethren) practice and was perhaps himself a member of that denomination.

3. According to *The Preston County Journal* of September 25, 1924, Charles Trembly was a cashier at the Terra Alta Bank. He also gave the address for the ceremony that marked the opening of the "hard" Terra-Alta-to-Kingwood Road that fall, linking Reedsville "to salt water."

4. Josephine Feather was a Preston County teacher. The person named was most likely Josephine Fay Feather (Wolfe) (Seal) born January 29, 1888, descended from Harvey Arlington and Georgia Etta (Jackson) Feather. She married Charles Henry Seal (1) and Roy Wolfe (2) (Rogers, 49). Her first use of the "Seal" surname was in the 1916 minutes. She died May 2, 1975, buried Sugar Valley Cemetery.

b 5. The "sixties" was a reference to The Civil War; the "war" in 1918 would have been World War I.

6. These two presentations would be tremendous resources to unearth. Unfortunately, *The Preston County Journal* gave no account of the reunion. There were many Titchenells listed in the *Feather Genealogy* book, but no Joel. From references in *The Preston County Journal,* we know he lived at Valley Point and Beech Run. He was a veteran of The Civil War, having served in the 17th W.Va. He was born in Pleasants County, W.Va., Aug. 23, 1848, and died May 15, 1928. He is buried at Mount Mariah Cemetery, Valley Point. His knowledge of the Feather family must have been substantial to be able to give a "spell-binding" address comparing the family's well-known men to those of the Bible. "Grandmother Feather" would have been Adam's wife, unless he was using the term to refer to his great-grandmother, who would have been Mary Connery (Connelly), wife of Jacob.

Reunion endnotes

7. Jane Virginia Feather was the last-born daughter of Jacob and Mary. She married Israel Shaffer (1810-1897) and had eight children. Gustavus C. was born in Preston County on December 24, 1844, and died December 19, 1927, in Temple, Oklahoma. He was a Methodist Episcopal pastor and was endowed with a personality and ability that enabled him to win more than 3,000 souls during his ministry. He served in Company B of the 38th Ohio Infantry during The Civil War. Rev. Shaffer is buried in the Center Grove Cemetery, Warren County, Illinois.

7. Brown's Park was created in 1907 with a donation of three acres of land on Kingwood's west side and along present-day Route 7. The community park and playground is maintained by Kingwood Parks and Recreation. It has playground equipment and covered pavilion with wood-burning fireplace, electrical service, restrooms, and off-street parking. The relocation of the reunion to Kingwood might have been driven by a lack of shelter at Wesley Chapel, the relative newness of Brown's, and the availability of motorized transportation that would have made it possible for attendees to travel farther distances to a location more than 10 miles from the Crab Orchard.

8. This would have been Effie L. Feather, born January 27, 1870, to Zaccheus M. and Nancy Metzler Feather (Abraham, John S., Jacob). Effie married Edward L. Teets and lived in Aurora. It is interesting to note that Zaccheus and Nancy named a son Walter H. and a daughter Jessie, names that were repeated by Walter and Estella Harsh Feather, who also lived in the Aurora area. Their youngest daughter, born August 31, 1915, was named Jessie (Edeburn); her older sister, Effie Olive (Biser), was born October 18, 1911. The names suggest that Walter and Estella were more than just casually acquainted with Effie and Edward.

9. The number of folks voting is indicative of very low attendance, especially when compared to the early reunions that drew hundreds of people. Perhaps only "true Feathers" were allowed to vote, but the attendance was nevertheless suffering from post-war out-migration, changing familial and cultural values, and the loss of a sense of heritage.z10.

10. Youngest daughter of James Walter Feather and his caretaker.

11. These two individuals died after the reunion,.

12. R. M. Gidley owned 29.2 acres on Crab Orchard with $1,730 in improvements. A second tract of 65 acres was owned on Roaring Creek and had no improvements. The second parcel could possibly have been the homestead farm.

Index

Female names are indexed by their maiden name with married surname in parentheses.

All places assumed to be in West Virginia unless otherwise noted

Symbols

3rd Infantry of Virginia 84
3rd Regiment, W.Va. Cavalry 114
6th Heavy Artillery of Pa. 92
6th W.Va. 47, 123
7th W.Va. 81, 102, 123
14th West Virginia 29
14th W.Va. 29, 52
17th W.Va. 34, 81, 93
38th Ohio Infantry 176
101st Airborne Division 127
377th Field Artillery 127
1870 U.S. Census 89
1880 U.S. Census 31, 77, 84, 89, 114
1900 U.S. Census 30, 47, 64, 89, 113
1910 U.S. Census 36, 110
1920 U.S. Census 30
1930 U.S. Census 36, 40, 43, 45, 64
1959 U.S. Census 137

A

acres 82
Adams County, Pa. 27
Adams, H. Z. 98
Addison, Pa. 57
Addy, W.L. 100
Afton 50
Aitken, Agnes 154
Albright, Amanda Jane (Feather) 34
Albright, Bernhardt 34
Albright Cemetery 19, 92
Albright community 18, 82, 89, 108, 118, 120, 123, 131
Albright, Daniel 34, 55
Albright, David 34
Albright Elementary School. 121
Albright family 27, 34
Albright, Mike 89
Alden, John 56
Aledo, Ill. 80
Allegany County, Md. 43
Alsace, France 41
Amish 68
Anderson, Verdia Blanche (Feather) 127
Andersonville Prison 29
apoplexy 55, 111
applesauce, making of 86

177

Index

Argabrite, Michael 130
Armstrong, Anna Bell (Livengood) 153, 160, 162
Armstrong, Annie Evelyn (Feather) 71
Armstrong, Bill 161, 163
Armstrong, Gerald 163, 164
Armstrong, Ike 160, 164, 170
Armstrong, Isaac 165
Armstrong, Jeanette 170
Armstrong, Linda 170
Armstrong, Mrs. Annie 152
Armstrong, Ronald 153
Armstrong, Ronald Allen 169
Armstrong, Ruby 164
Arnettsville 97
Arthurdale 120
Arthur H. Wright Funeral Home 49
Arthur Miller 100
Ashtabula General Hospital 136
Ashtabula, OH 136
Atkinson, Mary (Feather) 96, 98–99, 121
Atkinston, George Wesley 97
Aurora 107
Aurora Pioneer Cemetery 27
Aurora pioneers 107
Awman, Bruce 66
Awman, Elva 66

B

Ball, Franklin 98
Ballion farm 103
Baltimore, Md. 33, 46, 51
Baltimore & Ohio 32

Bavaria, Germany 34
Beatty branch 20
Beatty, Elizabeth (Snyder) 80
Beatty, Hulda Sarah (Taylor) 81
Beatty, Jacob 80
Beatty, James 20, 80
Beatty, John T. 80
Beatty, Louisa 80
Beatty, Lucy A. (Charlton) 81
Beatty, Martha Ann (Blicksenderfer) 81
Beatty, May C. 80
Beatty, Robert 80
Beaver Creek 50
Bedford County, Pa. 18, 28, 59, 91
Beech Run 175
Beech Run Cemetery 35
Beerbower, W. D. 17
Bell, Sara 167
Bell, Sarah 165
Bennet, Ralph 154
Berkeley County, Va. 41
Berkheimer, Johann Leonard 41
Berry, W.H. 112, 141, 142
Bethlehem Steel 133
Bigler, (Mrs.) Ethel 127
Biloxi, Mo. 132
Bischoff, Johannes Heinrich 27
Bischoff, Johannes III 27
Biser, Carl 171
Biser, Effie 171
Biser, Marrel 166
Bishoff, G.W. 149
Bishoff, Henry 27
Bishoff, Lydia Elizabeth (Albright, Miller) 27

178

Index

Bishoff, Ruth 159
Bishoff, Susan (Ringer) 27, 31
Bishoff, Walter 66
Bishop, Gay Alton 44
Bishop, Loretta Agnes 44
Black, Jean 162
Blamble, John 166
Blooming Rose region 43
bold-faced names 20
Bolinger family 104
Bolyard, Lyle 170
B&O Railroad 32
Bower, Lydia 35
Bowers, Thomas 143, 144
Bower, Thomas 147
Bowman, Hope 48
Bowman, Rick 48
Boylan, Elizabeth (Feather) 92
Boys Band of Kingwood 150
Braddock's massacre 113
Brand, Lydia 165
Brandonville 104, 114
Brandonville (Lutheran) Circuit 17
Brandonville ME Circuit 51
Brandonville Turnpike 27
Brandonville Turnpike (Pike) 18
Bright's disease 125
Brookside 107
Brooks, R.L. 98
Broomhall, Mahlon 116
Broomhall, Mary Jane (Feather) 30, 116
Browing, Dorcas (Kelly) 113
Brownfield, Alcesta Jane (Feather) 93
Browning, Effie 151
Browning, J.D. 154

Browning, Meshach 113–114
Browning, Mrs. Effie 146
Browning, Mrs. J.D. 148, 150, 151, 152
Brown's Park 148, 149, 151, 152, 176
Brown, W.G. 144
Bruceton Band 143
Bruceton Mills 113
Bruceton Mills Cemetery 81
Buck's County, Pa. 104
Burkhalter, Luella 125
butchering process 86
Byer, J.D. 153
Byer, Mrs. Isa 154

C

Cale, Janet Sisler 20
Cale, M. T. 73
Cale, Sara Elizabeth (Feather) 81
California, Feathers in 31, 165
Cambridge. Ohio 155
Camden 39
Camden, Maine 39
Camp Cody, N.M. 83
Camp Funston, Kan. 49
Camp Wiley, Wheeling 29
Camp Zachary Taylor, Ken. 83
cancer 77
canning of furits and vegetables 86
Carroll, Bruce 100
Carter, Joshua 129
Casseday, Pauline 131
Casselman, Pa. 11, 80
Casteel, Laura Effie "Laurie" (Stanton) 123
Casteel, Nathaniel 123

179

Index

Casteel, Solomon Wesley "Sol" 123
Castle, Emma Sybil (Feather) 57
cataracts 88
Centennary 27
Centennary Cemetery 59
Center Grove Cemetery 81, 176
Center Knob 110
chancery case, Adam H. Feather 30
Charleston 117
Charleston M.E. Circuits 98
Cheat Hill 99
Cheat River 18
Chidester, Deborah Ann (Feather) 52, 57, 74
Chidester, Harrison 53–54, 57
Chidester, John B. 57
Chidester, Savana (Falkenstine) 57
child burials 20, 30
  Lenox Memorial 73–75
Childs, Frank 166
Childs, Jud. 95
Childs, J. W. 95
Childs, Mary Lou 159
Childs, Orlena 95
Childs, Sarah 155, 156, 158
Civil War 34, 77, 84, 92, 93, 102, 114, 123, 176
Clark County 40, 47
Clarksburg 42, 43
Cleveland Heights, Ohio 31, 127
Cloyd's Mountain 29, 52
Coal Lick Road 12, 67, 118, 119, 122, 132
Coal Lick Run 83
coal mining 18, 39, 45, 64
coal mining deaths 60

Coffman, Myrtle Mae (Feather) 76
Cole, Bessie (Keener) 67, 118
Conner, Aretta M. (Crane) 112
Conner, Benjamin A. 112
Conner, Elizabeth (Forman) 113
Conner, Elma Ophelia (Martin) 112
Conner, Emma Mary (Wilson) 112
Conner family history 113
Conner, Frances C. (Wolf) 112
Conner, Grace 66
Conner, Grace Blanche (Layman) 112
Conner, Ida Arizona (Falkenstein) 112
Conner, Jane (Miller) 155
Conner, Jane R. (Greaser) 112
Conner, John M. 112
Conner, Lulu Bell Louissa (Lenhart) 112
Conner, Mary Ann (Feather) 66
Conner, William 113
Conner, William Jr. 113
Conner, William Zaccheus 112
Connery surname discussion 89
Connoly, Mary (Feather) 11, 78–81
consumption (tuberculosis) 30, 116
Continental Army 78
Cook-Walden Capital Parks Cemetery and Mausoleum 76, 85
Cottrill, Theodore Jennings 127
Courtship of Miles Standish poem 56
cousins marriages 19, 50, 63, 96, 136
Crab Orchard 11, 17, 18, 34, 36, 56, 69, 70, 90, 94, 107, 109, 113, 116, 121, 124, 139, 141, 142, 154
  celebrations 130
  events in 38–40

180

Index

farm life in 85–87
Feather exodus from 80, 81
social life 65
Craborchard Cemetery 19
Crab Orchard Lutheran Cemetery 19
Crab Orchard Road 18
Crab Orchard Run 18, 84, 114
Craig, A.D. 52
Cramer, Claud 66
Cramer, Derrill 66
Cramer, John 65
Cramer, Karl 157
Cramer, Orf 158
Crane, Clay 95
Crane, Darlene 165
Crane, Don 167
Crane, F. W. 66
Crane, Gay 161
Crane, Glen 160
Crane, Greeley 156
Crane, Iretta 161
Crane, James 155
Crane, M. L. 70
Crane, Myrtle 66
Crane, Nina (Forman) 104, 160, 161, 162, 163
Crane, Samuel D. 69
Crane, Scott 95
Crane, Smith 66, 95
Crane, Stanley 66, 130
Cranesville 34, 37, 114, 154
Crane, Virginia 66
Crescent Band, Bruceton 54
Cress, Catherine (Ervin) 61
Cress family house 89
Cress, J. C. 120

croup 74, 137
Cuppett, Jefferson 28
Cuppett, John 28
Cuppett, Parson 153
Cuppett, Virginia Ellen (Ringer) 27
Cuppy, John 28
Cuyahoga County, Ohio 31

D

Daily, Dr. W.F. 33
Damascus, Md. 113
Davis boys 100
Davis, Edna 151
Davis, Edna Rogers 151
Davis, Jess 100
Davis, Mildred 151
Davis, Sim 101
Davis, Tucker County 35, 123
Deahl, Julia (DeBerry, Feather) 35
Deal, Archibald J. 60
Deal, Ella Delmerrl (Feather) 133
Deal, John 60
Deal, Susannah Ella 60
DeBerry, Archibald J. 60
DeBerry, Clark Martin 35
Deberry, Delph 158
DeBerry, Gilbert 35
DeBerry, John Ray 60
DeBerry, Julia (Deahl) 35
DeBerry, Lucy Ann (Deal) 60
Decker's Creek 46
Deming N. M. 83
Dewitt, Archie 39
DeWitt, Junior 155, 160, 162
DeWitt, Marion 155

Index

DeWitt, Zuella 125
Dombrowolski, Paul 118
Doyle, Sara Jane (Feather) 74
Duckworth, Loretta (Bishop) 48
Dunham, Amos 41
Dunham, Catharine (Feather) 20, 80
Dunham, Catherine (Feather) 41–42, 75
Dunham, David 41
Dunham, Samuel Goodnight 41
Dunn, Matilda Jane (Welch) 116
Dutton, Sadie 168

E

Eddy, Mrs. Allie 127
Edison (world's best dog) 206
Egensperger, Margaret A. "Peg" Feather 31
Eglon 56
Eglon Community Cemetery 19
Eiseman, Grace 150, 151
Elkins 101
Eller, Barbara J. (Feather) (Hopkins) 206
Elliot, Paul 170
Elliott, John 100, 119
Elliott, Linda 126
Elliott, Max 126
Elliott, Maxine Alice (Feather) 119, 133–134
Elliott, Paul B. 124
elopement 124
Emery and Henry college hospitals 53
Engle, Albert 52, 148

Engle, Hannah (Feathers) 44
Englehard, Pauline 151
Englehart, George 66
Englehart, Hazel 143
Englehart, Wilfred 66
Englehart Woolen Mill 53
Engle, J. W. 33
Engle, Sarah "Salome" (Albright) 34
Engle, Sarah "Salome" (Albright)) 34
English, Eric 129
English immigrants 104
Ervin, Elizabeth "Betsy" (Feather) 20, 31, 60, 75, 80, 134
Ervin, Elizabeth (Feathero 115
Ervin, Eva 115
Ervin, Irena Ellen (Feather) 15, 30, 44, 75, 85
Ervin, Isaac 60, 61, 115
Ervin, Jacob 61
Ervin, John 75
Ervin, Julia A. Smith 75
Ervin, Mary 61, 75
Ervin, Mary (Feather) 19, 74, 80, 91, 115, 134
Etam 31
Etta, Georgia 67
Eve Catharine Feather 80
Everett, Gary 126, 129
Everett, Michelle 126

F

Fairchance, Pa. 127
Fairmont Creamery Duet 161
Fairmont Normal school 51
Fairview Cemetery 65

Index

farming, subsistence. *See* Feather family, occupations, farming
farm life described 1920-1935 85–87
Faulkner, T. R. 70
Fayette County, Pa. 41, 89, 102, 124
Fearer, Addyson 132
Feaster, Andrew E. (Feather) 34
Feather, Aaron E. 206
Feather, Abraham 29, 92
Feather, A. C. 153
Feather, Adah Blanche (Feather) 27, 44, 162
Feather, Adam 20, 28, 39, 74, 80, 108, 118, 121, 128
Feather, Adam H. 29, 45, 88, 116
  land 88
Feather, Adam (son of James) 44
Feather, A. J. 159
Feather, Alice 95
Feather, Alitia May "Allie" (Crane) 30, 155
Feather, Alva Clifton 30, 37, 89
Feather, Alyssa 68, 132
Feather, Amanda Jane Albright 34
Feather, Amanda Jane E. (Peaslee) 31–32, 88
Feather, Amos 42
Feather, Amos Conaway (son of Christian) 45
Feather, Amy Louella 53, 74
Feather, Andrew 66, 148, 160
Feather, Andrew Elias 34, 50, 77
Feather, Anna 163, 165
Feather, Anna Clarissa 49
Feather, Anna D. 162
Feather, Anna May Lee 35

Feather, Annie 155
Feather, Annie Evelyn 70
Feather, Ar(i)zona E. 74
Feather, Arnold 166
Feather, Arthur Klett 136
Feather, Artimus Milroy 93
Feather, Arzona S. 83
Feather, Barbara 163
Feather, Beatrice Lucille (Flynn) 50, 116
Feather, Belle 160
Feather, Benjamin C. 59
Feather, Benjamin Gilbert 37, 77
Feather, Benton Luther 84
Feather, Bert 66
Feather, Bertha Blanche (Moss) 111
Feather, Bertha B. (Moss) 31–33
  obituary 32–33
  wedding 31–32
Feather, Bertha Mildred 37
Feather, Bessie 95
Feather, Bessie Ada (Hayden) 30, 89
Feather, Beverly (McNabb) 129
Feather, Bill (William Lloyd) 88
Feather, Bob 160, 161, 163, 165, 167
Feather, Brantson Claude 164, 165
Feather, Brantson Claude (B. Claude) 27, 38–40, 63, 66, 75
  farm accident 167
Feather, Carl 167
Feather, Carl Dakin 45, 47
Feather, Carl E. 206
Feather, Carl T. 83
Feather, Casey 68
Feather, Catharine 104
Feather, Catharine Annie 44

183

Index

Feather, Catharine Jane (Welch) 69
Feather, Catherine Irene (Merkel) 76
Feather, C. D. 94, 153
Feather, Charles B. infant 74
Feather, Charles E. 75
Feather, Christena Summers 44–45
Feather, Christian 20, 29, 41, 44, 75, 80
  children of 42
Feather, Christian family
  descendants from in 1955 166
Feather, Clara Phelicia Guesman 46
Feather, Clarence Theodore 40, 45, 46, 123
Feather, Clarence Wade 48–49
Feather, Clarissa 50
Feather, Clarissa Jane (Welch) 43, 134
Feather, Clay 160
Feather, Clinton Daniel 34, 54, 56–57
Feather Construction 126
Feather, Cora Belle (Cramer) 94
Feather, Curtis Jesse 84
Feather, C. Wade 45
Feather, Dailey 66
Feather, Dale Lloyd 37
Feather, Dana Wilbur Mercer 50–51, 97, 116, 117, 143
Feather, Daniel C. 29, 52–54, 57, 60, 74, 134, 147
Feather, Daniel Wolfe 80
Feather, David 166
Feather, David O. 34, 54–55, 93
Feather, David R. child 74, 119
Feather, David Summers 44
Feather, D.C. 142, 153
Feather, Denny 160, 162, 163, 170

Feather, Dora 163
Feather, Dorothy Lee (Elliott) 124
Feather, Dressie M. 76
Feather, Edith A., teenager 74
Feather, Edna Leah Luman 75
Feather, Effie L. 176
Feather, Eliza V. 62
Feather, Ella Delmerrl Deal 60
Feather, Ella Lee (Livengood) 133
Feather, Ellis 74, 83
Feather, Elma 74
Feather, Elmer B. 38, 39, 63, 95, 96, 121, 141, 143, 144, 145, 146, 148, 151, 156, 157
Feather, Elmer Stanley 136
Feather, Emma Belle (Haun) 64, 77
Feather, Etta B. (McDonald) 93
Feather, Eugene Jarve 76
Feather, Eva Catherine 52, 61, 65, 134
  birthday celebration 65–67
Feather, Eve Catharine (Lewis) 20, 64, 80
Feather, Eve (Eva) Catharine (Lewis) 64
Feather, Ezecual. *See*
Feather, Ezekiel 29. *See* Feather, Zaccheus "Zack"
Feather, Ezekiel Clarence 80
Feather, Ezra 46, 100
Feather, Ezra A. 40, 74, 83
Feather family 102
  extent of 139
  first name choices 42
  land holdings 12, 52, 69, 100
    of Jacob's sons 19–20
  litigation 70–71

Index

longevity 29, 89
military service 29, 43, 52, 67, 77, 78, 81, 83, 92, 93, 102, 127, 132, 133, 141
musical talent 54, 160–161, 161, 163, 164, 168
occupations
  bank director 53
  blacksmithing 100
  board of education member 53
  business owner 81
  clergy 50, 95–99, 176
  coal mining 45, 60
  farming 14, 30, 35, 39, 40, 43, 45, 47, 63, 65, 70, 71, 77, 81, 90, 91, 101, 103, 110, 111
  shopkeeping 99–100
  teacher 90
  team master 92
orphans 30
pluralization of surname 18
Feather farm, William Larry 30
Feather, F.J. 37
Feather, Flora B. 83
Feather, F. Madeline farm 67
Feather, Frank 153
Feather, Frank A. 142
Feather, Fred "Freddy" Lynn 67, 74, 118, 133
Feather, Fred Lynn 60
Feather, Gay 155
Feather, George 167
Feather, Georgia Etta (McGinnis) 67
Feather, Gerald Spencer 76
Feather, Gilbert S. 83
Feather, Gilbert Woodrow 76

Feather, Gilbert Z., child 74
Feather, Grant 66
Feather, Guy 155, 160, 167
Feather, Guy Allen 93
Feather, H.A. 144, 146, 152, 154
Feather, Hanna Eliza (infant) 44
Feather, Hannah Catharine (Albright) 77
Feather, Harriet "Hattie" Belle (Metheny) 84
Feather, Harrison 43, 69, 93
Feather, Harry 95
Feather, Harry Kendall 76
Feather, Harvey Arlington 30, 67, 89, 115, 148, 156
Feather, Hazel 40, 47
Feather, Helen Mabel 56
Feather, Helen Mable 57
Feather, Henrietta, Mary (Johns) 115
Feather, Henry Clay 77
Feather, Henry L. 83
Feather, Howard 127, 163, 164, 165, 166
Feather, Hoy Jackson 58, 71
Feather, Hugh Clifton 71, 146, 153, 154, 159, 162, 165
Feather, Icie E., child 74
Feather, Ike 161, 167
Feather, Isaac B. 60, 62, 77, 134, 142, 143, 156, 157
Feather, Isaac Christian 77, 84
Feather, Isaac Emerson 45, 74
Feather, Isaac (son of J. Solomon) 93
Feather, Issac 159
Feather, J.A. 151
Feather, Jack 160, 162, 163, 166, 167

185

Index

Feather, Jacob 11, 29, 66, 139, 140
  children of 19–20, 80
  farm location 29
  homestead land 39, 63–64, 91–92, 119, 122, 141
  immigration 78–79
  main entry 78–81
  marriage 79
  redemptioner 79
  testimony of Daniel Martin 124
  wedding certificate 172
Feather, Jacob Adam 80, 82
Feather, Jacob Emery 43, 55, 82, 93, 107, 108
  farm 82
Feather, Jacob F. 60, 74, 83, 122, 134
Feather, Jacob F. infant 74
Feather, Jacob (III) 42
Feather, Jacob Jr. 20, 80, 118
  children of 80
Feather, Jacob L. 154
Feather, Jacob Luther 45, 84, 124
Feather, Jacob (of James) 84
Feather, Jacob Wesley 81
Feather, James 20, 42, 81, 84
Feather, James Christian Jr. 15, 45, 75, 85–89, 119, 130, 155
Feather, James Connery 30, 89, 109
Feather, James C. (son of J. Solomon) 55, 91, 107, 146
Feather, James C. (son of Norris) 31
Feather, James I. 154
Feather, James (Little Jim) 155
Feather, James (of John Solomon) 80
Feather, James Stephen Sr. 76

Feather, James Walter 16, 81, 116, 156, 157, 158, 159, 165, 166, 167, 176
Feather, Jane Blanche (Nethamer) 103
Feather, Jane Virginia (Shaffer) 20, 81, 176
  children of 81
Feather, Jared "Jurd" Allen 69, 90, 152, 156
Feather, J.A. & S.A. 73
Feather, J.B. 153
Feather, J.C. 95
Feather, J.C. Sr. 154
Feather, Jennie Virginia (Feather) 96
Feather, Jessie (Edeburn) 157, 166
Feather, J.H. 90
Feather, J.I. 153
Feather, J.M. 55
Feather, J. & N. 74
Feather, Jocelynn (Carter) 126, 129
Feather, Joe 158
Feather, John 29, 168
Feather, John B. 29
Feather, John D. 115
Feather, John F. farm 67
Feather, John H. 162
Feather, John Hartman 81
Feather, John Harvey 71, 90, 107
Feather, John M. 91, 108
Feather, John Mark 82, 157
Feather, Johnnie 160
Feather, John Quincy 74, 93
Feather, John S. 52
Feather, John Solomon 19, 28, 61, 74, 75, 80, 91, 108, 115, 134

Index

Feather, John Solomon (son of Christian) 45
Feather, John Summers 93, 94, 118, 129
Feather, John Wesley 44
Feather, Joseph B. 36
Feather, Joseph B. (of Jacob) 134
  children of 81–82
Feather, Joseph B. (Rev.) 20, 38, 63, 69, 95–99, 119, 142, 143
Feather, Joseph B. (son of Christian) 45
Feather, Joseph Czalmon 42, 84
Feather, Josephine Fay (Seal) (Wolfe) 71, 115, 143, 144, 145, 146, 151, 152, 153, 154, 155, 156, 157, 158, 161, 164, 166, 175
Feather, Joseph Marcellus 93
Feather, Joseph Wesley 84, 93, 153
Feather, Josiah 78, 82, 95, 104
  store robbery 100
Feather, Julie Ann 68, 131, 132
Feather, J.W. 54
Feather, Karl 169
Feather, Karl Ward 56, 57
Feather, Kathy (Dobrowolski) 118
Feather Lane 88, 119
Feather, Laura Rebecca (Tichnell) 84
Feather, Lena Alfreda 60, 67, 74, 133
Feather, Lena Blanche 40, 47, 74
Feather, Lessie 110
Feather, Lester 161
Feather, Letitia Olive (Blamble) 116, 167
Feather, Levi 93, 102
Feather, Levi Hess 69, 72, 75, 94, 103

Feather, Lilly 94
Feather, Lilly Catharine (Harned) 82
Feather, Linda (Friend) 48
Feather, Linda Joy 126, 129, 133
Feather, Linda Lucille 44
Feather, Lissa (Perrin) 129
Feather, Lona May (Hiles) 116
Feather, Louisa Jane (Forman) 93
  obituary 106
Feather, Lulu Blanche 74
Feather, Luther Martin 61
Feather, Lyda (Scott) 154
Feather, Lydia A. (Trembly, Goff, Park) 119, 128
Feather, Lydia (Bishoff) 92
Feather, Madalene 157
Feather, Mahala Catherine (Reckart) 108, 128
Feather, Malinda Jane (White) 84
Feather, Marcellus 107
Feather, Margaret Catharine (Michael) 81
Feather, Margaret Ella (Miller) 102
Feather, Margaret Jane (Forman) 62, 93
Feather, Mariah Ann Welch 108
Feather, Mark Lee 118
Feather, Martha (child) 83
Feather, Martha (Haigh) 156
Feather, Martin L. 143, 157
Feather, Martin Luther (of Zaccheus) 33
Feather, Mary 148, 150, 151, 153
Feather, Mary Anna (Teets) 44, 114
Feather, Mary Ann (Conner) 60, 80, 112, 134

Index

Feather, Mary Ann Kelly (Rodeheaver) 113–114
Feather, Mary Ann (McCabe) 133
Feather, Mary (Atkinson) 63
Feather, Mary Caroline 69
Feather, Mary Caroline (Rodeheaver, Godley) 69
Feather, Mary Catharine (Guseman) 93
  wedding 94–95
Feather, Mary Connoly 13
Feather, Mary (Core) 80
Feather, Mary Henrietta (Johns) 71, 115
Feather, Mary Jane 45, 75
Feather, Mary Jane (Falkenstein) 81
Feather, Mary Louisa "Lou" Mercer 117
Feather, Mary (Parnell) 119, 128
Feather, Mary Pearl 103
Feather, Mary Rebecca (Keener) 67, 118
Feather, Mary Sisler 118
Feather, Mary Waunita (Fike) 39
Feather, Mason L. 206
Feather, Matthew 68, 132
Feather, Mattie E. (Woodruff) 96
Feather, Melissa May 93
Feather, Melisssa Ellen (Bishoff) 77
Feather, Merle Clifton 76, 119–121, 130–131, 131, 132
  granddaughter's recollections of 119
Feather, Merritt 155, 156
Feather, Michael E. 75, 81
Feather, Michell (Everett) 129

Feather military veterans. *See* Feather family, military service
Feather, Minerva Bell (Feather) 38, 52, 61, 63, 96, 121, 134, 161
Feather, Minerva Jane (Shears) 84
Feather, M.L. (Martin Luther) 42, 53, 109, 109–111, 134
  obituary 111–112
Feather, Mollie 95, 161
Feather, Molly Letitia (Molisee) 74
Feather, Morris or Norris Stanhope 30
Feather, Mrs. Belle 161
Feather, Mrs. J.A. 94
Feather, Mrs. Jared 160
Feather, Mrs. Scott 160
Feather, Mrs. Tom 160
Feather, Mrs. Wesley 154
Feather, Mrytle Allie (Davis) 84
Feather, Nancy Maria (Stokes) 60, 122, 134
Feather, Nancy Wilhelm 74, 122
Feather, Naomi Leticia Engle 74
Feather, Narcissus Amelia (Fawcett) 80
Feather, Nechie Loye (Titchenell) 77
Feather, Nellie Pauline (Wiles) 133
Feather, Nora Ellla (Metheny) 84
Feather, Noral Faye (Fox) 103
Feather, Oakey Jarvis 76
Feather, Okey (Cornelius?) 164, 168
Feather, Olive 94
Feather, Oliver Andrew 16, 116, 162
Feather, Opal Jane (Funk) (Dick) 76
Feather, Ora Virginia (Stephanic) 76

Index

Feather, Orpha Christine (Cramer) 94
Feather, Orval 40, 47
Feather, Osa Grace (Lemmon) 76, 121
Feather, Paul 66, 160, 163, 164, 166, 169, 170
Feather, Paul & Anna 170
Feather, Paul Dana 37
Feather, Paul David 59
Feather, Paul Harold 35, 71, 115, 123
Feather, Pauline Virginia (Kelly) 39, 150, 151, 152
Feather, Perry Alva 40, 46, 171
Feather, Phillip 127
Feather, Rachel Rebecca (Wolfe) 45
Feather, Rachel Virginia (Scott) 93, 125
Feather, Rebecca (Kelly) 93, 125
Feather, Remington Charles Edward 77
Feather reunions 15, 139–174
Feather, Rev. Charley 153
Feather, (Rev.) Joseph B. 29, 50, 95–99, 109, 116, 117, 128, 139, 140, 146
  Methodist circuits served 98
  Methodist roots 97
  traits 99
Feather, Rhuea J. (Kelly) 83–84
Feather, Robbie (Fitzgerald) 129
Feather, Robert 166, 168
Feather, Robert "Bob" Lynn 119, 129, 133
Feather, Robert C. 165
Feather, Robin (Pape) 129
Feather, Rosa Lee (Chapman) 136

Feather, Rosalie Francine (Henry) 133
Feather, Roy Leland 83
Feather, Russel 81, 169
Feather, Russell Benton Jacob 77, 127
Feather, Sabra Jane (Rodeheaver) 119, 128
Feathers, Albert "Burt" 137
Feathers, Albert Franklin "Bert" 137
Feather, Samantha Jane (Rodeheaver) 69
Feather, Samuel Equatious 44, 84, 93
Feather, Sara Elizabeth 80
Feather, Sara Elizabeth (Kelly) 134
Feather, Sarah (Beatty) 20, 80, 88, 156
  children of 80
Feather, Sarah Catherine (Bishop) 84
Feather, Sarah Elizabeth (Childs) 45
Feather, Sarah (Kelly) 36, 154
Feather, Sarah (White) 118
Feather, Sarett Sue 153
Feathers, Arthur 136
Feathers, Charles B. 137
Feathers, Charles Wayne 136
Feathers, Cliff 71
Feathers, Clinton D. 135
Feather, Scott 160, 162
Feathers, Curtis Christopher 127
Feather(s), Curtis Earl 77
Feathers, Earl Smith 36, 91, 136
Feather, Season Lynn 126, 129
Feathers, Gay 159
Feather, Shannon (Friend) 48
Feather, Shawn 129–130
Feather, Sheri Mullins (English) 129
Feather, Shirley Ann (Shrout) 75

189

Index

Feathers, Iretta Marie 136
Feathers, Jessie Flo (Roby) 76
Feathers, L. H. 135
Feathers, Martin Luther (of Christian) 45, 110
Feathers, Mildred Irene (Cooley) 75
Feathers, Morris Stanhope 30
Feathers, Obediah O. "Obe" 137
Feathers, Okey Cornelius 137
Feather, Soll 158
Feather, Solomon Bell 62, 93
Feather, Sophia 80
Feather, Stanley 66
Feathers, Theodore 135
Feather, Susan F. (Nugent) 80
Feather, Syndee (Payne) 129
Feather, Teddy E. 127
Feather, Terry Alan 75
Feather, Thalbert Clairnton 82
Feather, Theodore Samuel 82
Feather, Thomas Jefferson 77
Feather trivia 54, 80, 83
Feather, Troy 161, 165
Feather, Troy A. 116
Feather, T.S. 108
Feather, Ulysses Simpson Grant 83
Feather, Verna May (Welch) 76
Feather, Viola 162
Feather, Violet Ann 75
Feather, Virgil Gay 75, 103
Feather, Virginia 66
Feather, Virginia E 37
Feather, Virginia Leda (Shirley) 133
Feather, Virginia Ruth Dils (Marcinek) 76
Feather, Virginia (Schaffer) 147

Feather, Wanda Ameta (Allen) 103
Feather, Wanda Ellen Hillery 119, 130
Feather, Wendy (Griffin) 129
Feather, Wendy (McLaughlin) 85, 119, 121, 131, 132
Feather, Wesley 153
Feather, William 45, 147
Feather, William "Bill" 131
Feather, William C. 116
Feather, William G. 119, 128, 131, 131–132
Feather, William Larry 68, 121, 131, 132
Feather, William Lloyd 68, 87–88, 130
  recollections of farm 120
Feather, William Victor 75
Feather, Willis B. 39, 75
Feather, Wilmeth "Bill" 119
Feather, Wilmeth Scott "Bill" 133, 133–134
Feather, Winfield Scott 60, 74, 82, 108, 133, 153
Feather, Zaccheas Allen 81
Feather, Zaccheus 115
Feather, Zaccheus M. 176
Feather, Zaccheus "Zack" 20, 31, 42, 52, 60, 65, 75, 80, 134–135
Feather, Zacheus 61
Feather, Zachial. *See also*
Feather, Zack. *See* Feather, Zaccheus "Zack"
Feather, Z. & E. infant 73
Fedder 139, 140
Felton, Anna (Feather) 83
Fike, A. R. 33
Fitzgerald, Robbie 126

Fitzgerald, Russell 126, 129
Flanagan, Rev. 117
Flynn, Dana Paul 50
Flynn, George Augustus 50
Flynn, Robert Michael 50
Forest Lawn Memorial Park 31
Fork Lick ME Circuit 98
Forman, Amanda Virginia (Nedrow) 104
Forman, Belle 95
Forman, Calvin Crane 104
Forman, Charles Waitman (C.W.) 104
Forman, Charlie 110
Forman family history 104–105, 175
Forman Gate school 120
Forman, John 104, 106
 obituary 105
Forman, June 105, 154
Forman, L.J. Mrs. 55
Forman, Louisa Jane (Feather) 104
Forman, Mary (Conner) 112
Forman, Mary Ellen (Hayes) 104
Forman, Maxie 94
Forman, Mollie 95
Forman, Mollie (Hayes) 106
Forman, Mrs. E. 95
Forman, Mrs. L.J. 94
Forman, Rhuea Belle (Hartman) 107
Forman, Rhuea Belle (Nedrow) 104
Forman, Robert 104
Forman, Samuel 104
Forman, Wade 105
Forman, Willey McGrew 104, 106
Forman, Willie 95, 158
Forman, Worley Klet (W. Klet) 38, 104–105, 148, 154, 157, 158, 159, 160, 161, 166, 168
Fortney, Ashel 73
Fortney, E.V. 151
Fortney, Rachel 73
Fortney, Vernon 148, 149
Forty-Four Years of the Life of a Hunter 113
France 41, 59
Frankenthal, Germany 11, 78
Frankhouser, Mary (Summers) 28, 118, 128
Freeland, Pearl 66
French immigrants to Preston Co. 42, 59, 60
Friend, Craig 48
Friend, Elizabeth Emmer (Feather) 44
Friend, H. E. 61
Friend, Sam 48
Friend, Sydney 48

G

Galloway, Rebecca Anne 168
GAR 53
Geneva, OH 108, 157
German immigrants 34, 57, 79, 108
 appeal of Alleghenies to 59
 in Preston County, W.Va. 27
Gersom Martin 124
Gibson, B.T. 147
Gibson, Carl 66
Gibson, Hazel 155
Gibson, Hugh 66
Gidley Property 169, 176

Index

Gidley, Richard M. 164, 176
Glade Farms 28
Glades, Great 113
Glasscock, William E. 33
Glenn L. Martin Aircraft 57
Glenville ME Circuit 98
Glover, Mary (Conner) 113
Goldenseal magazine 206
Goodnight (Gutknecht), Catherine Dunham 41
Goodnight (Gutknecht), Jacob 41
Goodnight, Jacob Mackey 41
Grace Hill, Iowa 81
Graham, Mrs. Jesse 148
Green County, Pa. 97
Green, John 27
Green River Group 48
Greensburg 30
Green's Run 80
Gregg, Elihu 54
Gribble, Virginia (Welch) 43
Griffin, Glen 126, 129
Griffin, Wendy 126
Gross, Elizabeth 73
Gross, John 73
Groves, Martha 158
Grucza, Marie M. 31
Guariglia, Amato 154
Guseman 34
Guseman, Christine Susan Wolfe 46
Guseman, Clara Pehlicia (child) 95
Guseman, Clara Phelicia (wife) 40
Guseman, Elmer Theodore 95
Guseman family history 46
Guseman, Henry Jacob 46
Guseman, Italia May 95

Guseman, Jacob Henry 46
Guseman, John Willie Jacob 95
Guseman, Lovina 95
Guseman (place) 53
Guseman, Private Abraham 46
Guseman, Theodore Jacob 94
Guthrie, Nancy (DeBerry) 60
Gutknecht. *See* Goodnight
Gutknecht, Christian 41

H

Haigh, Harry 156
Haigh, Joseph 162, 171
Haigh, Martha Elizabeth (Feather) 71, 154, 162
Haigh, Robert Browning 154
Hann, Foster 101
Hardesty, Crystal 48
Hardesty, Jamie 48
Harley & Gustkey 32
Harned, Lillie (Gray) 157, 158
Harned, Mrs. L. E. 108
Harrison County 30
Harrison, Ethel (Moss) 33
Harsh, Estella (Feather) 176
Hartman, Donald 66
Hartman, Frank 95
Hartman, Harlan 66
Hartman, H. Foster 66, 159
Hartman, Joseph 90
Hartman, Lydia (Feather) 20, 81
Hartman, Mack 95
Hartman, Malinda Ellen (Feather) 93
Hartman, Marguerite Helen (Collison) 107

Hartman, McClellan George 106, 107, 160
Hartman, Mildred 158
Hartman, Mrs. McClellan 148, 150, 161
Hartman, Nina Mildred (Hartman) 107
Hartman, Ruby 66, 150
Hartman, Sarah J. (Feather) 90
Hartman, Verna Louise 107
Hartman, Viletta Willard (Powell) 107
Harvey, Sarah M. (Feather) 93, 94, 129
Haugen, William 139
Hauger, Ezra 144
Hauger family history 58
Hauger, Mike 49
Hauger, M.W. 101
Hauger, Ruth 49
Hauger, Virginia Mary "Jennie" (White) 58
Hauger, William J. 58
Haun, Emma Belle Feather 64
Haun, George C. 64, 158
Haun, Margaret Jane 64
Haun, Norval Paul 64
Hayden, Annie D.M. (Feather) 56
Hayden, Bessie Ada (Feather) 30, 157, 162, 167
Hayden, Will 162
Hazelett, Barbara (Welch) 43, 108
heart disease 82, 84, 136
Heffelfinger, Edna 161, 169
Heffelfinger, Jean (Black) 162
Hefflefinger, Alfred 168

Herndon, Nettie 30
Herring, George Washington 59
Herring, Mary Jane (Livengood) 59
Herrney, Mrs. Geo. A. 150
Hesse 139
Highland M.E. Choir 150
Hile, Lona May 157
Hileman, Charlotte Dessie 31
Hileman, Martha Jane 60
Hileman, Sarah 66
Hill, Bernyce (Feather) 30
Hillery, Dailey 131
Hillery, Effie 131
Hillery, Floyd 131
Hillery, George 131
Hillery, Judson Gilbert 130, 131
Hillery, Wanda Ellen (Feather) 85, 130, 132
Hillery, Wilma 131
Hindman, W. L. 98
Hocking County, Ohio 57
hogs 86
Hope Town Cemetery 40, 47, 128
horses, use on farm 86
Hoty, Ralph 167
Houston, Mariah J. (Lovenstein) 37
Huffman, Bill 162
Hughes, Edith (Feather) 127
Hughes, Mrs. Dorothy 127
Hunt, Eve (Welch) 43
hunting prowess 113
Hyden, R.E. 169
Hyre, Gwendolyn (Feather) 120, 131
Hyre, Loren 68
Hyre, William 68
Hyre, Wilma 68

Index

I

Idleman, E. P. 52, 143
Illinois 40, 47
Independence 32
Indiana 41
infant and child burials 73–75
Inglewood Park Cemetery 95
Iowa 81, 162
Irish immigrants 113
Irish Meadow Lane 72

J

Jackson, D.R. 100
Jackson, Georgia Etta "George" (Feather) 67, 70
Jackson, James F. 153, 158
Jackson, Phil 153
Jacob Feathers
　problem with proliferation 83
Januketes, Carol Lynn 167
Jeffers Cemetery 102
Jefferys, Emily (Feather) 102
Jeffreys, Rachel (Forman) 104
Jenkins, Cora 66
Jenkins, Frank 66
Jenkins, Jean 169, 170
Jenkins, Karen Sue 165
Jenkins, Paul E. 169
Jenkins, Roamma (Rodeheaver) 109
Johns, Burgett Parker "B. P." 71, 115, 160, 170
Johnson Chapel Cemetery 128
Johnson, Jonas 121

Johns, Rosemary (Stephenson) 115, 164
Johns, Thomas P. 115
Johns, Tom & Margaret 169
Johns, Tommy 163
Jordan, L. H. 105
Josephine Furnace 27

K

Kansas 47, 49, 103
Kansas land 103
Kearney Cemetery 93
Keener, Archie 118
Keener, Edna (Gardner) 118
Keener, Floyd E. 67, 118
Keener, Lucy 118
Keener, Mary Rebecca (Feather) 118
Keener, Oliver 118
Kelley, Clyde 158
Kelley, Sarah 52
Kelley, Willis Hugh 154
Kelley, W. S. 66
Kelly, Abigail "Abbie" (Feather) 69
Kelly, Alfred 114
Kelly, Amanda Hyde (Matthews) 125
Kelly, Anna Sirissi (Feather) 36
Kelly, Annie R. (Feather) 91
Kelly, Carrie E. (Van Hoesen) 125
Kelly Cemetery 50
Kelly, Dallia (Feather) 34
Kelly, Dallie A. (Feather) 34, 50
Kelly, Elizabeth (Askins) 50
Kelly family in Preston County 35, 43
Kelly, John 50, 126
Kelly, John S. 158

194

Index

Kelly, John Solomon 125
Kelly, John T. 36
Kelly, John W. 64
Kelly, Joseph 50, 125
Kelly, Joseph M. 113
Kelly, Joseph Meshack Allen 50
Kelly, Margaret Malinda 64
Kelly, Mary Ann (Feather) 82
Kelly, Mary Catharine (Walker) 125
Kelly, Mary Elizabeth 148
Kelly, Odessee "Dessie" (Haun) 64
Kelly, Pauline Virginia (Feather) 75, 154
Kelly, Rachel B. (Ringer) 125
Kelly, Rebecca (Feather) 125
Kelly, Roy 114
Kelly, Ruth Annie (Feather) 69
Kelly, Sarah Adaline (Miller) 125
Kelly, Virginia Lenhamina "Jennie" (DeBerry) 125
Kelly, Walter J. 39
Kelly, William 50
Kelly, Willie 125
Kelly, Winfield Scott 36
Keota Cemetery 81
Keyser 30
Kiester, Edna 167
King of Prussia 78
King, Rev. 144
King, Spencer 106
Kingwood 18, 20, 27, 35, 78, 80, 81
  American Legion Post 56 132
Kingwood Band 149
Kingwood M. E. Church 105
Kingwood Parks and Recreation 176
Kingwood Turnpike 27

Knights of Pythias 53, 112
Knights of the Golden Eagle 53
Kondner, Minnette H. (Moss) 33
Korean Conflict 132
Kreps, Diana L. 171

L

Lancaster County, Pa. 57
LaSalle County, Ill. 40
Layman, Grace 159
Layman, J.N. 150
Layman, William 148, 152, 159, 161
Lee, Anna May (Feather) 123
Lee, Anna Rosa (Feather) 136
Lee, Nicholas J. 35
Lee, Samuel Ellsworth 35, 123
Lee, William F. 35
Legge, Dr. 33
Lemmon, Caleb Dorsey 76
Lemmon, Georgia (Joyner) 121
Lemmon, Martha (Abernathy) 121
Lemmon, Osa Grace Feather 85
Lemmon, Robert 121
Lenhard, Ray 161
Lenhard, Will 158
Lenhart, J. A. 83
Lenhart, Lou 151
Lenhart, Myrtle 159
Lenhart, Will 157, 159
Lenhart, W.L. 151, 156
Lenhart, W.M. 152, 153, 154
Lenox 26, 100–101, 122, 134
  Feather migration away from 16
  social life in 65–66
Lenox churches 17

195

Index

Lenox Community Center 16
Lenox Extension Homemakers. 131
Lenox Funeral Home 105
Lenox Homemakers 68
Lenox Memorial Cemetery
  history of 11, 17
  maps of 22-24
Lenox Store 22-24, 104
Lenox switchboard 101
Leonard, Harry 164, 166
Lewis, Ann Elizabeth (Reckart) 62, 108
Lewis, Brian 129
Lewis, Catharine Jane (Feather) 20, 81
Lewis, Catherine Jane (Feather) 84
Lewis, Christian F. 65
Lewis County 40
Lewis, Eve (Eva) Catharine Feather 64
Lewis, George Ludwig 108
Lewis, James A. 65
Lewis, Jane Dodge (Stemple) 65
Lewis, John 80
Lewis, Lydia 64
Lewis, Margaret 64
Lewis, Mary 64
Lick Run 18
Liston, Flo 148
Liston, Mary 165
Liston, Mrs. Wilber 154
Liston, Murhl 148
Liston, Sevilla "Savilla" 35
Liston sisters 146
Livengood, Annabelle 163, 170
Livengood, David Samuel 59

Livengood, Eddie 169, 171
Livengood, Effie E. (Feather) 37
Livengood, Ella Estella (Feather) 59, 126
Livengood family history 59-60
Livengood, Harland 165, 168
Livengood, Hope 171
Livengood, Johann Peter 59
Livengood, Nina 170
Livengood, Patrick 169
Livengood, Samuel Sherman 59
Livengood, Stanley Ward 133-134
Livengood, Virginia Crane 59
Logan, Ohio 52
Long Hollow church 147
Los Angeles, Calif. 57
Los Angeles County, Calif. 31
Los Angeles National Cemetery 133
Lostant, Ill. 40, 47, 128
Loudon Park Cemetery 33
Loudoun County, Va. 50
Lovenstein, Andrew 37
Lovenstein, Archibald 37
Lovenstein, Atta (Alta) (Feather) 37
Lovenstein, Bertha 37
Lovenstein, Charles 37
Lovenstein, David 37
Lovenstein, Esther 37
Lovenstein, Francine 37
Lovenstein, Hannah 37
Lovenstein, Marcus 37
Lovingstone, Alta (Atta) (Feather) 30
Lutheran Cemetery 19
Lutheran Church (Lenox) 15, 17
  history 17
  location 17

members 27, 28
Lutheran Church Road 12
Lutheran faith adherents 27, 28, 47, 53, 55, 92, 97, 100, 135
Lutz, Fla. 127

M

Manoun, Charley 152
Maple Spring Cemetery (Eglon) 19
Maplewood Cemetery 56, 57
Maplewood Cemetery (Kingwood) 19, 77, 124
Marion County 64, 67
Marion ME Circuit 99
Martin band 142
Martin, Daniel 124
Martin, Dempsey Ernest 35
Martin, Elma 66
Martin, H.M. 94
Martin, Isaac W. 124
Martin, Jacob B. 124
Martin, Phebe Jane (Feather) 84, 124
Martin, Taylor 144
Maryland 28, 90
Masontown 78
Masontown Cemetery 74
Matheny, Sara (Martin) 124
Mayfield Heights, Ohio 31
Mayfield, Mart 100
Mayflower passengers 56
McCabe, Maryann 126
McCarty, Rev. 82
McClain Printing 19
McClain, S.H. 100
McGinnis, Georgia 161

McGinnis, Georgia Etta (Feather) 67, 71
McGinnis, Harry Jesse 67
McGinnis, Keith 166, 169
McGinnis, Larry Keith 68
McGinnis, Larry Keith Sr. 67
McGinnis, Terry Lynn 67
McHenry, Md. 78, 122
McKabe, Lorata (Wilhelm) 122
McLaughlin, Casey 132
McLaughlin, Kyle 68, 132
McLaughlin, Robert 68, 131, 132
McLaughlin, Sarah 68, 132
McLaughlin, Stephen 68, 132
McLaughlin, Wendy 68
McManis, Bessie 167
McMullen, Mary Polly (Browning) 113
McNabb, Beverly 126
McNabb, Shawn 126, 129
Medsler, Ada Sharps 153
Medsler, Mary R. 153
Menear, Mary (Ervin) 61
Menota, Ill. 40
Menoun, Charles 153
Mercer, B.L. (Bertram Longfellow) 117
Mercer County, Pa. 27, 72
Mercer, E. E. (Elias Emery) 117
Mercer, Mary Louisa "Lou" (Feather) 50, 97, 117–118
Mercer, Susan Effie (Donaldson) 117
Messenger, Joshua 65
Messenger, Rebecca (Lewis) 65
Metheny, Doug & Paulette 170
Metheny, John 100–101

Index

Methodism 107
Methodism adherents 68, 69, 84, 93, 95, 107, 108, 121, 131, 132
Milford Township, Pa. 79
Mill Creek 155
Miller, Albert 102
Miller, Annie Susanna (Hartman) 90
Miller, Charles (Charley) 152, 153, 154, 155, 156, 161, 163
Miller, Enos 68
Miller, James J. & Sara Ann W. 68
Miller, Jane 66
Miller, Mary Jane 170
Miller, Nancy 165
mills 46
mineral rights 83
Missouri 40, 46, 47, 95
Molisee, Molly Letitia (Feather) 74
Monongalia County 18, 34, 46, 50
Monongalia Power 67
Moravian burial conventions 81
Morgan, Bruce 168
Morgan farm (William) 81
Morgan Mines 130
Morgan, Scott 154
Morris Park 141
Morris, Rev. 144
Morris, Squire 100
Morris, W.W. 52
Moss, Harvey C. 31, 111
Moss, Harvey Calvin
  wedding 31–32
Mother's Day 33
Mountain People in a Flat Land 206
Mount Calvary Cemetery 64
Mount Carmel 123

Mount Moriah Baptist Cemetery 76, 93, 102, 124
Moyer, Eli 48
Moyer, Matt 48
Moyer, Valerie 48
Moyer, Wyatt 48
Muddy Creek 11, 18, 46, 84, 99
Mullins, Priscilla 56
Mullins, Sherri 126
murder 56
Muskingum County, Ohio 50
My Fathers' Land book 12, 62, 81, 206

N

Naylor, Mary (Forman) 104
Nebraska 47, 93, 107
Nedrow, Elma Jane (Lee) 35
Nedrow, Jane (Lee) 123
New Hampshire 31, 122
New Jersey 79
New Ponca, Okla. 83
New Salem Church Cemetery 136
New Wilmot, N.H. 31
Nice, Martha Arminta (Shaffer) 107
Normandy American Cemetery 127
Normandy Invasion 127

O

Oak Grove Cemetery 65
Oakland, Md. 90, 124
Obama, Barack Jr. 42
occupations of Feather men.
  See Feather family, occupations

Odd Fellows 47, 53
Odd Fellows Cemetery 83
Ohio 31, 41, 50, 52, 57
Oklahoma 83, 130
Oneal, Fay 66
orphans
  Adam H. 88
  DeBerry 60
  Hauger 58
  Levi Feather 102
Orr, D.B. 142, 143

P

Palatine 98
Pape, Boyd 126, 129
Pape, Robin 126
paralysis 89
Park, Flora M. (Feather) 40, 47, 48, 74
Parnell Cemetery (Cuzzart) 19, 30, 35, 78, 113, 114, 128
Parsons 65, 66
Parsons City Cemetery 65
Partlow, Va. 129
Payne, Shawn 126
Payne, Syndee 126
Peaslee, Amanda 52, 65
Peaslee, Amanda E. 134
Peaslee, Amanda Jane (Feather) 31, 61
Peaslee, Benjamin Wells 31
Peaslee, Benjamin Z. 31, 66
Peaslee, Cora 66
Peaslee Family origins 31
Peaslee, Hepsibah Pike 31
Peaslee, Howard 66, 158

Peaslee, Howard Franklin 31
Peaslee, Jeane 159
Peaslee, Joan 158
Peaslee, John K. 31
Peaslee, Mable 66
Peaslee, Mae 159, 162, 165
Peaslee, Nita 38
Peaslee, Ray 66
Peaslee, Roxie 158, 159
Peaslee, Roy 66
Pennsylvania 11, 12, 18, 27, 28, 30, 34, 44, 57, 59, 71, 72, 74, 80, 97
Perrin, Lisa 126
Perrin, Michael 126, 129
Perry County, OH 60
Petso, Violet 166
Philadelphia, Pa. 28
Pleasantdale 119
Pleasant District 31, 35, 46, 90, 99
Pleasant Grove Cemetery 58
Pleasant Hill ME Circuit 99
Pleasant View Cemetery 75
Plymouth Colony 56
pneumonia 47, 58, 74, 88
Poling, Jenny (Albright) 34
Portland District 40, 45, 47, 63, 65, 70, 71, 82, 89, 110
Pounds, Phoebe Jane (Feathers) 77
pregnancy complications 32
Preston County 11
  early shopkeeping in 46
  land records, loss of 11
  migrations to from Pa. 27, 59–60
  unsolved murder 57
Preston County 4-H Camp 164
Preston County Association of

Index

Retired School Employees 68, 132
Preston County Board of Education 120, 132
Preston County Courthouse fire 54
Preston County Historical Society 68, 132, 139
Pruntytown 78, 99
Putnam County, Ohio 40

Q

Quakers 31, 104, 113, 116

R

Rankin, Sara Ann (Feather) 75
Reckart, Abraham 108
Reckart, Belle Nora (Miller) 108
Reckart, Earnest August 62, 69, 108
Reckart, Elizabeth (Feather) 62, 77
Reckart family history 62
Reckart farm 28, 91–92
Reckart, George Ludwig Lewis 62
Reckart, Henry Lewis 108
Reckart, John F. 108
Reckart, Lucille 168, 171
Reckart, Nettie Florence (Feathers) 74, 137
Reckart Saga 91
redemptioner 79
Red Stone Township, Pa. 89
Reedsville 120, 130
Reed, W.E. 52
Rembold, James David 157
Revolutionary War 46, 62, 139

rheumatism 45
Riley Lumber Co. 104
Ringer, Adah Blanche (Feather) 27, 38, 39, 75, 157, 167
Ringer, Amanda (Feather) 110
   wedding ceremony 110–111
Ringer, Amanda Jane (Feather) 31
Ringer, Augusta Florence (Heare) 72
Ringer, Emma E. 101
Ringer, Ezra 101
Ringer Family Cemetery 72
Ringer family history 72
Ringer, Flora Bell (Hillery) 130, 131
Ringer, George W. 73
Ringer, George W. Jr. 72
Ringer, Harrison 38, 39
Ringer, Harrison "Harry" 27
Ringer, Huldah Catharine (Feather) 72–73, 75, 103
Ringer, Isa 38
Ringer, Jacob 72
Ringer, John 27, 31
Ringer, Joseph 72
Ringer, Joseph R. 66
Ringer, Marshal 73
Ringer, Mary 73
Ringer mill land 27
Ringer, Noah 73
Ringer, Philip 27
Ringer, Vernie 66
Ringer, William 73
Roaring Creek 18, 34, 71
Roberts, L.W. 94
Roby, Clyde G. Sr. 76
Roby, Harold Lloyd 76
Roby, Helen Ruth (Funk) 76

Index

Roby, Jesse 168
Roby, Jesse Paul 76
Rodaheaver, Hillery W. 101
Rodeheaver, Benton 168
Rodeheaver Cemetery 78
Rodeheaver, Christopher (Christian) Columbus 78
Rodeheaver, Col. John 109
Rodeheaver, Hillery W. 114
Rodeheaver, Homer 148
Rodeheaver, Isabelle (Feather) 78, 99, 101
Rodeheaver, James B. 113
Rodeheaver, Jared A. 109
Rodeheaver, J. Frank 95, 109
Rodeheaver (John) Cemetery 114
Rodeheaver, John F. 113
Rodeheaver, Martha (Kelly) 36
Rodeheaver, Martha V. 30
Rodeheaver, Martha "Virginia" (Feather) 89, 109
Rodeheaver, Mary Ann Kelly Feather 113
Rodeheaver, Missouri Olive Welch 114
Rodeheaver, Mrs. Samantha 154
Rodeheaver, Samuel Patrick 78
Rogers, Edna (Davis) 19
Roosevelt Memorial Park 57
Rubenstein Market 16
rug making 86
Ryland, Malinda (Kelly) 50

S

Saint Mark's Evangelical Lutheran 135
Salem 50
Sallaz, Rev. 109
Samuel (ship) 41
Samuel ship 28
Saxony, Germany 34, 107
Schaeffer, Mary Elizabeth (Trowbridge) 81
Schaeffer, Nancy Maria (Shaw) 81
Schaefferstown, Pa. 107
Schaffer, Jacob F. 81
Schaffer, Sarah Jane (Wilson) 81
Schneider, Dewalt 59
Schneider Family Cemetery 11, 19, 49, 80
Schrupp, Elisabetha (DeBerry) 60
Scott, Dr. B.F. 33
Scott, Equatious V. 125
Scott, Flora B. (Sisler) 125
Scott, John 154
Scott, John Wesley 125
Scott, Lydia 168
Scott, Nathan 125
Scott, Sarah Margaret (Feather) 44
Scott, Willie John 125
Seal, C.H. 156
Seal, Paul H. 156
Shady Grove Union Cemetery 39, 60
Shafer, Adam Johann 107
Shaffer, Israel 20, 81, 147, 176
Shaffer, Jacob Rhodes Sr. 107
Shaffer, Jacob Thomas "Jake" 107
Shaffer, Madeline Florence (Feather) 90, 107

Index

Shaffer, Rev. Gustavus Cresap 81, 147, 150, 152, 176
Shaffer, Susanna Katherine (Wilson) 81
Shaffer, William Morgan 81
Shaw, Bertha (Haun) 64, 162
Shaw, Opal 153
Shaw, Opal M. 64
Shay and Elliott Cemetery 119
Shiffertt, John 166
Shipley, Nora 168
Shirley, Patricia 157
Shoresite 129
Shultz, W. M. 69
Shultz, W.M. 117
Siggens, Mary (see Silgens, Mary) 80
Silgens, Mary (Feather) 20, 80
Simon, Cameron 166
Simon, Michael 166
Sines, Catharine (Wilhelm) 122
Sisler Cemetery 123
Sisler, Leeta May 31
Sisler, Mary Anne (Rodeheaver) 78
Sisler, Mary (Feather) 20, 80, 82, 118
Sisler sisters 156
Smith, Catherine (Feather) 104
Smith, Jacob 104
Smith, Mahala "Hallie" I. (Forman) 104
Smith, Mrs. Mary 127
Smith, Nellie B. 97
Smith, Ruth (Evans) (Feather) 206
Smith, S.C. 54
Snider, Samuel W. 102
soap production at home 86

Somerset County, Pa. 11, 12, 18, 28, 44, 57, 59, 61, 72, 74, 80, 141
  migration from to Preston County 28, 61
  Palatines' migration to 59
South Dakota 47
Speck, Anna Maria (Albright) 34
Spencer, Thomas Patrick 64
Spiker, Frances Jean 159
spinal disease 76
Spotsylvania, Va. 126, 129
Stanton, James Thomas 123
Stanton, Ora F. (Feather) 45
Stephenson, Thomas 168
Sterling Faucet 120
Sterling Rockwell International 132
Steuben, General von 62
St. George 34, 65
St. Mary's County, Md. 123
Stokes, Benjamin Frank 122
Stokes, Blaine 66
Stokes, Charles 66
Stokes, Charles Edward 122
Stokes, Cyrena E. (Davis) 122
Stokes, Etta M. 122
Stokes, Floyd Herbert 66
Stokes, Jacob C. 122
Stokes, Jerry 66
Stokes, John E. 122
Stokes, Nancy 66
Stokes, Nancy Maria Feather 122
stomach cancer 37
Stone, Olive 169
Strawser, Alfred 49
Strawser, Ira B. 49
Strickland, Mrs. Viola 127

Index

string music 160
stroke 34
Sugar Valley 73
Summers, Christeen (Feather) 20, 81, 84
Summers, David R. 128
Summers, John 28, 118, 128
Summers, Mary 80
Summers, Mary (Feather) 20, 28, 118, 128
Summers, Sabra Eusebia (Feather) 20, 28, 74, 80, 118, 128
Sunset Memorial Gardens 75
sunstroke 36
Sypolt, Darwin Wayne 76
Sypolt, Everett Clifton 76
Sypolt, Floyd Homer 76
Sypolt, Malinda Theodothia "Mollie" (Feather) 76
Sypolt, Opal Mae (Peaslee) 76
Sypolt, Pearl Virginia (Cox) 76
Sypolt, Ralph William 76
Sypolt, Sarah Ann (Casteel) 123

T

Tampa, Fla. 127
Taylor County 65
Teets, Albert 44, 114
Teets, Anna Hazel (Bishop) 44
Teets, Edward L. 176
Teets, Effie 148, 150
Terra Alta 30, 37, 43, 46, 47, 48, 53
Terra Alta band 53
Terra Alta Cemetery 37, 40, 44, 59, 125
Terra Alta High School. 48
Terra Alta M.E. Church 33
Terra Alta Park 166
Terra Alta Quartet 142
Terra Alta Republican newspaper 140
Terra Alta singing band 142
Thomas 16
Thomas, Janett 162
Thomas, Mary Waunita (Feather) 75
Thomas, Ward Fike 39
Thorn, Annette 170
Tipton County, Ind. 41
Titchenell, Hazel (Feather) 115, 163, 169, 170
Titchnell, Joel 146
tragedies 37–38, 39, 44, 47–48, 49, 51, 56, 58, 63, 83, 94, 95, 100–101, 102
Travis County, Texas 76
Trembly, Charles 143
Trembly, Matta 161
Trembly, Russ 168
Trenton, N.J. 79
Tressler, J. L. 17
Troxell, Margaret 107
tuberculosis 30, 81
Tunnelton 163
Turner, Gene 49
typhoid fever 105

U

Uniontown, Pa. 71

Index

V

Valley District 130
Valley Forge 62, 79, 108, 124
Valley Point 28, 42, 106, 124, 127, 175
VanMeter, Martha Ellen "Mattie" (Feather) 44
Vansickle, Joseph 156
Vatter, Anna Clarissa (Clara) (Schneider) 11
Vätter, Jacob. *See* Feather, Jacob
Vätter, Joseph Christian 11, 79
Virginia 18, 50

W

Walker, Joel 126
Ward, B.D. 149, 151
Ward, Mrs. B.D. 151
War of 1812 91
Warthen, Lecretia 65
Watkins, Mrs. Gathel 127
Watring, Brenda (Feather) 48
weddings 38, 94, 110
wedding traditions 32
Welch, Andrew Jackson 43
Welch, Barbara E. 49
Welch, Beck 154
Welch, Catharine Jane (Feather) 49, 69
Welch, C. F. 66
Welch, Clarissa Jane (Feather) 49, 60
Welch, Dayton 101
Welch, Dorotha Alfreda (Folk) 76
Welch, Dr. Charles Darrel 76
Welch, Earl 76, 159

Welch, Elizabether (Broomhall) 116
Welch, Frank 153, 156, 157, 160
Welch, Goldie 101
Welch, Herman 66
Welch, Ida M 49
Welch, Jacob 43
Welch, Jacob H. 102
Welch, Jacob Harrison 43
Welch, Jacob Wesley 49, 116
Welch, Jainie 49
Welch, John F. 43, 108
Welch, Joseph 95
Welch, Joseph Brice 101
Welch, Joseph J. 43, 108
Welch, Kathryn Elaine "Kay" (Rose) 76
Welch, Lillie 159
Welch, Madalene 153
Welch, Mariah "Annie" (Feather) 43, 82, 108
Welch, Marila A. 43
Welch, Mary Jane "Mollie" (Feather) 50, 116, 117
Welch, Matilda Jane (Dunn) 50
Welch, May 95, 158, 159, 160
Welch, McClure 49
Welch, Nita 153
Welch, Olive 101
Welch, Persis A. (Childs) 43
Welch, Rebecca 154
Welch, Roama 49
Welch, Thomas G. 66, 160, 163
Welch, Thomas Jefferson 43, 49
Welch, Tresia Lucretia 58
Welch, U.S. 95
Welch, Willis Hugh 76

Wesley Chapel 114, 131, 176
  members 40, 121, 132
  photo of 14
  restroom facility 168
  reunions held at 142, 143, 145, 147,
    151, 152, 153, 154, 155, 156, 157,
    158, 159, 161, 162, 163, 165, 168
Westmoreland County Memorial
  Park 30
West Virginia
  statehood 18
West Virginia Births 30
West Virginia National Cemetery 78
Wheeling 29, 93
Wheeling Intelligencer 38
Whetsell, H. S. 103
White, Alva James 58
White, Dora Ellen (Feather) 58, 71
White Family Cemetery 118
Whitehair, Hugh 66
Whitehair, W.A. 65, 66
White, John Nelson 84, 84–85
White, Malinda Jane (Feather) 42
White, Maude (Hyre) 68
Whitesell (Whetsell), Coral 161, 162
Whitsell (Whetsell), Lillian 144, 148
Wilhelm, C.P. 157
Wilhelm, Edna 157
Wilhelm, Jacob 122
Wilhelm, Jeff 122
Wilhelm, Kelly (Andrews) 122
Wilhelm, Nancy (Feather) 83, 122
Wilhelm, Peter 122
Wilhelm, Solomon Sr. 122
Willey 29, 104, 105
Williams, Carney 152

Williams, Millard 152
Williamstown Cemetery 47
Williamstown, Mo. 40
Wilson, Rebecca 167
Wilson, Rosa May 77
Winfield District (Marion County)
  64
Wismanns, Marie/Maria (Vatter/
  Feather) 11, 78
Wolfe, Boyd Christian 123
Wolfe, Christine Susan 46
Wolfe, Edith Virginia 123
Wolfe family Portland District 43
Wolfe, Fanny 158
Wolfe, Jim 169
Wolfe, Lucille 171
Wolfe, Orman 169
Wolfe, Roy 168
Wolfe, Susan Mah (Feather) 20, 80
World War I 83, 145
Wotring, Abraham 107
Wotring, Catherine Elizabeth (Shafer) 107
W.Va. Calvary 114
Wymps Gap, Pennsylvania 41
Wyoming 49

Y

York 34
Yorktown 79
Youghiogheny River 43
Young, Harry 40

Index

Z

Zion Lutheran 58
Zion Lutheran church 17
Zion Lutheran (Lenox) 82
Zook surname 128

Reader notes

About the Author

Carl E. Feather and bonded canine partner, Edison.

Carl E. Feather is a seventh-generation Preston County resident; his fourth great-grandparents, Jacob and Mary Feather (Vätter), settled at Crab Orchard in 1803. He is descended from Christian's line. The story of his German-Swiss Palatinate immigrant ancestors and their relationship to the Allegheny Mountains is told in *My Fathers' Land*, also by Carl. His book, *Mountain People in a Flat Land* (Ohio University Press), relates the story of migration from West Virginia to Ohio in the post-World War II years.

Carl is married to Ruth Evans Feather, a Certified Ophthalmic Technician originally from eastern Pennsylvania. Carl and Ruth have been Bruceton Mills, West Virginia, residents since 2020. Carl has a son, Aaron E., by Barbara J. Eller (Hopkins, Feather), and grandson, Mason L. Feather.

A retired journalist and professional photographer, Carl has freelanced for West Virginia's traditional life magazine, *GOLDENSEAL*, since the mid-1980s, and more than 100 of his stories have been published on its pages. He continues to write and shoot for the quarterly. Follow his adventures and video at his website/blog, thefeathercottage.com.

www.ingramcontent.com/pod-product-compliance
Lightning Source LLC
Chambersburg PA
CBHW020232170426
43201CB00007B/398